# THE CLUBWOMAN AS FEMINIST

# The Clubwoman as Feminist
## True Womanhood Redefined, 1868–1914

## Karen J. Blair

### Preface by Annette K. Baxter

HOLMES & MEIER PUBLISHERS, INC.
NEW YORK ■ LONDON

First published in the United States of America 1980 by
Holmes & Meier Publishers, Inc.
30 Irving Place
New York, N.Y. 10003

*Great Britain:*
Holmes & Meier Publishers, Ltd.
131 Trafalgar Road
Greenwich, London SE10 9TX

**Library of Congress Cataloging in Publication Data**

Blair, Karen J
  The clubwoman as feminist.

  Bibliography: p.
  Includes index.
  1. Women—United States—Societies and clubs—
History. 2. Women in public life—United States—
History. 3. Feminism—United States—History.
I. Title.
HQ1904.B56    301.41′2′0973    79-26390

ISBN 0-8419-0538-X


Manufactured in the United States of America

*To my parents,*
*Josephine LeVanda Blair and Henry A. Blair*

# Contents

# Acknowledgments

Researching and writing a book can be a difficult task, but my path was eased considerably by the assistance of many kind and talented people. Great numbers of creative clubwomen, archivists, and librarians discovered valuable sources for me. I would especially like to thank Nancy Chudacoff of the Rhode Island Historical Society, Susan Boone of the Sophia Smith Collection at Smith College, and Shonnie Finnegan at the State University of New York at Buffalo. The Inter-Library Loan staff at SUNY/Buffalo was enormously helpful.

Ellen DuBois was an unmatchable dissertation adviser, whose enthusiasm for the subject of women's history and women's clubs was contagious and whose verve and tact as mentor is deeply appreciated. For intellectual stimulation and encouragement, I am also indebted to Jane Weinstein Berman, Gail Dickersin, Virginia Drachman, Anne Filiaci, and the other members of the SUNY/Buffalo Graduate Women's History Group. Mari Jo Buhle, Alice Clement, Mary Grant, David Hollinger, Sally Gregory Kohlstedt, Jesse Lemisch, Anne Firor Scott, and Charles Trout are scholars who offered valuable criticisms. I want to thank Margaret Grey and the Friday Morning Club of Los Angeles for use of the photograph which appears on the cover. I am indebted to Mary Granger, Donna Gietscheir, and Lynne Schlinger, who typed the drafts of the manuscript, and to Bronwyn Mellquist for her help in editing it. I also received help from Cynthia Blair, Donna DiPaolo, Constance Metcalf, Barry Rubin, and Susan Young. I owe particular thanks to Charles Beyrer who twice interrupted this project but restored my vision, and for his skills I am especially grateful.

The Skinner Fellowship of Mount Holyoke College and the Woodrow Wilson Doctoral Dissertation Fellowship in Women's Studies provided financial assistance.

Finally, I acknowledge all the women, then and now, who have worked to build a better life for themselves and for the rest of us.

# Preface

Sisterhood is an idea long dormant and now once again alive in the American psyche. The women's movement has done this, clearly and irrevocably. When internal differences among feminists arise, they are now almost universally felt as double-edged: usefully advancing the dialectic, but also posing a potential danger to unity. In again making sisterhood a trust, the contemporary movement has generated a revival, in several senses of the word. Sisterhood is at once a drama of self-discovery reenacted, a faith in womanhood reawakened and an historical consciousness repossessed. It is this last sense of sisterhood that Karen Blair has explored through this exhaustive and richly suggestive study of the clubwoman, feminism's forgotten ally.

Scholars like Carroll Smith-Rosenberg, Blanche Wiesen Cook and Keith E. Melder have alerted us to some of the specific structures, as distinct from ideologies, within which nineteenth-century and early twentieth-century sisterhood was nourished. But the club as a structure, with a persuasive legitimacy of its own, has been neglected. Perhaps this is because clubs, contrasted with other forms of association, are traditionally seen as occupying a select sphere buffeted from what are deemed to be undesirable influences. This perception has been reinforced by the exclusionist aims and policies that some have regularly embraced. Far from offering a retreat, however, most clubs, particularly the woman's club, served as a vehicle of entry into the main stream of public affairs. The resulting impact of clubwomen on the evolving shape of American ideas and institutions in the twentieth century has previously been indicated in the work of only a few discerning scholars, Mary Beard, for example, and in more recent times, Sheila M. Rothman. Now it is meticulously examined by Karen Blair against a background of relevant contemporary scholarship. Her work confirms our growing realization that women did more than enter the main stream of social and political innovation; they frequently remained to direct it.

Recently Professor J. Stanley Lemons has described women in the reactionary 1920s as the solitary champions of Progressivism in an uncongenial age. It is easier to see why this was so in the light of Blair's illuminating study. The reforming zeal of the turn-of-the-century Municipal Housekeepers who were the immediate predecessors of these latter-day Progressives was rooted in powerful internal drives that the attainment of suffrage could hardly satisfy. These drives went deeper than the political need to participate; they arose from an emotional need to express one's identity and make a lasting contribution.

In *The Clubwoman as Feminist* we see this need surfacing in the beginnings of Sorosis and the New England Woman's Club; developing cohesion in the Association for the Advancement of Women and extending its reach in the literary clubs that proliferated from Providence to Kansas City; achieving further definition in the efforts to cross class barriers in the Boston and Buffalo Women's Educational and Industrial Unions; and finally acquiring serious public recognition in the massive organizational appeal of Jane Cunningham Croly's General Federation of Women's Clubs. The message of this growth and success is clear: whether dedicated to social reform or to self-improvement, women's clubs had in common their power to afford women a more complete, and therefore a more authentic, self-expression.

Female self-expression was effectively thwarted by the prevailing conventions of American society in the last half of the nineteenth century. Women's defiance of these conventions, in their antislavery, suffrage, and temperance agitation, as well as in many of the lesser reform movements they helped populate, was made palatable through the agency of Domestic Feminism. According to its precepts women's domestic nature, to which men attributed moral superiority, entailed special responsibilities that might justify occasional altruistic forays beyond the family circle.

This disarming defense of women's activities outside the home most often functioned successfully in religious and educational work. As an example, a new study by Anne Firor Scott offers ample evidence of its role in the realization of Emma Willard's Troy Female Seminary. Willard, according to Scott, built "a highly successful career by using for her own ends social stereotypes about woman's place." And, as Blair vividly illustrates, such a defense made possible a variety of escapes from unadulterated domesticity, among them the escape into larger cultural and intellectual arenas.

What lends special piquancy to the saga of the clubwoman as Domestic Feminist is the ingenuity with which she bridged her two worlds. In their appeals to the opposite sex, women found that it required greater skill to rationalize club activity on the grounds of self-improvement than it took to explain their participation in social welfare and humanitarian reform. Men had barely sanctioned escape from the kitchen and nursery for the more compelling reasons of missionary work, educational endeavors, and health care. How could they be expected to tolerate such desertion for a closer familiarity with the poetry of Robert Browning?

Citing male complaints at the decrease in homemade pies consequent upon the growth of women's clubs, Blair hints at the immensity of the gap between male and female perceptions of the vital role clubs played in women's lives. Such trivialization of the club movement by men suggests the threat women's clubs represented to the stability of the male-female equilibrium of the late nineteenth century. Contemporary jeremiads, disguised as tracts, like the Reverend John Todd's *The Daughter at School*, testified to a generalized male fear of collective desertion of the maternal role by young women and the inevitable decline in the quality of the next generation of men. Sporadic but increasing defection from the home was making men edgy.

In the face of this anxiety, it is no surprise that men did little to help women overcome the limitations of their training and environment. Following the logic of their prejudices, they systematically excluded women from experiences that might assist their intellectual growth. Exclusion by males was frequently the precipitating factor in the coalescing of a women's group. The origins of the suffrage movement are to be found in women's exclusion from participation in the London World's Anti-Slavery Convention and, later, women's colleges were to arise in response to the exclusion of women from educational opportunities in the leading men's colleges. It is less well-known, though equally telling, that the birth of Sorosis was inspired by an act of exclusion: only males were invited to the New York Press Club dinner for Charles Dickens.

But retaliation at male exclusiveness hardly furnished more than the initial motive for organization; it was the rewards of sisterly communion that offered the incentive for continued association. It is significant that the *New York Herald* censured the ladies of Sorosis, shortly after its founding, for meeting simply to take toast and tea rather than engaging in socially useful activity. One can hardly imagine like censure being directed against a male club. Indeed, as Blair observes, female self-improvement was evidently more threatening than social activism.

If the club served the cause of cultural enlightenment for masses of women, it clearly served another purpose as well: it taught women the value of their own autonomy. Like today's women's groups, whether as diffuse in character as the National Council of Women, or as concentrated as the women's caucuses of professional societies, clubs strengthened collective confidence and afforded their members a more complete sense of individual identity. And they inevitably had the effect of cultivating in women an appreciation of each other. Sisterhood was the predictable outgrowth of such regular collaboration in sociability. Blair's study documents the genesis of these sentiments in a variety of surroundings and circumstances.

What it also documents is that, through these clubs, women were beginning to experience what the historian Mary Ryan has in another connection called a primary female bond. In the films of the 1920s, she notes, "Female friendship appeared as a supportive by-product of heterosexual relations, not as a primary female bond." It was this defensive form of female friendship that seems to have been revived in the suburban coffee klatches of the 1950s. In the late nineteenth century, by contrast, women learned to cultivate friendships with other women for mutual growth, not simply as a hedge against sexual betrayal or marital crisis. Pooling their resources in the club led to a heightened awareness and a more confident estimate of the qualities which, for lack of more precise language, were variously to be labeled the feminine perspective, the feminine scale of values, the feminine style. These women had no need of psychological studies to certify the differences between male and female orientation and behavior. They expressly acknowledged those differences and, through the instrumentality of the club, rapidly came to honor them.

Blair's analysis of the club movement subtly projects the clubwoman's awakening consciousness of the possibilities for cultural transformation in the recognition of women's distinctive outlook. She shows how clubwomen advanced from their early assertion of the civilizing value of artistic and literary culture when transmitted by women to the "offices and market places" of the male world, to the more aggressive female-inspired civic programs of later years. The climax of this progression was an open male concession in 1914 that the clubs were a desirable force on the American scene. This concession, which surely was intended to stave off more ominous challenges, signified the triumph of Domestic Feminism.

As long as female difference could still be accommodated to domesticity, even if it were no longer identical with it, women could indulge the habit of sisterhood. But with the official recognition of equality that suffrage brought not long after, difference, in a seldom acknowledged yet fundamental way, would cease to be politically respectable. It followed that organized female attempts to alter the texture of American society through social welfare, labor reform, and peace efforts during the first decade of full suffrage ended equivocally.

One of the most important contributions Blair makes through this study of clubwomen is to underscore what Gerda Lerner has asserted in other contexts: the lack of parallelism between women's history and the orthodox components of the history within which it exists. The striking difference in women's and men's perceptions of social ills at the start of the twentieth century is notable enough, for example, in the vigor with which women initiated the settlement movement. In striving to identify with a more rational and just society, clubwomen too were in the advance guard of Progressivism, and out of step with the prevailing politics of men. Furthermore, middle-class men, immersed in the battle for economic well-being, had little energy to spare for cultural pursuits. Despairing at the materialism of the age, critics like Henry Adams and Henry James saw women as the only credible custodians of culture. Thus in seeking a closer familiarity with the literary and artistic, clubwomen returned to a past whose achievements were often little known to their husbands and brothers and, when known, often rejected. The clubwoman illustrates in her own history the disjunctions in the experiences of men and women within the same class at the same period.

All the while, paradoxically, these women were seeking a greater measure of equality and a share in the rights and privileges of males, especially so after their endorsement of suffrage. Men reluctantly permitted them to do so only because of their acceptance of the premises of Domestic Feminism. Club-women held the middle ground between women like Charlotte Perkins Gilman, whose analysis of their plight would have mandated a radical break with social norms, and the overwhelming majority of their sex who contentedly played out their conventional roles or suffered in silence. Domestic Feminism was simultaneously a philosophy they calculatedly used and one with which they concurred. Like women throughout history, they could not finally opt for the autonomy they had come to savor.

Thanks to Blair's indefatigable scholarship, the intricacies of the club-women's adventures are set forth for women at a time when they are once again in touch with the primary female bond. Like the clubwomen, women today need to feel the compelling force of their female difference if they are to make an impact upon a society, shaped by the apathy and occasional cynicism of both sexes, that promotes violence, worships objects, and abandons culture. Yet they must not disavow their right to equality in that society lest, like the women of the New England Woman's Club, they find their own power to function as a sisterhood endangered by the invariable reach of male dominance.

Unlike the clubwoman, today's feminist cannot rely on Domestic Feminism as a vehicle of change. The dialectic of contemporary feminism has discredited the idea of the home as the exclusive precinct of woman, and even men have begun to suspect the stereotypes from which such an idea springs. But the weakened link between women and domestic virtue leaves an ideological vacuum for today's feminist. Surely she must continue to seek new strategies for linking her female identity to her private and public persona. Only thus can she realize her fullest capacities in a world that, increasingly, calls for the best from both sexes.

Annette K. Baxter
Barnard College

# Introduction

The true history of nineteenth-century feminism is only beginning to be written. The tendency to identify feminism with women's rights has led to the mistaken idea that most nineteenth-century women were safely and happily ensconced in a cotton-wool world described as "the Domestic Sphere." Leaving aside the fact that the majority of women were farmers' wives or factory workers for whom life was never easy, this description is inaccurate even for the women of the growing middle class, those Victorian ladies who loom large in fiction and image.

This book, by focusing on the woman's club, a realm in which proper ladies flourished, will demonstrate beyond argument that many of them were feminists under the skin, developing a significant and popular strategy for achieving autonomy, however much they may have maintained their ideological cover. This fact helps explain the surge of support for women's rights beginning about 1910, as the daughters of the women discussed here grew to maturity and carried the whole matter a step further. If feminism, like heat, could be measured in some analog of British Thermal Units, the total to be found in women's clubs would have been much larger than that in suffrage organizations, because so many more women were engaged in the former.

An understanding of clubs demands a familiarity with the ideology of the "lady": the belief that every woman was a moral and domestic creature who embodied the desirable traits of loving maternity, intuition, and sensitivity. This was one of the foundations of nineteenth-century middle-class American society.[1] Most nineteenth-century women would have been offended if they were not described as ladies. Exactly what being a lady meant and what traits were assigned to her, however, changed during the course of the century. In the early 1800s and during much of the previous century, the definition of an "ideal lady" applied only to the upper classes in society and resembled a type that had existed among the aristocracy of western Europe for several hundred years. She was leisured and ornamental, absorbed in learning the niceties that would render her amusing and enable her to beautify her home. Wealthy young women learned to dance, sing, embroider, make wax flowers, paint china, and play the harpsichord.[2]

For the remaining social classes, this style of life was hardly typical. In preindustrial America most women's labor was essential to the success of the farm and the survival of the family. But as industrialization gained momentum during the first half of the century, individual wealth increased and the application of the "ideal lady" concept broadened. As more and more middle-class men could afford to support their wives, women became economically inconsequential homebodies. To be sure, a woman worked hard in the home—keeping house, cooking, gardening, canning, sewing, and raising the children—but, unlike her husband, she did not earn a wage for her labors. Because the house-bound woman no longer contributed directly to the family income, she was incorrectly labeled "leisured" and endowed with other traits of the upper-class, ornamental, ideal lady. Unlike her wealthier counterpart, however, the middle-class lady was judged not only by her amusing charms. She was defined by her supposedly natural qualities of domesticity and morality.[3] The lady's function of embellishing her family's environment was expanded into being the moral guardian of the home.

The widespread acceptance of this "ideal lady" ideology was ensured by the sermons and popular literature that justified and explained women's role. God—said clergymen, medical men, and popular writers—created woman with natural or biologically moral superiority over man. Her ability to create a happy and wholesome environment for her family grew from her instinctive sanctity and sweetness. Thus, woman's ability to dispense goodness uniquely qualified her as a moral caretaker.[4]

In order to better prepare herself, woman should concentrate on the perfection and application of her God-given gentleness and delicacy to the exclusion of other traits. The Reverend F. D. Fulton, one of many clerics who outlined the proper deportment of the lady, praised her for her "childlike" love of "all that is beautiful in nature." Pleased that "no coarseness was mingled with her plainness of speech; no boisterousness with her zeal," he urged a nurturance "of her charming and unaffected manner."[5] The Reverend Hubbard Winslow told women to observe their "appropriate sphere" by remaining quiet in church and by paying deference to all men and reverence and homage to their husbands.[6]

Doctors told women that they could not expect to be successful at extra-domestic tasks because of biological deficiencies. This argument won wide support, bringing Reverend Fulton to insist: "Women cannot compete with man in a long course of mental labor. The female mind is rather quiet and timid than fiery and driving. It admires rather than covets the great exploits of the other sex."[7]

Writers on the female condition justified the restrictions of ladydom by asserting that a woman should be sufficiently gratified by her indirect ameliorating influence on husband and children. Reverend Winslow found that "she is capable of exerting a benign and almost irresistable dominion over the affections and the conduct of the other sex; but she can do it only by observing her appropriate sphere and putting forth her characteristic graces."[8] Alexander H. Sands reminded graduates of the Hollins Female Institute to radiate their special influence with moderation and tact:

For your brothers you will ever have a kind word of encouragement, when right, but not a word of reproof when wrong. If you should unfortunately be afflicted with an intemperate brother or husband, you will find his habit not cured by a harsh or bitter tone, but rather by persuasion and the tenderness of affection, which a sister or a wife only can feel and appropriately express.[9]

Mrs. John Sandford echoed the belief that woman should be content with her own selflessness. "It is not to shine, but to please, that a woman should desire; and she will do so only when she is graceful and unaffected, when her wish is not so much to be admired as to contribute to the gratification of others."[10]

While woman was charged with the responsibility for the home, man commanded the public realm and was active in the market place. With spreading industrialization during the mid-nineteenth century, man's public and woman's domestic spheres grew apart. She had little knowledge of his workplace and he had little knowledge of domestic routine and child care.[11] Cities, technology, and industry all continued to expand while the lady concerned herself with the establishment of a good home, physically removed from the activity of economic development. Furthermore, woman's concentration on the passive qualities required of the domestic lady, coupled with male antagonism to any other role for her, precluded her entrance into and success in man's world. Thus, the effect of the ideology of the lady, which had permeated all levels of society, was the virtual banishment of women from the public sphere.

Despite the centrality of the domestic sphere to nineteenth-century women's history, however, historians of women originally looked elsewhere. Accepting the traditional male definition of "activity," scholars examined woman's political work—specifically, the 1848–1920 struggle to win the suffrage. Although these studies reveal much of importance, they leave us with a partial view of resistance among nineteenth-century women to incarceration in the home.[12] In order to understand the true nature and extent of nineteenth-century feminism, it is necessary to look closely at women's domestic sphere.

The very boldness of the suffrage movement limited its appeal. Only a small percentage of women were strong enough to ignore the teachings of the sermons, popular magazines, novels, beauty guides, health manuals, fashions, and even phrenology[13] which instructed them to stay home and practice meekness, passivity, and subservience. Yet many women too timid to scandalize their kin by clamoring for electoral power still chafed under the multitudinous restrictions ladydom imposed. Likewise, women who avoided what they considered radical suffrage campaigns did not necessarily acquiesce in the doctrine of ideal ladydom. They railed against it from its inception in the early nineteenth century and demanded the autonomy which was central to nineteenth-century feminism.[14] In both the political world of the militant suffragist and the domestic world of the homemaker, women responded with anger to the limitations placed upon them. They differed, however, in their approach to the solution. American ladies could have been victims of self-effacement and martyrs to selflessness, but many of them found ways to evade society's restrictions. This book is a study of their struggle to leave the confines of the home without abandoning domestic values.

Through a study of the General Federation of Women's Clubs, and the literary clubs of which it was composed, this work demonstrates the relationship between the feminism of the suffragists and that of the clubwomen. The literary or culture club, devoted to the systematic study of literature, history, the arts, and current events, provided a significant alternative route toward women's self-development. Yet while numerous women's organizations have been studied—such as the National American Woman Suffrage Association, Women's Christian Temperance Union, Women's Trade Union League, National Consumers' League, abolition societies, and female auxiliaries to the Socialist Party—literary clubs have been ignored, dismissed as trivial or frivolous, or, at best, have been misunderstood as simply some of the many organizations formed at the turn of the century which were devoted to civic reform and improvement.[15]

Literary clubwomen, like most American women, were isolated, schooled only for service to others, powerless, and denigrated, even as they were revered. But as active agents, nineteenth-century women utilized the domestic and moral traits attributed to the ideal lady to increase autonomy, assert sorority, win education, and seize influence beyond the home in the forbidden public sphere. These women met together regularly in their clubs, developing friendships, confidence and knowledge. They demanded respect for the supposedly natural traits of morality and domesticity, not for the purpose of imprisoning themselves at home but in order to enlarge woman's sphere.

This book examines women's literary organizations as a form of Domestic Feminism. Daniel Scott Smith first used the phrase Domestic Feminism in 1974 to describe a growing autonomy which he perceived nineteenth-century women developing within the home, most notably by limiting sexual intercourse with their husbands.[16] Women justified their rejection of husbands in the bedroom by skillfully emphasizing the lady's traits: in order to be a good mother, a true woman, a conscientious lady, women had to limit sex and therefore children to improve the quality of the child care they could provide.[17] But Smith's phrase Domestic Feminism has far wider applications. Despite public criticism, thousands of nineteenth-century women effectively employed the lady's traits to justify their departure from the home to exert special influence on the male sphere. By invoking their supposed natural talents, women took the ideology of the home with them, ending their confinement and winning influence in the public realm. Domestic Feminism resulted when women redefined the ideal lady.

Before the Civil War, there were women who were struggling to embody the traits of the ideal lady, but who found the restrictions intolerable. In trying to adapt to the model, they altered it. The seeds of Domestic Feminism lay in the very ideal to which women aspired, for to maintain the viability of ladydom necessitated its transcendence. The work of Carroll Smith-Rosenberg on Moral Reform Societies demonstrates that women who sought to fulfill conventional moral expectations found themselves arriving at public influence when they contested the double standard inherent in widespread prostitution.[18] Nancy Cott has shown that the successful rationale for improving women's minds "was founded on, not opposed to, women's domestic occupation and material destiny."[19] The preservation of conventional appearances in the implementation of Domestic Feminism permitted the opening of new public avenues to women.

The politicization of Domestic Feminism, whereby women nurtured pride in the lady's special qualities and confidence to reach out into the public domain, began with the founding of Sorosis and the New England Woman's Club in 1868. These two women's clubs, begun simultaneously in New York City and Boston, were the first influential literary clubs of their kind—not rejecting the traditional imagery of the lady, but consciously building upon it. Their modifications made the role more palatable, for clubwomen transformed ladydom by providing an intellectual and social self-improvement program outside the realm of the household, designed to nurture the skills that would enable women to demand reforms for women and for all people in a society that had relegated them to the sidelines.

Early literary clubwomen expanded their numbers greatly in the late nineteenth century through speeches, conferences, federations, and varied programs which attracted women from all corners. That clubwomen endorsed the federal suffrage amendment in 1914 attests to their unfailing determination and success at providing women with vehicles for public decision-making. Although their ideology of Domestic Feminism did not totally reject traditional images of the lady, their espousal of the lady's special talents did not preclude radical political activity. The paths of clubwomen and suffragists united in 1914. Club support of the most forward-thinking branch of the era's feminist movement was the logical culmination of club ideology. The story of the literary club from 1868 until 1914 is also the examination of the movement to render obsolete the nineteenth-century cliché, "Woman's place is in the home."

## CHAPTER ONE

# Origins of the Culture Club Movement, 1800–1868

Before 1868 only a handful of women overtly rebelled against ladydom through woman's rights, abolition, and temperance movements. Most women tried to live up to the ideal lady image, but many resented its restrictions. The efforts of these less political women to break the bonds that held them in the home foreshadow the formation of literary clubs in America.

Domesticity and morality, however entrenched in the American ideal of womanhood, nevertheless became vehicles whereby ladies could alleviate the repression of domestic confinement. Woman's responsibility to set and maintain moral standards for her loved ones provided a loophole whereby she not only could but had to leave the home and exert influence on the public sphere. In her quest to fulfill her role as upholder of the good life, she, of necessity, had to supervise the moral standards of her community, or wickedness would destroy the home she had uplifted. In her quest to carry out her responsibilities thoroughly, she discovered routes to the mitigation of oppression on which postwar women would build the culture club movement.

With woman's supposedly natural inclinations toward morality, religious activity became the obvious way for a good woman to leave the home to exert some influence on the world around her. Her church activities expanded beyond attendance and domestic preparations for church functions to include weekly meetings for Bible reading called "mite societies." Every week, each member would contribute a penny to a fund which, at the end of the year, was used to purchase Bibles and tracts, or given to domestic missions, the poor, or a young man attending theological school. Women also began to distribute tracts and to run Sabbath Schools, which often provided children with the rudiments of an education in addition to religious instruction.[1] Thus, woman experienced a gradual but steady introduction to organizational work.

Some of the women engaged in this wider church participation began to feel a kinship with female coworkers and to develop a pride and confidence in the superior moral characteristics they shared. The solidarity which grew among women in church organizations spurred them to think of imposing their standards beyond the domestic sphere into the male public domain.

In the name of virtue, women in New York and New England who were enraged about moral decay set up Moral Reform Societies to abolish prostitution. The first society originated in 1834 in New York City's Third Presbyterian Church in response to a report that the city had ten thousand prostitutes. Moral reformers tried to rescue fallen women and failed, but their monthly newspaper, *The Advocate of Moral Reform*, with a national circulation of 16,500 by 1837, printed the names of men frequenting brothels. The embarrassment caused a diminution of prostitution wherever the program was established.[2]

The attempts by these women reformers to exercise a moral influence developed into a successful attack on some central aspects of male culture and led to the beginnings of Domestic Feminism. Women challenged male prerogatives by consistently applying the standards of the lady to the larger society. In the process, women learned to cooperate with each other, to organize, speak out at meetings, publish newspapers, and wield influence in the public sphere. With sorority came the recognition of woman's potential for protesting male abuses through political action which yielded women new influence.

Some of the Moral Reform Society members went on to more political feminist causes. Moral reformers like Clemence Lozier and Lucretia Mott later worked in such areas as abolition and suffrage. Most of the society members, however, did not move into radicalism, but became Domestic Feminists who concentrated on applying their moral qualities to the world at large through self-improvement and reform. These are the women who, in increasing their own autonomy without abandoning those qualities attributed to ladies, anticipated the literary club women of the late nineteenth century.

Just as efforts to embody ladydom through church work developed into reform movements, attempts to teach ladydom in the schools contributed to the growth of higher education for women. Although the admission that one needed to learn to be a lady seemed to go against notions that the role was natural to women, schools arose without fanfare to instruct young females in domestic and ladylike skills. Among the pioneers who elevated this branch of learning into a solid higher education for women were Emma Hart Willard, who established the Troy Female Academy in 1821, Catharine Beecher, who opened her Hartford Female Academy in 1823, and Mary Lyon, whose Mount Holyoke Seminary was opened in 1837.[3]

Included in the curriculum of these three schools was training in household accomplishments. Willard and Beecher were more explicit about this than Mary Lyon, who claimed, "I have thought that, in the proposed seminary, it would be well to have the domestic work done by the members, not as an essential feature of the institution, but as a mere appendage."[4] Whether or not she truly saw the program as a money-saving device or as a concession to society's norms is unknown, but there is no doubt that Mount Holyoke's domestic work made the innovation of higher education for women more palatable to a skeptical audience.

The schools placed many restrictions on women. The authoritarian teachers, rigid schedules, school bells, demerit systems, and heavy moral emphasis have led one historian to dismiss them as "masks of oppression."[5] To be sure, the presence of the fashionable ladylike elements of docility were real. Yet such schools simultaneously provided women with invaluable skills. Women studied such subjects as ancient languages, science, math, theology, philosophy, geometry, and anatomy, which previously had been denied to them. These educational reformers strove to secure endowments, scholarships, libraries, laboratories, equipment, and better teachers in order to turn the schools into stable and respectable centers for learning that could compete with men's colleges in facilities, curricula and teaching. They dared to provide physical education for women when more conservative supporters of ladydom doubted that the female anatomy could withstand exercise. The schools produced many teachers and missionaries and a few feminists, but more importantly, they provided girls with models of self-sufficient unmarried women and with firm friendships, self-confidence, and ambition.[6]

Not surprisingly, the coupling of higher education with domestic and moral training impressed many as befitting women. C. C. Smith, a book reviewer, wrote that although no one would "desire to see any woman enlisted in the fierce and angry strife of politics, or bending under the weight of cares designed only for the sterner sex," women should develop their minds because education would enhance their characters.[7] The Reverend Hubbard Winslow, who opposed women dealing with public issues, urged eight hours a day for study, arguing that it was important to diffuse knowledge as well as moral influence upon the family.[8] Women who did not expect to alter the traits which constituted ladydom but only to enhance them, nevertheless contributed modification of the ideology. They had begun to extend woman's influence outside the home through their increasing knowledge and self-confidence.

As hundreds of women in New York and New England participated in religious and educational endeavors that foreshadowed the development of the late nineteenth-century club movement, those women who were to become the actual leaders of the movement were becoming politicized by the discrimination they were experiencing as they pioneered new careers for their sex. Whether working of necessity or for fulfillment, women in the middle of the century pushed into teaching, medicine, ministry, journalism, and writing. The attraction of careers was great despite strong resistance to woman's participation. Freedom, adventure, independence, responsibility and, not unimportantly, salary, were great incentives. "It is impossible to forget the sense of dignity which marks the hour when one becomes a wage-earner," said Elizabeth Stuart Phelps,[9] a successful novelist. These were women who not only felt the constraints of ladydom in the home but were also victims of the slights inflicted upon budding career women in the public arena. Their own experience, with the restrictions imposed by misconceptions about ladies' abilities, developed in many women doctors, teachers, writers, and ministers a determination to somehow alter woman's subordinate status.

The early pioneers in careers for women found that the accepted traits of ladies could be used against them. Woman medical students were particularly vulnerable because of the undue importance placed on female modesty by men and women alike. When Elizabeth Blackwell attended medical school, she had to fight for the right to attend classes in anatomical dissection, which were considered indelicate for a gentle lady.[10] In contrast, when Harriet Clisby, later the founder of the Women's Educational and Industrial Union, attended the Bellevue Hospital Clinic in New York City, she complained that a male doctor was trying to humiliate her and other women students by telling a male patient to undress in front of them.[11] The problems did not cease once the students became physicians. Women doctors like Sorosis member Dr. Anna Manning Comfort were subjected to innumerable unnecessary irritations.

> Male physicians declined to consult her, druggists refused to put up her prescriptions, her signs were torn from her office door, she was often summoned on false calls. Her early patients would ask to see her diploma and catechise her on irrelevant subjects, and, the most vital of all, would exclaim: "What! Do you mean to say that you ask me as much as a man doctor?"[12]

Other career women encountered similar evidence of sexism resulting from the popular image of the lady. Suffragist and New England Woman's Club member Lucy Stone replaced her brother at the head of the classroom, but the salary was cut from thirty to sixteen dollars per month.[13] When the Reverend Anna Howard Shaw went to preach in a northern lumber camp, her nighttime travel caused the stage driver to assume that she was a loose woman since no lady traveled alone. She responded to his threats by holding a gun on him until he delivered her safely to camp.[14]

Most women were not willing to demand respect at gunpoint. More typically, women tried to win acceptance by emphasizing their commendable feminine traits. The method used by Women's Educational and Industrial Union supporter Ellen Richards, the first woman to do graduate work in chemistry at the Massachusetts Institute of Technology, plainly illustrated the pattern other career women would follow in the club movement.

> I hope in a quiet way, I am winning a way which others will keep open. Perhaps the fact that I am not a Radical or a believer in the all powerful ballot for women to right her wrongs and that I do not scorn womanly duties, but claim it as a privilege to clean up and sort of supervise the room and sew things, etc., is winning me stronger allies than anything else. Even Professor A. accords me his sanction when I sew his papers or tie up a sore finger or dust the table.[15]

Rather than denying the domesticity assigned to ladies, Richards employed it to make her presence tolerable in a field heretofore hostile to women. Her self-conscious use of ladylike qualities is an early example of Domestic Feminism—women winning a place outside the home using domestic credentials.

With this same technique, Richards would later become a pivotal figure in the home economics movement.

Women writers independently discovered Richards' strategy to facilitate their entrance into the literary market. Particularly attractive because it did not necessitate direct conflict in the male sphere of hospitals or laboratories, writing allowed woman to labor in her own sphere and receive compensation for her efforts. Also, the creativity of writing was thought to be well-suited to the lady's intuitive sensibility. Women authors often got their start by writing about housekeeping, the topic they were supposed to know best. Thomas Wentworth Higginson judged that "it seemed to be held necessary for American women to work their passage into literature by first compiling a cookery-book."[16] These works generally taught women how to accomplish their household duties more efficiently so they could relieve the drudgery of their chores.[17]

Many women enjoyed extraordinary success by writing for women about their common experiences.[18] Critics were harsh on them for their obsession with domestic detail and their distance from high art. But in these books were female characters who used their domestic and moral traits to step out of their traditional roles. Fanny Fern, the penname for Sara Willis Parton, was particularly able in using this technique in her numerous books.[19] A feminist and suffragist, Fern scorned the leisured antisuffragists who failed to see how the ballot would especially help wage-earning women. "She may never see or hear of those other women, who may be lifted out of their wretched condition, of low wages and starvation, by this very lever of power."[20] Yet like many women before her, she urged their cautious expression of discontent. In *Life and Beauties of Fanny Fern*, she said on female rights: "...Better policy to play possum, and wear the mask of submission. No use in rousing any unnecessary antagonism...I shall reach the goal just as quick in my velvet shoes, as if I tramped on rough-shod as they do with their Woman's Rights Convention brogans."[21]

Fern's writings well illustrate the trend in popular literature of this period to portray woman as the undeserving victim. She records countless incidents of insensitive, oafish men. In "Mrs. Cracker," the wife who does not want her husband under foot must urge him to stay home because she knows he always does the opposite. "A Lady on Money Matters" immortalizes a woman who slaves over a sick husband and then, after asking for fifty cents, is quizzed about how she spent the last sum he gave her. In "The Widow's Trials," a man refuses to hire his widowed niece on his newspaper but steals her work and then brags about her when she later becomes famous without his help. "Aunt Hetty on Matrimony" best sums up the philosophy of the author, who suffered three unhappy marriages. "It is the hardest way on earth of getting a living."[22]

Fern scorned the slavish devotion to housework that was lauded by proponents of ladydom. "Nobody will thank you for turning yourself into a machine. When you drop in your tracks, they will just shovel the earth over you and get Jerusha Ann Somebody to step into your shoes."[23] And instead of idealizing maternity, she advocated abortion for some women. Calling guides for young wives "Moral Molasses":

> I would like to write a book on some kinds of legal murder; that is if really *good* people had not such moonshine notions about "delicacy." This class are really the drags on the wheel of reform.... What of the ten or twelve, even healthy children "who come," one after another, into the weary arms of a really good woman, who yet never knows the meaning of the word *rest* til the coffin lid shuts her in from all earthly cares and pain?[24]

Her message urged women to exert moral power. In "Kitty's Resolve," the belle of the ball is able to exude such charm that the intemperate lawyer abstains from alcohol. Yet attainment of power and influence did not preclude ladylike behavior. Career women, for instance, could be good women. In both "A Practical Blue-Stocking" and "A Chapter on Women," the surprising endings reveal a woman writer who is also a loveable homemaker.[25]

It is not surprising that Fern and writers like her, as well as other career women, wholeheartedly supported the club movement. Club goals were compatible with their goals. Both groups sought to gain women power as moral homemakers and as sensitive career women not by breaking out of their prescribed roles but by stretching them a bit and circumventing them when necessary. In 1868 these career women would found the most influential clubs in the history of the literary club movement.

Literary clubs had begun to spring up even before 1868. Suffragist Elizabeth Buffum Chase recorded her participation in a prewar Female Mutual Improvement Society in New England. In this group girls met each week to read useful books and to exchange original compositions.[26] As early as 1800, women in Chelsea, Connecticut, in addition to their charity and temperance work, founded a literary society "to enlighten the understanding and expand the ideas of its members, and to promote useful knowledge" by reading such works as *History of Columbus*, Watts's *Treatise of the Mind*, and Trumbull's *History of Connecticut*.

These were only two of many clubs.[27] Throughout the United States, women, including Sorosis founders Alice Cary, Mary E. Booth, and Kate Field who formed the Hearth Stone literary society between 1852 and 1858,[28] were establishing antecedents for the late nineteenth-century trend toward women's clubs.

These women were budding feminists, critical of women who spent too much time on clothes when the mind needed adorning. They were defensive about the accusation that inquisitiveness was a stigma on women. Curiosity, they claimed, was the source of all knowledge. "The idea of woman's incapability is entirely preposterous," the clubwomen asserted, there being "no summits in the broad field of literature which a female cannot explore."[29]

Although literary clubs were largely in abeyance during the Civil War, the war years contributed to, rather than stifled, the club spirit. The conflict provided a unique opportunity for women, predominantly among the affluent,[30] to strengthen the skills they had acquired in their antebellum religious and educational reform efforts. Patriotism legitimated women's participation in the Sanitary Commission, a voluntary association which raised about thirty million dollars to purchase food, uniforms, and medical supplies for the Union soldiers. The group also screened nurses for the army hospitals, competed with men for government contracts for the manufacture of army clothing, and hired the wives of volunteer soldiers to make the uniforms. Sanitary Commission women coordinated huge fairs in every big northern city, raising millions of dollars by selling donated gifts, and providing entertainment, refreshments, and exhibits. They set up free "hotels" for soldiers in transport—entertaining six hundred thousand men, serving four and a half million meals, and providing one million nights' lodgings.[31] While such work in serving the army could be likened to the self-sacrificing service they were expected to practice in the home, women gained for themselves further experience in working with other women, and a pride in the organization's massive accomplishments.

After the Civil War ended, literary clubs developed rapidly. Self-consciously political feminists began to build their own philosophy of woman's role from their own career experience and expanded it with the support of women such as those who worked in prewar religious and educational institutions and in the Sanitary Commission. These were women who tried to be ladies but created, in the process, a new and broader role for women. The efforts to become truly domestic and moral ladies yielded in practice an influential Domestic Feminism.

CHAPTER TWO

# Sorosis and the New England Woman's Club

The founders of Sorosis and the New England Woman's Club (NEWC) first effectively articulated and implemented the ideology of Domestic Feminism as a philosophy for clubwomen. Both organizations were established in 1868. Although not the first of their kind, they were the most influential forerunners of the widespread culture club movement of the late nineteenth century. While their location permitted them to assemble some of the most extraordinary women in America, women everywhere could emulate their format and copy their programs as they tried to inspire American womanhood to abolish the constraints on the growth of women's talent. The members were self-conscious, indeed, self-interested individuals who were ambitious for themselves and their sex. Beyond the sisterhood and self-confidence inspired in the membership, the clubs provided a forum where the demand for women's rights could be expressed. Members justified both self-improvement and action to erode sexism by invoking the domesticity and morality ladies were supposed to embody. Not at the expense of the wholesome family, but because of the talents nurtured there, would clubwomen collaborate. They based their efforts to provide alternatives for women on the assurance that such work would make them better ladies rather than deserters of the home. This philosophy won enormous support among women. The appeal of Domestic Feminism lay in its redefinition of the ideal of ladydom while it affirmed its soundness.

The founder of Sorosis was Jane Cunningham Croly, the single most important figure in the woman's club movement. A determined feminist and journalist whose work was widely syndicated under the pen name Jennie June, Croly was born in Leicestershire, England, in 1829. She became acquainted with controversy early in life when her father, a Unitarian preacher, tried to hold classes to educate workers, much to the anger of their neighbors. The family emigrated in 1841 to New York state. Jane attended public school and later became a teacher while keeping house in Massachusetts for her minister brother and writing a small semimonthly newspaper for his congregation.[1]

In 1855, a year after her father's death, Jane Cunningham went to New York and sold her first article to Charles A. Dana, assistant editor of the *New York Tribune*. Soon she was writing a ladies' column for several newspapers, which made her one of the first syndicated woman columnists in America.[2] In 1856 she married David Goodman Croly, an Irish immigrant on the staff of the *New York Herald*. Three years later they bought a weekly newspaper in Rockford, Illinois, and began publishing the *Rockford Daily News*.

David Croly was editor and publisher of the paper, but there are indications that Jane Croly was also involved in the venture. She wrote a column, "Gossip with and for Ladies," later called "Home Department," but this apparently was not her only duty. The *Rockford Republican*, a rival newspaper, included in a report on her husband's progress: "Jenny, like a true woman, has joined him in his labors and toiled incessantly."[3] One Rockford resident even declared, "She edited the paper and he played chess."[4] The newspaper ceased publication on 30 April 1860, and they returned to New York, where both began working for the new *New York World*. By 1862 David was managing editor of the paper. Meanwhile, Jennie June managed the *World*'s Woman's Department from 1862 until 1872 and contributed women's and cultural news to other publications.[5] In 1860 she began her twenty-seven-year association with *Mme. Demorest's Mirror of Fashions* (later *Demorest's Monthly Magazine*), which she coedited for many years. She also wrote for *Frank Leslie's Weekly* and *Graham's Magazine*. In addition, she prepared sewing manuals for the Demorest pattern company, edited three homemakers' guides and numerous magazines, and wrote several books: *American Cookery Book* (1886); *Talks on Women's Topics* (1869), which was a collection of her articles; *For Better or Worse: A Book for Some Men and All Women* (1875); *Thrown on Her Own Resources* (1891), and the *History of the Woman's Club Movement in America* (1898).[6]

While writing, she was also raising four children. In the mornings Croly took care of the family and the domestic duties. At noon she went to her office to write.[7] There was also time in her busy schedule for associations with many of the literary celebrities of the day. The Crolys entertained Louisa May Alcott, Oscar Wilde, poets Alice and Phoebe Cary, poet and journalist Ella Wheeler Wilcox, and also the famed agnostic, Robert Ingersoll.

Necessity, in addition to ambition, prompted Jane Croly's astounding efforts. From 1879 until his death in 1889, David was sick with Bright's disease, so Jane began to support the family. Soon after her husband's death, she became the first woman in the United States to teach newswriting. Columbia University opened a school called Rutger's Woman's College where Croly taught journalism.

It was through journalism that Croly most clearly articulated her response to woman's inferior status in America. By her ability to express feelings that women all over America shared, she made herself the force from which the Sorosis membership and, indirectly, all clubs drew direction. Jennie June Croly's analysis of women's oppression derived from her observations about her own struggle and those of her friends, many of them career women. Although her vision concentrated on skilled women, much that she articulated was applicable to women of all social strata.

In assessing the ways in which women had been shortchanged, she recognized the two separate spheres of nineteenth-century America, the public and the private. While the bulk of her remarks criticized the prevailing standards of the domestic world in which women spent most of their time, she also wrote against women's exclusion from the public realm. Change must take place on both fronts, Croly insisted, for women to lead satisfying lives. Women's work in the home should neither be scorned nor abandoned; it should be elevated. And women should use their domestically nurtured talents to influence the world outside the home. Croly's refusal to relinquish the domestic sphere and her attempt to reconcile it with public influence yielded the Domestic Feminism that club members practiced.

Croly's writing traced the roots of women's difficulties in society. She focused on the faulty upbringing of girls, which produced unhappy, unhealthy, and unskilled women. From the start, the young girl's behavior was curbed until she learned to stifle her spontaneous inclinations in order to protect her physical features and her image as a fragile being.

> The little girl must not play out of doors when she is little, because it will spoil her complexion. She must not run when she is older, because people will think her a tom-boy; whatever her faculties are, she must only put them to use in a certain way, because there are only a few things that society admits a woman can do, or will tolerate her doing.... No wonder women are ill-formed, ill-made, half-made, and not at all grown into natural womanhood—the wonder is, that there is anything left of them at all. If nature had not been stronger than conventionalisms, nothing would have been left of them.[8]

Not only did firm restrictions on natural behavior patterns outrage Croly, she viewed the young girl's formal education as hampering the productivity of most women. Croly dismissed the ornamental arts as frivolous and condemned women's "jingling on the piano, her faint watercolor sketches."[9] Significantly, she simultaneously rejected the advancing efforts to provide girls with higher scholarship. It is not that she failed to recognize the importance of serious intellectual endeavor, but rather that she simply considered it impractical for women whose reality in America during the 1860s was marriage and motherhood.[10]

The inhibition of physical freedom and the useless education girls received naturally hindered women from developing worthwhile talents. Their minds were diverted toward the pursuit of clothes, presents, and parties, empty attractions for which women had to further demean themselves by relying on fathers, beaux, and husbands. "She does not realize for sometime, perhaps, the sort of obligation under which she has placed herself; to what extent she has sold her freedom, her peace of mind, her self-respect, her truth, and loyalty, for this mess of pottage,"[11] Croly warned her readers. The faulty upbringing inevitably produced not only a deformed human being, but also one who depended on men for support and approval.

Like Fanny Fern, Croly realized that despite training for a pampered existence, most women were called upon to demonstrate great strength in marriage. Lack of preparation did not prevent many strong women from summoning great vigor and common sense to boost the males who failed to shield the supposedly frail sex from life's problems. A great many women rose to the occasion while seeming to remain deferential and charming.

> They must shine equally in the parlor and in the kitchen; they must be indefatigable as baby–tenders; prudent and lynx–eyed as housekeepers, they must be ten Bridgets rolled into one, while their husbands are poor; they must be able to entertain princes and appear as the most brilliant and accomplished of women when he becomes rich; they must be the traditional ivy; trusting, tender, confiding, gentle, and passive, while he is speculating away the future, and the oak, when, as so often happens, he sinks under the pressure of his reverses.[12]

The role of motherhood assumed an important part in Croly's thought, as it did in the daily life of most women who married in an era without reliable birth control. Maternity seemed to be the greatest barrier to the admission of women into the enticing public sphere. The realization that woman could enjoy public influence only through her sons was the cruel culmination of a life of deprivation. "The unformed and inexperienced mind and heart of the young girl will not accept this conclusion; her aspirations are all toward the realization of her dreams, in her own proper person. Why should she not be counted in the list of the world's great ones?"[13]

Childbirth and child-raising, however, were inevitable for most women in the mid-nineteenth century. Not only did Croly accommodate to this reality, she, like a true lady, elevated the function until it became superior to any work men could accomplish. "The young wife about to become a mother should look upon herself as, in a manner, consecrated to the Divine will and purpose in humanity. She may be poor in purse, her house may be narrow, her wardrobe destitute of silks or jewels; but she is about to bring into the world an heir of all the ages."[14]

Yet Croly's sanctification of women's biological functions did not preclude their entrance into the public sphere. It merely established women's superiority over men. The maternal sensitivity, moral superiority, and domestic ability which she ascribed to women made them all the better equipped to influence the public sphere. That women be permitted to use this knowledge was essential, Croly insisted, because families did not provide sufficient purpose for women. Child-raising was not mission enough. "The objectless lives that most women lead, are responsible for nine-tenths of the 'nerves,' the 'low spirits,' the 'depressions,' the 'liver complaints,' and the 'general debility,' that American women especially suffer from."[15] Leaving the home to make an impact on the public sphere, through a job or some clubwork, was her solution.

Croly had little regard for the men who dominated the society which oppressed women. She did not expect most men to assist ladies in breaking out of the home. Rather, she supposed women must work around men and hope to win approval when female influence yielded a richer society for all. Thus, because women failed to take initiative to demand change, Croly held them responsible for the sorry state of their own position. Her solution was a simple one; women must take control of their own lives and work together to demand the specific changes they desired.

The kinds of change women needed were varied. In order for women to enter the public sphere, the work in the domestic world must be handled with utmost efficiency. A new education was required that would enable women to understand "chemical composition of food and the physiological reasons for clothing." She should have botanical and health care information at her fingertips.[16] Systematic housekeeping and freer clothing for the easy operation of the home must be achieved before women could consider leaving their homes. Croly expected women to continue to run their houses smoothly, but with minimal effort. Once this was achieved, women must spend the rest of their energies and talents on improving the public sphere, both by applying their sensitivity to solve social problems and by acquiring the education which would permit them to enter satisfying occupations heretofore closed to women.

Croly experimented with a number of plans to foster woman's entrance into the public sphere. In 1889 she began the Woman's Press Club of New York City. She was vice-president of the Association for the Advancement of Medical Education for Women. She was president of the Women's Endowment Cattle Company, organized to earn profits for women. The company had a capital stock of one and a half million dollars and controlled two million acres of grazing land in New Mexico with thousands of head of cattle. But her most effective strategy for creating a united effort to alter public deficiencies and to attain education, skills, and positions in male-dominated careers was the founding of women's clubs. Clubs could nurture a pride in woman's special domestic and moral abilities and could serve as a gathering place for discussing women's perceptions of personal and social problems. Finally, these associations would provide a way for women to leave the home and create a force to rectify the ills they had identified.

Croly might have turned to the growing woman suffrage movement to voice her concerns about woman's place in America. Many women, in the aftermath of the Civil War, looked to one of the two new suffrage organizations—the National Woman Suffrage Association based in New York City and led by Elizabeth Cady Stanton and Susan B. Anthony, or the more moderate, Boston-based American Woman Suffrage Association—to achieve change for women. Certainly Croly felt women should not be denied the franchise. But, political equality for women was an explosive issue because it challenged woman's place in the home and demanded for them "a kind of power and a connection with the social order not based on the institution of the family and their subordination within it."[17] Seeking redress of grievances through overtly political means scared off male and female supporters of limited change who feared they would be supporting abolition of the home. Croly wanted to attract the large numbers who shared her complaints. Her club movement with its Domestic Feminist ideology enabled her to do that without contesting, indeed, by elevating, woman's place in the home. While she did not avoid public criticism, she did win more supporters than suffrage did.

Thus, armed with a dismal view of women's lives, but a firm conviction that women could improve them, Croly launched Sorosis in April 1868. The immediate cause for the founding of the club was the exclusion of women from a New York Press Club dinner for Charles Dickens during his lecture tour of the United States in March. When Jane Croly applied for a ticket to the affair, many Press Club members thought it a joke that she should dare to propose to make this a "promiscuous" social occasion, despite the fact that her husband headed the executive committee. Yet James Parton, the husband of Fanny Fern and another journalist on the committee, thought women deserved serious consideration. His wife soon added her application to Croly's, and other women followed. *New York Tribune* editor Horace Greeley supported the female applicants and refused to preside at the occasion unless "the women had a chance." It was not until three days before the affair that the committee finally told Croly that "if a sufficient number of ladies could be found willing to pay fifteen dollars each for their tickets, to make a good showing, and prevent each other from feeling lonely," they would be permitted to attend the dinner for Dickens. Croly refused to be assuaged and declined, saying the "ladies had not been treated like gentlemen."[18] This incident inspired Croly to form the organization which she felt was needed to improve women's status.

Not surprisingly, she called upon her friends, largely writers, to initiate the club experiment. Among them was Kate Field, writer and newspaper reporter. Anne Botta wrote for the *New York Mirror* and poet Josephine Pollard wrote for the *New York Ledger*, and wrote monosyllabic books for children. Charlotte Beebe Wilbour wrote *Soul to Soul*. Ellen Louise Demorest coedited *Mme. Demorest's Mirror of Fashion*, a leading fashion magazine, with Jane Croly and Mr. Demorest for years. Alice and Phoebe Cary were poets, Ella Dietz Clymer would publish three books in the late 1870s and 1880s, and Celia M. Burleigh became a minister shortly after the club began.[19]

After two preparatory meetings at Croly's home, the first meeting of the club was held at Delmonico's Restaurant on 13 April 1868. The organization challenged the status quo by the very meeting place it chose. One member later explained, "Prior to this, no woman, even in daylight, when unattended, could procure a meal at a first-class restaurant in New York. Neither could she get a room in a reputable hotel. Grievous restrictions hedged about evening amusements, lectures, and concerts. The greater liberty of action heartily enjoyed by women today [1893] is primarily due to women's clubs."[20]

Almost immediately, a conflict arose over a name for the club. The women were self-conscious about the impression they wanted to create and felt that an organization so vulnerable to abuse had to choose a title with utmost care.

Many names were suggested, including "Order of the Pen" and "Blue-stocking," which were rejected as sounding too literary. To some, "Women's League" sounded too political and masculine.[21] Then Croly and Wilbour happened upon "Sorosis" in a botanical dictionary. The term, which referred to plants with an aggregation of flowers that bore fruit, well suggested the women's determination to turn supposedly frail and lovely ladies into vital presences in the public sphere. The selection of this value-free title eliminated fears about appearing offensively "strong-minded" and also prevented confusion with organizations of different goals.

The club met twice a month, on Mondays, at Delmonico's. Members paid a five dollar initiation fee and were expected to take a pledge of loyalty. Meetings were devoted alternately to business and to social matters. On social days, lunch was followed by papers, entertainments, or speeches. Attendance was higher[22] and guests also boosted audience size on social days. Not surprisingly, professional responsibilities, child care, bad weather, travel, and illness influenced attendance, but since much of the work of Sorosis was carried on through committees, projects developed at a steady pace.

Membership in Sorosis was not open to all. The founders sent invitations to the earliest members. Later, a committee of Sorosis officers reviewed applications from potential candidates. Three blackballs excluded any hopeful from membership. In addition, Sorosis was determined to prohibit the admission of all men. Croly said women should work and work alone "because men would overpower them if they tried to work together."[23] Sorosis maintained its aloofness from men throughout its history. It saw its work in the association of women, not in integration. The only formal contact Sorosis had with men concerned the New York Press Club's apology over the Dickens affair. On 13 June 1868 the men invited Sorosis's members to a breakfast. Although they meant well, the men never let their guests utter a word during all the speeches and toasts. The women responded in kind at a tea for the men on 17 April 1869. Sorosis members took over the proceedings and allowed the men no participation in the occasion.[24] Finally, a dinner was held by the two groups. Croly boasted that it was the first great public dinner at which women ever sat down on equal terms with men, paying their own way and sharing the honors and the services.[25] One newspaper remarked, with surprise, that "the fair speakers were not a bit embarrassed,"[26] thereby crediting Sorosis with a breakthrough for women's advancement.

The women who joined Sorosis were, by and large, career women who had become keenly aware of sexism in their struggle for professional success.[27] Many, especially in the early years, were writers and journalists such as Hester M. Poole, Mary "Marion Harland" Terhune, Caroline Soule, Elizabeth Akers Allen, Eliza Archibald Conner, Rebecca Morse, Helen Campbell, Phebe Hanaford, and occasionally out-of-towners May Wright Sewall and Jane Grey Swisshelm. But women of many careers belonged to Sorosis. Late in the century, Christine Hayley Higley published a club woman's magazine, *The Woman's Cycle*. Ella Dietz Clymer turned to the stage, as did Kate Field.

Catherine Weed Barnes was a pioneering photographer. Singers Madame Clara Brinkerhoff, Clara Stutsman, and Vienna Demorest, stepdaughter of Ellen Demorest, were Sorosis members. The architect of the Connecticut Building of the 1893 Chicago World's Fair, Miss Elizabeth B. Sheldon, belonged. Teaching absorbed the attention of Anne C. Botta, May Wright Sewall, Clara Brinkerhoff, Phebe Hanaford, and Jennie Lozier. Kate Field and Celia Burleigh were lecturers.

Women in the arts and cultural fields did not monopolize Sorosis. Phoebe Couzins was the first woman admitted to law school in America. Several physicians were counted among Sorosis numbers—Anna Dinsmore French, Georgina M. Crosby, Helen S. Lassen, Harriet C. Keating, and two relatives of the feminist physician Clemence S. Lozier—her niece, gynecologist Anna Manning Comfort, and her daughter-in-law, Jennie de La Montagnie Lozier. Jane Grey Swisshelm had been a Civil War nurse. M. Louise Thomas was a botanist and agriculturalist. Mrs. Zilpah Plumb established the Light Gymnastic School for Women in New York City. Phebe Hanaford, cousin of Lucretia Mott, became a Universalist minister in 1868, and went on to serve as the first woman chaplain in a state legislature. Caroline Soule was also a Universalist minister. Celia Burleigh was ordained the first woman Unitarian minister. Ellen Demorest ran a department store and a dress pattern company in addition to her magazine. When Croly reported that Sorosis had eighty-three members after one year of existence, she proudly enumerated, "Among them were six artists or workers in art, twenty-two authors, six editors, one historian, eleven poets, nine teachers and lecturers, eight well-known philanthropists, two physicians, four writers on science, besides others who were contributors to periodicals."[28] When Sorosis grew,[29] still more professional women would be attracted.

Many of the members had entered careers not by choice but because they had been thrown on their own resources. Caroline Soule, who was widowed at the age of twenty-seven and left with five young children, became a writer and a minister. Fanny Fern tried writing only after sewing and teaching paid too little to support her two surviving children when her marriage failed. Swisshelm left her husband. Hanaford was divorced. For numerous club members, reliance on a male breadwinner was impossible.

Many women who joined had also been active in various reforms. In addition to maintaining careers, Rebecca Morse, Jane Grey Swisshelm, the Cary sisters, and M. Louise Thomas had been staunch abolitionists. Mrs. Ella Dietz Clymer lived at the Utopian community of New Harmony along with her aunt and fellow Sorosis member, Mrs. Robert Dale Owen, wife of the community founder. Ernestine Rose, a Polish Jew, tried living at a Utopian community in Skaneateles, New York.

Like so many nineteenth-century reformers, many of the members also were deeply involved in women's rights. Among the active suffragists were Phoebe Cary, Phoebe Couzins, Jane Grey Swisshelm, Anna Manning Comfort, Isabella Beecher Hooker, Ernestine Rose, Charlotte Wilbour, and Dr. Mary

Putnam Jacobi. In 1872 Hooker spoke before the Senate Judiciary Committee with Susan B. Anthony in support of the federal suffrage amendment. In 1869 Rose helped Stanton and Anthony turn the Equal Rights Association into the National Woman's Suffrage Association. Wilbour was an early president of the New York Woman's Suffrage Association, and Jacobi would write *Common Sense Applied to Woman Suffrage* in 1894.

Most of the members were adventurous women. Whether motivated by circumstance or uncontainable talent and energy, they were driven to explore avenues unknown to most women. Even so, they could not disregard the difficulties of maintaining both their femininity and self-respect while they tried to reconcile their careers and their private lives. Their discomfiture pushed them into the club in hopes of finding succor, edification, and concrete solutions to their predicament. The professional writers, doctors, and ministers who met in Sorosis needed to create a respectable place for themselves in a society that disdained ambitious women.

In founding Sorosis, Jane Croly wanted to create a harmonious environment for women which would foster unity through their common experience with injustice. To that end, she discouraged discussion of potentially incendiary topics, notably suffrage and religion. Although the bulk of the membership agreed with her basic analysis of woman's oppression and her Domestic Feminist strategy for correcting it, the diverse women who joined Sorosis sometimes brought dissenting impulses that ran contrary to Croly's plans. There was a movement to assist New York women typesetters in unionizing to which Croly did not subscribe. Members initiated some charitable programs such as fund-raising for victims of disease and disaster throughout the world which were all too reminiscent of traditional work for women. Sorosis's history is not a story of total conformity, yet members shared a dissatisfaction with woman's place in society and a need for support and cooperation from other women.

Sorosis served as a forum for mental stimulation among these women. Croly's followers sought women "hungry for the society of women, that is, for the society of those whose deeper natures had been roused to activity, who had been seized by the divine spirit of inquiry and aspiration, who were interested in the thought and progress of the age, and in what other women were thinking and doing."[30] The Sorosis constitution defined its purpose this way:

> The object of this association is to promote agreeable and useful relations among women of literary and artistic tastes.... It recognizes women of thought, culture and humanity everywhere, particularly when these qualities have found expression in outward life and work.
>
> It aims to establish a kind of freemasonry among women of similar pursuits, to render them helpful to each other, and bridge over the barrier which custom and social etiquette place in the way of friendly intercourse.
>
> It affords an opportunity for the discussion among women, of new facts and principles, the results of which promise to exert an important influence on the future of women and the welfare of society.[31]

Less abstractly, Sorosis's first president, Alice Cary, expressed hope that this association would foster confidence in women. Sorosis should make them able to "open out new avenues of employment to women, to make them less dependent and less burdensome, to lift women out of unwomanly self-distrust, disqualifying diffidence, into womanly self-respect and self-knowledge."[32] The club founders further "proposed the inoculation of deeper and broader ideas among women, proposed to teach them to think for themselves, and get their opinions at first hand, not so much because it is their right as because it is their duty."[33]

Although the officers meant that woman's first duty was to herself, they believed that it was wiser public relations to stress the collective benefits rather than the personal gains for women. Consequently, Sorosis members tended to temper their interest in self with a vision of altruism. They insisted that concern for others, not for self, prompted women to join Sorosis. They also assured the public that any gains which benefited women would in turn benefit everyone. Thus, outsiders should view Sorosis's ultimate goal as helping all human-kind—work that had long been assigned to ladies.

In spite of the members' efforts, the fact that Sorosis in practice concentrated on self-growth and refused to align itself with any particular concern caused many observers to question the club's altruism. The members' selfishness baffled even liberal newspapers like the *New York World*, of which Croly's husband was managing editor. After greeting the club's formation nervously—"Woman has laid down the broomstick to pick up the club"—and then applauding Sorosis for its antagonism to gossip and fashion,[34] the *World* became disgruntled when the club formally refused to respond to Susan B. Anthony's invitation to support the Working Women's Association. This organization, an alliance between suffragists and female wage earners for the purpose of forming women's trade unions, appealed to some Sorosis members, but was not attractive to Croly and the other women who preferred to examine their own problems rather than associating with wage-earning women. While the *New York World* gave extensive uncritical coverage to the meetings of the Working Women's Association and the Boston Working Women's League,[35] it chastised Sorosis. "If the organization was designed solely to meet for 'toast and tea,' why form a conspicuous club to do so?" the *World* asked.[36] Upon Sorosis's first anniversary, the *New York World*, in an editorial entitled "A Sigh for Sorosis," declared the club a failure. "If we are to take them at their own word, the lovely ladies of the Sorosis have not done nearly so much as we had hoped they might towards improving and elevating the sex to which it is their duty, as we hope it is their pleasure, to belong."[37]

Croly defended Sorosis's preoccupation with self-growth for members, to the exclusion of any other priorities. "It is not the province of a Sorosis to identify herself with any special reform, but to give encouragement and inspiration to all reforms,"[38] she insisted. Her advocacy of self-help and personal growth was not inconsequential.

Suppose...that some of us did begin to realize that we were growing more and more stupid, and more and more "dull," and more and more "inane" every day, and determined to do something to help ourselves, and that something was Sorosis, would not even that be accomplishing a little? It takes a certain length of time for a model woman to learn even to go to Delmonico's and pay for a lunch to eat her own self...[sic][39]

Yet she admitted this was a more threatening program than acceptance of the self-sacrificing route. "Had Sorosis started to *do* any one thing, from building an asylum for aged and indigent 'females' to supplying the natives of Timbuctoo with pocket handkerchiefs, it would have found a public already made...."[40]

If the *New York World* chose to express wonder at Sorosis for its narrowness, other newspapers found different reasons to criticize the new organization. Some were skeptical about the ability of mere women to congregate in harmony. A *New York Times* editor, after prophesizing an early death for Sorosis, wrote that many men would have to recant their opinions with regard to women if the club lived a year.[41] The *London Queen*, a woman's periodical, begrudgingly wrote, "We hope that Sorosis may be able to hold well together, if only to prove that women are not destitute of the power of acting harmoniously together when they choose to do so." Generally, it expressed incredulity at their audacity by maintaining, "The idea is a ludicrous one."[42]

The novelty of women meeting together and potentially neglecting their homes for a few hours each month outraged the influential *Harper's Weekly*. In the 15 May 1869 issue, cartoonist Charles G. Bush characterized his view of Sorosis meetings by illustrating nervous husbands caring for their babies on the stairs while the wives orated and carried on in a most masculine, political fashion.[43] The cartoon implied that self-interest was incompatible with ladydom. Club members, however, were not convinced that their self-interest was alien to ladydom. Since they still considered themselves ladies, they proceeded to seek means of self-growth in areas that had been traditionally linked with them, particularly with the arts.

Sorosis's business was conducted, at first, through four basic committees, reflecting the cultural interests of the membership: literature, art, drama, and music—all part of their training in ladydom. Partial explanation for the members' interest in culture lies in their level of sophistication. Most Sorosis clubwomen had been well-educated, even if self-taught, and had sometimes traveled in Europe. In addition, since many members earned their living as writers, literature and aesthetics were a part of their daily life. But more important was the idea that women had an inherent interest in culture.

Croly felt, as her friends did, that "women have special sympathy for this culture for culture's sake."[44] While this did not mean that they endorsed the antebellum association of "lady" with dilettantism—Sorosis's program was a far cry from ornamental embroidery and sketching—still, the clubwomen's

"Sorosis, 1869," from *Harper's Weekly*, May 15, 1869, drawn by Charles G. Bush.

affinity for culture was related to the traits of the stereotypical lady. A strong bond existed between the spirituality attributed to the lady and her comfort in the spiritual realm of the arts. If ladies were supposed to be naturally other-worldly and intuitive in their care for others, it was logical that they were well-suited to explore the abstractness of the arts. Furthermore, the compatability of the moral lady and the uplifting quality of the arts made their coexistence probable. Sorosis members discussed, "Is the influence of the nude in art upon public taste healthful or hurtful?" They debated whether "the theatre should be made a school of taste, culture, refinement and morals." The arts, potentially, could uplift everyone, much as women were supposed to do. Women and the arts belonged together.

Culture study attracted hundreds of thousands of clubwomen, adhering to the belief that learning uplifts the ignorant and enhances social status. They hoped that acquaintance with tested cultural disciplines would reinforce their attempted arrival on the cultural scene. Thus they did not challenge the classical standards of art. What they were seeking was the same cultural authority formerly reserved for men. This use of culture study for their own ends set the club movement on the path to Domestic Feminism. A lady's command of the arts was related to her innate sensibility, but it was not related to her home. Her assertion of proficiency in a new world stretched her jurisdiction beyond the domestic sphere.

Although preserving tradition can be considered a conservative action, Sorosis members viewed the pursuit of culture as a forward-looking move in the context of women's rights. They felt they were emulating the salonieres of Europe by bringing together influential women to be admired by feminists. Margaret Fuller had already made some effort to replicate the havens of inquisitiveness and the clubwomen knew of her "Conversations." Sorosis founders Anne Lynch Botta, the Cary sisters, and, to a certain extent, Croly, had earlier hosted regular gatherings of New York literati in order to enjoy the excitement of intellectual exploration. Again and again, women used culture to soften the reality of sexism. "The arts everywhere encompass us with a cloud of beauty and comfort," Mrs. Emily Crawford would tell the 1893 Chicago Exposition.[45] Croly said the same: "Literary culture...endows us with the refinement and breadth and beauty of a better world, where the pin pricks of daily life cease to hurt us."[46]

Yet if the arts protected women, they also provided a superior stance for an attack on men's aggressive, competitive, acquisitive, and materialistic values. Suffragist and clubwoman May Wright Sewall deplored the "man of action" as "hero of the practical world."[47] Another clubwoman damned the college education that urged boys to become greedy, practical, and businesslike at the expense of developing "a love for the beautiful or any of the finer endowments of the spirit." She complained that young men were being trained to fill their short lives "with the feverish seeking for things that can never satisfy."[48]

Men were neither biologically able nor environmentally trained to commune with the beautiful. Thus, contempt and perhaps jealousy were expressed for ostentatious male philanthropists who created cultural institutions. At the 1893 Columbian Exposition, Sewall implied that any woman could know more about the arts than Carnegie himself: "The humblest lover and devotee of culture has a claim upon immortality which cannot be won by those who build even the proudest altars in her honor, if they have spent their own lives in worshiping [sic] at other shrines."[49]

The regular study of the arts by countless clubwomen who were inspired by Sorosis solidified the relationship between women and culture. As women cultivated the association, it strengthened their claim on the spiritual. Clubwoman May Rogers spoke on "The Novel as the Educator of the Imagination,"[50] and demonstrated that women not only could claim oneness with culture because they possessed the qualities of the lady but also could become better ladies because they associated with culture. By the late nineteenth century, women's grasp would be so firm that a new claim on the arts would be expressed. One writer, describing the attitudes of his mother's circle, observed, "The idea that men could share cultural matters on a basis of equality did not occur to many women."[51]

Even though clubwomen complained about the male veneration of utility, they still emphasized the practical need for arts. Sewall defended the tangible benefits.

> Culture turns the fruit of practical careers into soil and seed, which shall insure the enlargement of her harvests. Culture has repeated these object lessons so often that practical minds are beginning to see the corollary of them, and are wisely using culture as an instrument in forwarding their plans for the conquest of the material world.[52]

Her ultimate goal, however, was that women should wield enough influence to temper male behavior. "Culture...will never be satisfied with the tribute of temples and altars from the practical world until that world shall carry into its offices and market places the spirit and methods to be learned only at her feet."[53]

Although clubwomen felt that art enhanced everyone's life, it was particularly useful for women in examining their own place in society. Sorosis members were anxious to determine the impact culture had on their sex. Such efforts were a genuine aspect of members' developing self-consciousness.

> We do not want to paint pictures, perhaps, but we want to know all about those who do, and, if it is a woman, what kind of pictures she paints. As a club we do not get up dramatic entertainments, but we want to know how the drama affects the interest and welfare of women, socially, mentally, morally, physically, and pecuniarily, and whether we want to train our daughters in that direction for a livelihood.[54]

Members gave papers on "Women as delineated by the Old Masters"; "Has literature been elevated by the writings of women?"; "Is the woman given us by women novelists more true to life than the woman drawn by men?" Croly spoke on "Women as Writers." The art committee gave reports on pictures by women artists at the Academy of Design. The literature committee reviewed books written by women. Croly wrote to the Academy of Art, urging them to allow women to study in the proposed school.

Also significant to Sorosis was the source of employment that the arts offered women. Clubwoman Mrs. August Raymond Kidder, drama critic for *Belford's Magazine*, recalled how the first thing she ever wrote for pay was about Muldoon, the wrestler, and she spoke of how startling it appeared in print, and how different that money looked from any ordinary everyday greenback she ever saw before.[55] Sorosis members worked to create opportunities for women in culture-related professions by purchasing paintings by women artists and by establishing scholarships for female art students.

As attention to women in the arts grew stronger, consideration of women in other areas developed. As membership and interests multiplied, the number of committees grew to include Philanthropy, Science, Education, House and Home, and Business Women. Invariably, the club concerns centered around women and women's needs within each of the areas.

Despite Croly's public call for the teaching of the practical domestic arts for the average woman, higher education was discussed with particular interest in Sorosis because it was considered a vital route to financial independence for women. Sorosis members debated "Does the present system of education, in both public and private schools, sufficiently prepare the pupils for self-support?" In 1876 the club petitioned Columbia College and New York University to admit women. At one meeting, a report was given on the winners of the Girton College prize, a scholarship for English women. Clubwomen created the Emma Willard Fund which awarded a study grant to a poor but deserving girl. They spoke of assisting Columbia College to build its Woman's Annex. At their twenty-fourth birthday celebration, the members invited Elizabeth Cady Stanton to speak on Yale's admission of women to its post-graduate programs.

Financial independence could be gained only if education prepared women for a career and, in the process, increased alternatives for women. At social meetings, Sorosis members discussed such problems as the "Pulpit as a sphere for women"; "Will the entrance of women into business pursuits produce a beneficial influence upon civilization?"; "Does society properly recognize and protect business women?"; "In which profession can a woman do the most good: that of the ministry, the law, pedagogy, or medicine?" In 1878 they debated "Does business life for women destroy qualities and virtues which are the peculiar power and charm of her sex or is business life inconsistent with woman's best development?" It was pointed out that Massachusetts had sixty-seven thousand more women than men and New York had seventy thousand more. Most women *had* to earn their own living; the shortage of husbands necessitated it.

The concern for women's education and careers coexisted with a vast range of issues relating to women. "Properly systematized and understood, the work of the club will become the history of what is being done by women, as well as a record of new events in the world of intelligent activity," Croly predicted.[56] And the club, indeed, pursued the woman question with a vengeance. In 1869 there were papers on the "Sphere of Women" and "Women of the Last Century and Women of Today." No subject relating to womanhood was left untouched. The club even explored the possibility of turning household responsibilities into a career by dignifying domestic work with payment. "Whereas, it is universally conceded that the cares and duties appertaining to the Home are the natural employment of women. Therefore Resolved, that these occupations should be among the compensated Industries of civilized nations."

Medicine interested Sorosis members when it related to women's concerns. On 5 February 1872 a lecture with charts was given on the process of foeticide, or abortion. Later, the clubwomen discussed "The Moral Aspect of Foeticide." Dr. Anna Densmore French spoke to the members on the physiology of women, and several health lectures were given. Dress reform, too, was taken up because the fashions of the day threatened the health of women. The Freedom of Dress Committee included Ellen Demorest, famed fashion arbiter. Croly condemned the long trailing dress for street wear as a germ collector. By 1878 Sorosis members were urging physicians to consider the problem. They sent the *Woman's Journal* resolution that women of science should instruct milliners, dressmakers, hairdressers, and shoemakers in how to design their respective articles of women's clothing so as not to endanger health, ease, or grace.[57]

The seemingly disparate elements of Sorosis life—the social, the intellectual, the support for women's education, careers, dress reform, health, the pride in special domestic and moral capabilities, even charity work, all converged in support, both moral and material, for the career women of Sorosis. Each member of the group took from it a sense of helping herself and all women by sharing and growing together.

These women had had lives of change, but it seems likely that it was Sorosis that gave them strength for still more. After trying an acting career in New York in 1874, Kate Field moved on to head a cooperative dress association and also lobbied for government support to the arts. In 1890 she began a journal known as *Kate Field's Washington*. Ella Dietz Clymer tried writing poetry in 1873 and then headed for the stage. Celia Burleigh's careers as a lecturer and a minister were a direct result of the support Sorosis gave her. In 1871 Helen Campbell had the strength to leave her husband, study the conditions of working women, join Bellamy's first Nationalist Club, and become absorbed in the Home Economics movement. Phebe Hanaford, too, turned to the ministry in the 1870s, after she left her husband. True, not all members were strong enough to resist the pressures put upon them. When Anne Botta's husband insisted she stop her Sorosis activities, she quit.

Celia Burleigh best expressed Sorosis's contribution to its members:

> I believe I express the sentiment of every one who has been for any length of time a member of Sorosis when I say that the debt we owe it is beyond our power to

estimate.... One of the greatest needs of women is motive for mental activity—
an hospitable entertainment of their thought. For me Sorosis met precisely this
want; it afforded me an atmosphere so genial, an appreciation so prompt, a faith
so generous, that every possibility of my nature seemed intensified, and all its
latent powers quickened into life. If in the years to come I do any worthy work,
speak any word that has power to help a despondent soul, shed any gleam of light
on the dark and dreary ways that so many women are called upon to tread, it will
be to Sorosis, that it will be due in large measure—to this school where I have
been educated to better hopes, to nobler aspirations, and a larger life.[58]

The study of culture and of women gave strength and optimism to many of the
Sorosis members. For numerous clubwomen who would quickly emulate their
program, the results would be the same. The new attention to the arts and the
resulting justification of women's public activity in America would have a
significant impact on the Woman Movement of the nineteenth century. In
raising women's self-consciousness, articulating dissatisfaction with the
constraints of ladydom, and providing a nonmilitant outlet for action through
Domestic Feminism, Sorosis set styles.

Like Sorosis, the New England Woman's Club, formed in Boston in 1868,
met the needs of women who sought ways to exert influence outside the home
and who insisted "we were glad to prove also our loyalty to the first and most
important institution of humanity, marriage and family life."[59]

The NEWC was the brainchild of Caroline Severance—wife of banker and
reformer Theodoric Severance, mother of five, and worker for abolition,
temperance, dietary reform and women's suffrage. In 1855 the Severances
moved from Cleveland to Boston. Desiring the stimulation and companionship
of active, political women with social consciences, Caroline Severance
plunged into the reform activities of the city. She joined the original Board of
Managers of the New England Hospital for Women and Children. There she
met vital women who "made more evident the need for a quiet and central
place where friends might meet informally, and thus avoid the waste of time
and strength involved in going from one suburb, crossing the city in a slow
omnibus, and catching a train to another suburb, perhaps to find a friend going
through the same useless process."[60] Among the people Severance met at the
hospital whom she would tap for support of her club were Dr. Marie
Zakrzewska, a Berlin-born physician who had studied in Cleveland and in
New York City; Lucy Goddard, president of the hospital; Ednah Dow
Cheney, secretary and later president of the hospital; lawyer Samuel E. Sewall
and poet Harriet Winslow Sewall, parents of Lucy Sewall, a physician at the
hospital.

Throughout the city, via such organizations as the Radical Club and the
Free Religious Association, she met interested men and women who would
participate in her new club, an experiment to tap the collective energies of
women who wanted to study together, widen their friendships, and act to alter
social inequities. A sociable and gracious person, Severance was talented at

organizing like-minded women. Throughout her long life, she would continue to enjoy her greatest successes not in lecturing or writing but in bringing people together for action.

The first organizational meeting of the NEWC took place in February 1868, one month before Croly initiated the formation of Sorosis. In formalizing a purpose for the club, the founders hoped to create "a larger home for those who love and labor for the greater human family. Its plan involves no special pledge to any one form of activity, but implies only a womanly interest in all true thought and effort on behalf of woman, and of society in general, for which women are so largely responsible."[61] The NEWC's first mass meeting was held on May 30 and its regular weekly meetings began in November.

Although the purpose of the NEWC was similar to that of Sorosis in hoping to increase extra-familial influence, the backgrounds of NEWC members differed from those in Sorosis. Most NEWC members were less career-oriented and did not see themselves as pioneers in literary fields. They were primarily reformers of American life. Blue-blooded Julia Ward Howe, president of the NEWC from 1871 until her death in 1910, was the dominant spirit behind the club due to Severance's frequent travels and her move to Los Angeles in 1875. Like Severance, Howe had the ability to create a comfortable atmosphere that encouraged others to engage in productive activity. Howe had been active in a variety of reform movements. Writing only borrowed some energy from volunteer work for the Sanitary Commission, the peace movement, suffrage, and various other forms of women's rights, all of which profited from her serious and steady contributions.[62]

Although clubmember Ednah Dow Cheney wrote several books, she devoted most of her life to working for the improvement of society, not only for women but for blacks, in education, and in religious thought. Cheney helped found the Free Religious Association. She attended Margaret Fuller's "Conversations" for three seasons during the 1840s and she lectured at the Concord School of Philosophy in 1879. Cheney started the Boston School of Design to teach women art-related trades. She managed the New England Female Medical College in 1859. In 1862 she was secretary of the New England Hospital for Women and Children and was its president from 1887 until 1902. An active abolitionist, she organized a program to send teachers South for the Freedmen's Bureau from 1867 to 1875. With Lucretia Crocker, another NEWC member, she traveled through the South as an official government inspector of the Freedmen's Schools. Cheney was also active in the Massachusetts Woman Suffrage Association and the New England Woman Suffrage Association. She sent her only child to gymnastic classes and to early kindergarten. Such interests were typical among the NEWC membership.

Howe and Cheney were joined by countless other reform-minded women who were involved in an impressive number of concerns, including transcendentalism, abolition, Civil War work, temperance, education, dress reform, and cooperative housekeeping.[63] A preoccupation with experiment and a willingness to act were unifying factors among these women of diverse causes. Elizabeth Peabody was an advocate of Friedrich Froeble's kindergarten. She wrote *Moral Culture of Infancy, and Kindergarten Guide* with her sister, Mary Peabody Mann. Mary, wife of educator Horace Mann, produced books on botanical subjects and established a Cambridge Cooperative Housekeeping Society, an experiment which hoped to alleviate the tedium and expense of household care.[64] Mrs. Abba G. Woolson was a dress reformer as well as a writer.[65] Temperance attracted Mary I. Livermore and Louisa May Alcott among others. Kate Gannett Wells supported the Normal Art School in Boston to foster women's influence in public education and art education. Livermore, Woolson, and Howe were frequent lecturers on topics of interest to women.

In addition to Howe and Cheney, other NEWC members were active in the American Woman Suffrage Association—Lucy Stone, Mary Livermore, Lydia Jackson Emerson, Marie Zakrzewska, Louisa May Alcott, Caroline Severance, and Harriot Hunt. Livermore was vice-president of the suffrage association and an editor of the *Woman's Journal*. Alice Stone Blackwell edited the *Woman's Journal* and would be instrumental in merging the two suffrage organizations in 1890. Elizabeth Peabody and Harriet Hanson Robinson also were suffragists, as was Abby May, cousin to the literary Alcotts, president of the Massachusetts School Suffrage Association, and executive of the New England and Massachusetts Woman Suffrage Associations. Even those members like Kate Gannett Wells who opposed suffrage nevertheless considered themselves feminists.

The reform heritage of the NEWC members made them, unlike their Sorosis counterparts, amenable to the inclusion of a few interested male supporters. The men who joined the club came from the same reform movements as the women and were often those who matched wits with the NEWC members at the Radical Club and the Free Religious Association. They included novelist Henry James, poet John Greenleaf Whittier, Bronson Alcott, Brook Farm founder George Ripley, Judge Samuel E. Sewall, Dr. Dio Lewis, physical culture reformer, and Unitarian ministers Reverend O. B. Frothingham, Reverend James Freeman Clarke, Reverend John Weiss, and Thomas Wentworth Higginson, abolitionist and women's rights advocate. The men agreed to be supportive at a distance, without privileges of full members. Like Croly, Severance recognized the possible danger to women's growth if men gained dominance. "We admit our husbands, sons and friends, as associate members, to our literary gatherings and our recreations. We welcome their counsel and sympathy and receive most valuable and generous help from them. But, since woman pre-eminently needs the benefits of such an organization and of practice in directing it, we wish them to be free in debate and in executive detail from the constraining presence of their more experienced brothers."[66]

Members' participation in social movements of the era is the key to NEWC's importance to Domestic Feminism, just as the journalism of Sorosis founders is the key to their attachment to culture study. Reform efforts provided the New England women with an alternative vision for American society and the skills to attempt it. When they wed their sense of sisterhood with their talents for reform, they expanded the ideal female role of creating a moral society. Domestic Feminism, as NEWC practiced it, channeled the collective energies of women to modify the individualistic, competitive male world. They worked in such specific areas as education, politics, careers, and clothing, and portrayed this modification of the public sphere by women as a means to enhance the lives of all women and all humankind. Both the reformist ideals of NEWC and the self-improvement goals of Sorosis were vital to Domestic Feminism, but only when they were combined in the 1890s by the General Federation of Women's Clubs would Domestic Feminism reach its fullest potential.

When the official meetings got underway in November 1868, there were 118 female and 17 male members. Like Sorosis, the NEWC had to go through growing pains. The women were anxious to organize themselves into a congregation known as a "Club," which would disassociate themselves from the good-works societies and associations that women had long joined. But there arose the problem of the word "club," which held too masculine a connotation for ladies. Still, members were determined to override those difficulties. The use of the word became one of their earliest means of breaking tradition.

The NEWC members, like their New York City sisters, conducted meetings for social and cultural purposes. They shared a critique of sexist society. They both gave awards or memorial meetings to people they respected. They invited speakers, gave papers, and held classes. The membership was equally stellar and had the same wide sympathy for women's rights and an ambition to improve women's education, career opportunities, health, and fashions. The NEWC members suffered the same type of criticism Sorosis had, the *Boston Transcript* declaring, "Homes will be ruined, children neglected, woman is straying from her sphere."[67]

The reform efforts of the NEWC members, however, resulted in a bolder plan than Sorosis women developed for improving the quality of women's lives. The controversial reform of woman suffrage quickly became an accepted part of the NEWC program even though the issue was introduced with caution. Harriet Hanson Robinson recorded in her 1872 diary: "I was surprised to see how the club had grown in the matter of woman suffrage. The subject was hardly spoken of two years ago. Now the majority present look favorably on it."[68] To the experienced New England reformers, that a group devoted to the strengthening of woman's place should commit itself to supporting the franchise seemed logical.

In addition, NEWC members immediately set up specific projects that would benefit women directly. They undertook the founding of a horticultural school to open a new field of labor to women, the establishment of a store where women could buy sensible garments, and finally, the formation of a lobby for the election of women to the Boston school board in an era when women could not even vote for school board members. All these programs were justified by a Domestic Feminist argument as woman's proper work. Horticulture could be viewed as a career employing the lady's special sensitivity to nature. Dress reform enabled the lady to function more efficiently as an aid to loved ones. School suffrage enabled the maternal instincts to direct the course of children's education.

The Horticultural School was a pet project of Cheney,[69] who was determined that women should break into new, sustaining, and fulfilling careers. In January 1869 she secured the sanction of the long-established Massachusetts Horticultural Society and the following year began to rally support for a school in Newton which would teach women to support themselves through the sale of potted plants, fruits, and flowers.

The NEWC Horticultural School Committee handled the details of setting up the school. They desired a one-hundred-acre tract, and a dozen or two men and women, preferably women if they could be found, including a matron, scientific gardener, farmer, and teachers, to run the school. In addition, the bylaws stated that half the officers of the school should be women. The female students were to be over the age of sixteen and would study botany, vegetable physiology, agricultural chemistry, horticulture, and sciences. Electives were landscape gardening, agriculture, French, German, drawing, and painting fruits and flowers.

The school opened in February 1870, with six beds for boarding students, a dining room, sitting room, schoolroom, dayroom for nonboarding scholars, all supervised by a matron. Sunday was a day of quiet and order, and girls were requested to attend church at least once during the day. Donations to the school were generous and contributions were vast. The Ames Shovel Works, referred to as the Ames Plough Company, for example, donated various garden plant roots for five pupils. Tuition was set at one hundred dollars per year, and the NEWC raised ten thousand dollars to provide facilities and train the twenty-five pupils who attended the school in the three years of its existence.

Despite impressive resources, however, when the Bussey College for Horticulture in West Roxbury opened its doors to women on equal terms with men, the NEWC decided their school was unnecessary. The final 1878 report said everything had been sold to use the money to help finance girls in their study of horticulture. In fact, the club had run out of women willing to attend their school[70] and had reached only a handful at enormous expense.

NEWC members recognized the importance of Dress Reform to the increased productivity of women. A committee on the subject was formed after Elizabeth Stuart Phelps delivered a lecture to the club. The members defined the evils of existing styles and corresponded with women throughout America who were interested in change, including Sorosis President Charlotte Wilbour. They urged healthful, beautiful, serviceable, and simple garments.[71] They were most insistent that the heavy skirts worn by women needed to hang from the shoulders instead of the hips. Custom must be broken. Committee Chair Abba Woolson warned that women were "weaker than men in physical strength, from a lack of exercise in youth, and from an indoor life." Weighty garments were nearly certain to bring discomfort to her stomach and intestines, pain and even death in childbirth, and inferior babies.

Another member insisted women's clothing challenged good taste. "Its excessive ornamentation; and farther, its introduction of senseless, and glaring deformities, [is] disgraceful to the wearer, demoralizing to the community, and an outrage to good taste, and common sense universally."[72]

The committee claimed that it was religious duty to be proud of the body as it was, not as the fashion deformed it. Whenever club demands threatened to shake public opinion into outrage, God's name was invoked. The ladies assured all observers that He was on their side.

> Let women guard with intelligent care that marvelous body which came to her from God's hands, shaped according to his perfect designs. He committed it to her, not only strong and serviceable, but fashioned in exquisite beauty; let her hold it a crime to weaken its powers, and deform its fair proportions. When she learns to respect it as she ought, she will no longer cramp and burden and freeze and disfigure it by the garments in which she clothes it to-day.[73]

The garments that were designed under the auspices of the NEWC first were displayed in church parlors and vestries. By 1874 the club had a store on 25 Winter Street that employed women who made and sold the specially designed flannel undergarments, skirt supporters, stocking supporters, and brace and skirt supporters combined. Orders were taken from all over the country, but obstacles were great. Mismanagement caused garments and patterns to be poorly made. A hostile elevator boy who continually gave false directions to possible customers was fired only after the committee threatened to find another location for their store. In 1875 the NEWC found a new agent to handle the business and relinquished direct control over it.

The success of the third major project was augmented by the NEWC's overlapping membership with the Massachusetts Woman Suffrage Association. The NEWC Education Committee[74] worked from 1872 until 1874 toward the election of women to the Boston School Committee. They justified women's participation in school decisions by emphasizing the lady's natural capacity to know, love, and determine the needs of children. Thanks to this campaign, Boston had the first school suffrage law allowing female members, even though it would be 1889 before Boston women could vote for these officers. The club divided the city into wards, found women who would run for office, secured legal opinion on the women's eligibility, and in December 1873, saw four women win places on Boston school boards. Although the action was hotly debated, the Massachusetts legislature allowed them to be seated in December 1874.[75]

NEWC ideology and work enabled the club to provide for the nurturance of the members in a substantial way, as it had for the Sorosis women. Like their New York City sisters, the NEWC members treasured the sorority. Julia Ward Howe wrote to Ednah Dow Cheney: "I am anxious to get back to the Club.... To stay away from the Club seems like losing the comfort of one's family, and still it seems very formidable to think of meeting with so many, even of one's friends."[76] Cheney agreed: "I cannot express sufficient gratitude for the constant pleasure and comfort it has given me, the tie between the members was very strong, and we loved to be together, in the times of sadness as well as of joy and merriment."[77]

As with the Sorosis members, however, unlimited charity toward one another in the NEWC was impossible. Harriet Hanson Robinson wrote in her diary of a disappointing meeting after Thomas Wentworth Higginson read his translations of Sappho's poetry.

> Mrs. Cheney, as usual, made a few feeble remarks, and took up the time so that no one else would speak and called on Mrs. Howe, as if to say that she was the one to respond to any thing said of a poet.... The snobbishness of some of the ladies at the club is very irritating to me. Abby May, whom no one particularly likes, has been elected President of the club.[78]

In general, however, a supportive sisterhood prevailed, and Sorosis and the NEWC members shared the enormously significant goal of establishing similarly supportive clubs everywhere. At the first anniversary of Sorosis, Charlotte Wilbour stressed the need for clubs to grow in every community.

> There is no use in women hanging back, God intends to use them to accomplish his purposes, and he is fitting them for it. Men have had the sole control of affairs long enough, and a pretty mess they have made of it. God calls women now to the work of purification, and if they can sink selfhood, ideas of personal aggrandizement, and come singly and solely to the work of human redemption, they will be blessed beyond what women have known before.[79]

Both the NEWC and Sorosis made every effort to start women's clubs and associations throughout the world. Dr. Emma Brainerd-Ryder, a Sorosis member, began Sorosis clubs in Bombay, Ceylon, and Australia, carrying Croly's words, "Tell them the world was made for women also." Sorosis inspired the creation of the Inter-Collegiate Sorosis, an organization including young women from the University of New York and the University of Michigan.[80] Rebecca Morse of Sorosis organized a Nantucket Sorosis. Mrs. Celia Burleigh started the Brooklyn Women's Club. Boston's NEWC members were particularly active in starting clubs in the Boston vicinity. The Melrose Club, Home Club of East Boston, Winchester Club, and clubs in Providence, Danvers, and West Newton were either begun by NEWC members or styled on its plan.[81] Julia Ward Howe inspired the establishment of San Francisco's Century Club. Through these clubs it was expected that progress would be engendered for all women. In 1869 Charlotte Wilbour reminded Sorosis:

> The eyes of the world are on us, and their willingness to do us justice and even urge our claims should give us a hint to perform something to justify their kindest appreciation. There will arise opportunities for external work, demands for our united efforts, not as propagandists of any new gospel, but as co-workers with the struggling souls of our human sisterhood. Activity is the Mother of Power.... We have power. Let us use it.[82]

In addition to increasing this united power through club work, Sorosis and NEWC members wanted to hasten the process by creating an association of the clubs, where cooperation would stimulate progress still further. From the moment they started their own clubs, they looked forward to a federation or an associations of women's clubs through which they could rally greater strength. They started to build one immediately.

CHAPTER THREE

# The Association for the Advancement of Women

The early clubwomen realized that their potential for influence would be heightened if they could inspire other women to form organizations of their own and then unite into a strong federation. This had been a priority since the founding of the Boston and New York City clubs, even though they would not be successful until 1873 when they formed the nationwide Association for the Advancement of Women. Sorosis members took the lead in attempting to create an association of clubwomen. Among the first topics Sorosis discussed in April 1868 was "What means shall [we] adopt for the formation of accessory Leagues throughout the country?"[1] On 1 June 1869 Jane Cunningham Croly issued a notice inviting delegates to a preliminary meeting of a Woman's Parliament in New York City, in October, "to represent women upon all subjects of vital interest to themselves and their children."[2] She saw the Parliament as a permanent project for Sorosis, "the Club to act as the center of a great united womanhood, whose branches should extend all over the country, that these should be representative, elect their own officers, send delegates to an annual session, having its permanent home in New York, and its representative organ."[3]

Croly acted at a time when some of the leaders of the woman suffrage movement were causing alarm. Susan B. Anthony and Elizabeth Cady Stanton had published the first issue of their suffrage newspaper *The Revolution* in January 1868, and in May, they had formed the National Woman Suffrage Association. Suffrage conventions were held in many cities, and the newspapers, in apprehension, gave them wide coverage.

Croly's plan provided a less threatening alternative to women. Indeed, since she knew that suffrage was still greeted with horror in most circles, she was too impatient to wait for it to become acceptable. Referring to her plan to start a woman's legislature dealing with domestic-related matters, she said, "There is no need of waiting till men give us a vote, we take it without asking, and we apply ourselves at once to an examination of the causes of the evil we deplore, and of the remedy to be applied."[4] Four months later, she spoke even more angrily.

> I, for one, see no advantage in waiting, like the enchanted princess in the fairy tale, for a lover, in the shape of a vote, to set us free and transform us into living, breathing, acting women. The ballot is at best only one agency; it cannot do everything.... Two weapons women are free to use—either of them mightier than the ballot—the tongue and the pen. These can keep up a perpetual warfare....[5]

Her plan called for women in every community to form into legislative bodies of their own which would make decisions on all subjects "of vital interest to themselves and their children."[6] Croly announced:

> There is no reason why women should not elect their president and the entire corps if they choose, of official representatives. They should keep a cabinet or standing executive committee, always in session. They would soon have official organs, and might erect a Capitol of their own in New York City.[7]

Croly had firm supporters. Reformer Melusina Fay Peirce pointed out that for women to ask for the right of regulating their own affairs was "simply ridiculous. They possess it already—not, it is true, as men do over each other, by virtue of brute force, but by virtue of the irresistible influence that they, as women, possess over men."[8] She endorsed Croly's plan for a women's legislative body.

Croly insisted her parliament was milder than any plan the suffragists had devised. As one Sorosis member insisted, "It is not more than a parlor conversazione, where a few well-informed women of position and polite culture will discuss the best methods of training young children, of economical housekeeping and hospital affairs—things which most intimately belong to woman's sphere."[9] While Croly did not condemn the suffrage outright, her decision to juxtapose her own plan with it did nothing to allay public alarm. Instead of working for the vote, Croly ingeniously urged her followers to accept their responsibility for woman-related issues. She made it appear that her program would engage dutiful women, not rebellious ones. In effect, she tried to disassociate her work from that of the suffragists. "The Woman's Parliament," she wrote,

> affords women the opportunity of showing their desire is for the benefit and elevation of mankind at large and not a personal striving after place and power. With this view it will be understood that the Parliament has nothing to do with the demand for "Woman's Rights," so-called; it simply recognizes women's duties, and proposes a way to perform them. The champions of women's rights are doing a work which we thankfully and gladly acknowledge, but its discussion and demands would be out of place in the deliberations of an existing Woman's Parliament.[10]

Croly and her Sorosis supporters [11] were not entirely successful at providing assurance that the plan for a female congress was less threatening than suffrage demands. When Sorosis voted on whether to give the convention its support, only days before the Woman's Parliament was to take place, the measure was defeated by one vote.[12] The *New York Tribune*, edited by Horace Greeley, had feared that the Woman's Parliament would not avoid militancy. Greeley was relieved when the majority refused to endorse Croly's plan, which he mistakenly likened to the radical politics of leading suffragists. The *Tribune* opined:

> The chances seem to be that the celebrated Sorosis is almost on the eve of disruption; that about half a dozen self-elected leaders are determined to commit the society to the extremely advanced views of Mrs. Henry B. Stanton and Miss Anna Dickinson, neither of whom is a member; while the great majority are equally determined that they will not train in any such company.[13]

The Sorosis response to the *Tribune* comment reveals the Domestic Feminist orientation of the club members. Shirley Dare wrote a letter to the editor that disclaimed all association with suffragists and insisted that the Woman's Parliament was merely an extension of Sorosis's elitism. It was not a public arousal of feminist aspirations at all, as the suffrage conventions were thought to be.

> Sir: Sorosis is *not* in the least danger of disruption. None of its members are in favor of committing the society to the "extremely advanced views of Mrs. Henry B. Stanton and Miss Anna Dickinson," but the reverse. Sorosis desires to hold itself aloof from political claims and discussion. The Woman's Parliament is neither more nor less than a select convention of ladies of talent who meet *by invitation* to discuss questions of social science which properly interest their sex....[14]

Dare did not deny Sorosis support for suffrage work and explained that President Croly had not asserted or denied the right of women to vote.[15] She instead reinforced the strategy of relegating the suffrage cause to a less significant position behind Croly's tamer program. "Sorosis is neither a set of politicians in petticoats, nor of termagants in long trains. The society earnestly desires that people shall keep its name distinct from any political or fashionable ambition."[16]

The *Tribune* immediately apologized in an editorial after realizing that Sorosis's Woman's Parliament was a welcome alternative to the threat of suffrage agitation. "A Woman's Parliament, as described by a sprightly defender of Sorosis in another column, would be an excellent thing. We hope indeed to see it tried on a broader scale than there suggested, and with wider, if not higher, aims."[17] When the public likewise realized that the Woman's Parliament planned to work within woman's sphere rather than challenge it, the organization lost its ominous air and the newspapers changed their criticism to praise.

Seventy women, including many Sorosis members, attended the Woman's Parliament, which was held on October 21, 23, and 30, 1869, in New York City. Among the numerous speakers that addressed the group were Elizabeth

Peabody, who spoke on Kindergartens, Dr. Anna Dinsmore on "Hygiene and Sanitary Reforms," and Mary F. Davis on "Reform in Prison Discipline."[18] Croly also delivered a speech. She asserted woman's superior ability to correct problems affecting women and children in public education and in prisons and reformatory schools. Fostering hygiene in schools and public institutions, securing vocational training and proper remuneration for labor, improving domestic economy with cooperative households and public laundries, and combatting corruption in public life were goals for which women could work. "The function of the Parliament is to crystallize the intelligence and influence of women into a moral and reformatory power, which will act definitely upon all the varied interests of society," she had written before the convention and now urged through the Parliament program.[19]

In discussing work, Croly indicated her wider interest in urging women into new careers.

> Work that pays, women have been taught to regard with peculiar horror. Men might work for themselves, but women must work for others. Self-sacrifice was their special virtue, and they have been flattered into thinking it much more of a virtue than it really is. Notwithstanding the efforts to discredit labor, women have not been idle, but they have worked principally as the founders and sustainers of the family and of society. Men hold all the positions of emolument. Nine tenths of the women are absolutely dependent upon them for the bread they eat. This destitution of women is not because they do not work, but because their labor is not acknowledged—in other words, is not *paid*.[20]

Her plea was not for the vote, the absence of which she saw simply as one of many disabilities, but for money, which would materially and concretely improve woman's condition by ending her hateful dependence.

Throughout the meetings, the predominant message, summed up by the president of the Parliament, Melusina Peirce, was the need for women to correct those abuses resulting from male dominance that directly harmed the domestic realm. One paper reporting her views said:

> She thanked God that she was not a man to have one day to stand before God's high judgment seat and answer for a share in the dread crimes of strength against weakness, of armed might against defenselessness, of knowledge against ignorance, of lust against innocence, that must stamp man in the eye of his maker.[21]

Peirce insisted that women, one-half of the population, should take on one-half of the responsibilities of the world. She urged the formation of organizations paralleling men's political organizations, but with every woman participating, not represented by districts as men were. All women over the age of twenty-one should meet in their own towns and cities to make their own decisions on household education, health and social reform, pauper and criminal issues, fine arts, gardening, and newspapers and magazines for women.[22] "We propose to bring the moral force of all good women to bear in given directions," Croly explained.[23]

The Woman's Parliament adjourned with plans to form a Woman's Council comprised of New York women who would carry out the goals of the conference on the local level. Nevertheless, the *Tribune* resumed its initial skepticism about the ability of these Domestic Feminists to avoid the threatening ways of the suffragists.

> These worthy ladies snub the Suffrage Women by saying that they have "no connection with the shops over the way." That is all very well; but we shall see whether the Suffrage people are so easily snuffed out. They have great perseverance—we'll be sworn to that—and it will require the strongest logic of the Parliamentarians to convince them that they cannot come in.[24]

Greeley had not put his finger on the real problem, however. Unrealistic expectations doomed the program before it was organized. Croly had naively expected large numbers of American women to share her ambitions for the use of women's sphere. The success of Sorosis had misled her, and she failed to realize that most women could hardly justify their own legislature on the basis of their acquaintance with the domestic arts. Similarly, her vision of woman's power in the public sector was quite simplistic. In her eyes, women could attain influence by merely forming themselves into a congress. The new congress would be an improvement over male representative bodies since all women, not just representatives, would participate in this very direct democracy. Sheer numbers would have made this impractical. In addition, women who had been encouraged to defer to others and to avoid initiating their own plans were hardly prepared for legislating their own decisions. When Sorosis members met in November to discuss the need for classes in women's physiology in the high schools, the program died from lack of interest.[25]

The failure of the 1869 Woman's Parliament plan taught Croly that most women were not as ready as she was to politicize grievances, even in a ladylike way. Undaunted, however, Croly set about trying once more to convince Sorosis of the wisdom of a Congress of Women. Her vision of a body of women working to improve society through Domestic Feminism would garner more support as the suffrage movement appeared more radical than ever to supporters of limited change after 1870.

In the early 1870s the National Woman Suffrage Association, through a temporary alliance with Victoria Woodhull, became associated in public opinion with loose morals and free love. In November 1871 Woodhull scandalized American society when she publicized the Reverend Henry Ward Beecher's affair with Elizabeth Tilton. In 1872, when Woodhull tried to engage the National Woman Suffrage Association in her free love presidential campaign, the National Woman Suffrage Association suffered from the attempted partnership.

One newspaper described the result of the Woodhull-suffrage alliance. "Justly, or unjustly, the taint of the abominable free-love doctrine enunciated so unblushingly by certain female agitators has become attached, in the public mind, to some degree at least, to the whole 'woman movement.'"[26] This blot on the New York suffrage campaign may well have contributed to Sorosis's favorable response in 1873 to a resurrection of Croly's old plan.[27]

The demand for the franchise appeared to forecast the demise of the family and the integration of women into the heretofore male-dominated world of politics, business, and the professions. Contemporaries of the woman suffrage movement feared the upheaval of the world as they knew it; that is, the home as woman's sphere, the rest of the world under male control. Even suffragist clubwomen shared with more conservative members the realization that the radical implications of the franchise frightened potential supporters of the broader women's rights. The Domestic Feminism which Sorosis introduced attracted many thousands of women who recognized their own subordinate status but were not willing to go so far as the demand for suffrage to rectify injustice. Supporters of less overwhelming demands rallied around clubs to achieve changes in countless directly political realms.

Charlotte Beebe Wilbour, Croly's successor as president of Sorosis, revived the idea of a Woman's Parliament in the spring of 1873. Now the time was right for an organization to stimulate recognition of the need for less radical agitation for women's rights. In July 1873 Sorosis issued a "Messenger," announcing an autumn Woman's Congress.[28] It bemoaned "the absence of fellowship and concerted action among women . . . solitary and isolated," and urged recipients to rectify the sorry situation by supporting the new Congress. Little spontaneous interest must have been expressed by the recipients of this announcement because soon a circular, "The Messenger," was sent to women's organizations and to three hundred professional women—"woman preachers, teachers, professors, physicians, artists, lawyers, trading capitalists, editors, authors, practical philanthropists, and those who by their example inspire others not only to covet earnestly the best gifts, but to labor earnestly for them."[29] By 23 August 1873, one hundred and fifty-two career women and reformers appended their names to a second "Call," which was sent to sixteen-hundred American and European women.

Among those willing to lend their names to sponsorship were almost three dozen Sorosis women.[30] The New England Woman's Club also provided impressive support.[31] Other important women, representing a wide spectrum of interests within the growing Woman Movement, were attracted to the new organization as well. The *New York Times* correctly described them as "ladies who have become identified with every movement tending toward the progressive amelioration of women."[32] Sarah Grimke, the aging abolitionist, put her name to the "Call." Mrs. E. D. E. N. Southworth, an enormously popular writer of fiction, and Hester Pendleton, president of the Free Medical College for women in New York, responded. So did Emma Marwedel, supporter of kindergartens, the Reverend Antoinette Brown Blackwell, and Rebecca N. Hazard, who started her public work through the Industrial Home for Girls, then worked in the Sanitary Commission and became the president of the Missouri Woman Suffrage Association.[33] Frances Dana Gage, Ohio abolitionist and vice-president of the National Woman Suffrage Association, lent her name to the budding Congress.[34] Also, Frances Willard was a cooperative worker. No doubt teacher Willard picked up ideas that she would use to build the Women's Christian Temperance Union in later years. Finally, even Elizabeth Cady Stanton, the suffragist, put her name to the new ranks of supporters.

Wilbour let it be known that this new organization would not resemble the more fiery suffrage associations. "Deliberations will be earnest and intellectual and will [be] conducted in such a calm, rational, temperate and Christian spirit as to compel the respect of the world at large," she told a meeting of Sorosis.[35] By implication, she was divorcing the Congress from the suffragists whose deliberations did not compel the respect of the world at large. The Sorosis members' fears were assuaged and they voted to donate one hundred dollars to the First Congress.

On 15 October 1873, Sorosis created the nationwide Association for the Advancement of Women (AAW) "to consider and present practical methods for securing to women higher intellectual, moral, and physical conditions, with a view to the improvement of all domestic and social relations." Although later histories claim that Sorosis had no intention of guiding this new association,[36] Wilbour told AAW guests to the 20 October 1873 meeting of Sorosis that the club "should no longer be satisfied to follow the lead of others but should herself inaugurate more great movements in the best interests of women."[37] The AAW was thus an organization designed to transmit the beliefs of the Sorosis members to larger audiences of like-minded women. Throughout its twenty-five-year existence, AAW members propagated Domestic Feminism at annual conferences, known as the Congress of Women. An elaboration of the Sorosis and New England Woman's Club ideology underlay all the papers delivered by AAW members at the congresses, the belief that women were special and should bring their moral sensibilities to bear on the social problems in America.

The object of the association was not to secure a large membership, but to remain an elite body.[38] The AAW started with three hundred well-known names and its membership never rose past four hundred thirty-eight, a body of like-minded career women striving to educate audiences of ladies in the need for Domestic Feminism. Seventy of the original one hundred fifty-two signers of the "The Call" attended the First Congress. Some of these members presented thirty-five papers on a wide variety of topics, a format similar to suffrage conventions and the 1869 Women's Parliament. As in Sorosis, the plan was that "no one subject shall receive undue attention,"[39] and it was followed throughout the twenty-five-year existence of the AAW. The First Congress papers were delivered on subjects ranging from motherhood to women's colleges[40] to a New York City audience of four hundred women. Gentlemen were welcome at evening meetings, but few attended in 1873. The AAW was more successful than the Women's Parliament in distinguishing itself from female radicalism. After the New York Congress won praise from the press, the organization found itself not feared, but applauded. The *New*

*York Herald* found

> The Woman's movement has taken a new and surprising departure. The public may not be thoroughly conversant with the fact that for some time past the more violent woman's rights people headed by Victoria Woodhull, Susan B. Anthony, and others of the same stripe, have been diverging so widely from the accepted conventionalities of society as to compel a certain number of lady agitators who have membership in the Sorosis Club of the city to organize a new movement of women which was to be erected and maneuvered by the leaders of Sorosis, to the utter destruction of the free love party.[41]

One of the main reasons the First Congress of Women was successful was because its goals were more modest than those of the 1869 Parliament. Work proceeded, not in simultaneous congresses everywhere, but through a single annual congress that continued the work of educating responsive women to the relationship between the expansion of women's vistas and social regeneration. Sorosis's minutes recorded this goal.

> The press, in spite of its natural impulse to cast ridicule upon the "Petticoat Parliament" should at last recognize the dignity, purity, and success of the movement. What wonder that we regard this association for the advancement of women as a step toward the coming millennium. God grant that woman with her refinement, her love, and her religion may be the means in the hands of God of helping the weak, ennobling humanity and converting the world.[42]

The influx of women like many New England Woman's Club participants, however, had also introduced the belief that suffragism and Domestic Feminism were compatible and could coexist for the growth of women's activism on many fronts. They succeeded in using the AAW for a program Croly never envisioned as a school for suffragism at the same time that women were learning there that they should impart their domestic talents to the solution of world problems. The AAW became a proving ground that strong-minded suffragism and Domestic Feminism were not mutually exclusive.

Contrary to Sorosis's expectations and manipulations, the association decided to hold its Second Congress not in New York, but in a different city.[43] This plan effectively squelched Sorosis's hopes for domination and created a precedent for visiting a different city each year.[44] The most influential clubwomen in each of the host cities housed AAW members, royally feted them at club receptions,[45] and took them sightseeing. Not only did they renew old acquaintances, but they developed a network of like-minded women for friendship or to help in future causes, and most importantly, they enjoyed an exhilarating sense of collective camaraderie. Harriet Townsend noted, "There was an unusual sense of comradeship about the AAW women, delightful to recognize, each strong in her own convictions, but ever ready to listen and defer."[46]

The audience that attended AAW Congresses included the members, professional women of each community, clubwomen, many husbands, both skeptical and supportive, babies, reporters, and students. In Grand Rapids, high school girls attended the presentation of a paper on women in colleges. In Springfield, Mount Holyoke College students were admitted to a lecture on sociology. In some communities, the schools were closed for a day so that teachers and students could benefit from the program. Clubmember Maria Mitchell described the Syracuse crowd in 1875: "It was a grand affair, and babies came in arms. School-boys stood close to the platform, and school-girls came, book in hand. The hall was a beautiful opera-house, and could hold at least one thousand seven hundred. It was packed and jammed, and rough men stood in the aisles."[47] One Buffalo reporter portrayed the 1881 Congress as more sedate and refined:

> The ladies, literally and figuratively in high feather, looked on approvingly, enthusiastically, and with pardonable pride at being, for once at least, the dominating presence in an affair of magnitude. The men, nearly sunk in the exultant sea of femininity, sat with humble knees and deferential elbows, and bearing on their faces meek apologies for being men.[48]

There can be no doubt that the audience was responsive. Widespread newspaper coverage indicates that speeches were interrupted again and again with applause. When an Indiana high school teacher mentioned that eight of nine departments in her school were headed by girls, her statement brought loud approval from the audience in Rhode Island.[49] The newspapers frequently noted that the audiences grew each day, no doubt in response to the fact that the dailies often reprinted entire speeches and the comments made afterward.[50] It was not unusual for the papers to report on the third day of the Congress, "The building was densely packed, many being unable to find standing room."[51]

Host clubs devoted much care to details which would impress the public that the AAW was serious, but not revolutionary. The newspapers often noted that the local sponsor clubs began on time. These were not silly women, invariably late for appointments. To show they were still ladies, the dais was often decorated in a pleasing feminine manner. "The stage was handsomely set, brightly lighted, and the speaker's desk was adorned with vines and bouquets."[52] But, of course, the center of importance was the papers and their authors. Only AAW members could make presentations at the Congresses, thereby assuring some control over the content. Anna Garlin Spencer characterized the members as constituting "The First Who's Who of Women."

> It was a union primarily of achieving personalities. It showed the capacity of individual women, who, in spite of obstacles, had obtained higher education, had entered successfully into the "learned professions," long the monopoly of men, and had already taken high positions in education, reform, and social service...Mary A. Livermore, Maria Mitchell, Julia Ward Howe, its early presidents, were of intellectual stature to be seen across the continent, and known by women leaders in all countries. The service of Charlotte B. Wilbour, and that of Mary Eastman, and of Alice C. Fletcher and many others exceptionally gifted, made the Association for the Advancement of Women, unique.[53]

Sorosis members were present in large numbers,[54] as were the New England Woman's Club members.[55] They were joined by other ambitious career women and reformers: Catherine Beecher, Frances Willard, Harriet Beecher Stowe, Elizabeth Cady Stanton, Emma Marwedel, Emily Blackwell, Clara Barton, Anna C. Garlin, Elizabeth Stuart Phelps, educator Lucinda H. Stone, antislavery agitator and suffragist Elizabeth Buffum Chase, suffragist and educator Emily Howland, her niece Isabel Howland who was secretary of the AAW for many years and secretary of the New York Woman Suffrage Association, black writer, lecturer, abolitionist and suffragist Frances E. Harper, and Lily Lord Tifft, active in Buffalo charity and philanthropy, the first woman on the city's Board of School Examiners.[56]

The papers that they delivered resembled those given in Sorosis and the New England Woman's Club meetings. There were a few on the arts, on the sciences, and on current events. The bulk of the papers, however, educated women to the possibilities of Domestic Feminism. Most papers took for granted that women possessed a special moral excellence. Some directly stressed woman's capacity as mother—"Enlightened Motherhood," "Inviolable Home," "An Ideal Home," "The Legal Guardianship of Children," and "The Status of the Mother." But they also maintained that it was woman's duty to extend this quality beyond the home. From the

> ...sure footing of the family affections, we women are able to go on to the recognition of extended relations to humanity. The slave, the barbarian, the criminal, the outcast, claim our compassionate care and regard. And the very intensity of our feeling for home, husband, and children gives us a power of loving and working outside of our homes, to redeem the world as love and work only can.[57]

Speeches on the "Relation of Woman's Work in the House to Work Outside," and "Woman as Guardians of the Public Health" demonstrated the possibilities of the extension of woman's sphere.[58]

This woman's work was not as self-seeking as woman suffrage was said to be by its detractors. Domestic Feminism would aid everyone. Sorosis welcomed the AAW to New York City in 1887 with the words: "May you, in the future, be given still greater opportunities for doing good, not alone to women, but to the world."[59] Such work would not take women out of character, but make them even better women.

Morality would not be abandoned but reinvigorated as women solved secular problems and at the same time extended their own freedom. Papers on "Temperance," "Social Purity," "Moral Culture," "High Life and High Living," "Needs of the Religious Nature," "Festivals—Their Power as a Means of Moral Culture," and an attack on the double standard evoked wide interest. There developed such a sense of woman's supervision over morality that Abby Morton Diaz even criticized the Bible. She contended that the extensive use of the Old Testament in Sunday schools was harmful because it taught wrath, vengeance, and brutality to children.[60] Her attack created unusual apprehension in a Congress marked by agreement. A special session was held to discuss her statements, and one clubwoman sent a letter to the *Providence Journal*[61] attacking Diaz's presentation. Although clubwomen surely formed a self-consciously moral audience, most hesitated to go so far as to tamper with the Bible.

Indeed, AAW members emphasized the religious overtones of woman's duty and insisted that women striving toward justice would hasten the coming of the millennium. The club members regularly sang "The Battle Hymn of the Republic" in deference to their president, Julia Ward Howe, who wrote the lyrics, in a celebration of patriotism, and because the song invoked memory of women's bold activity in abolition and their own dreams of emancipation. But a more important reason was that the "Battle Hymn" suggested the coming of Judgment Day, facilitated by the earnest work of women. For the Fifteenth Congress, Grace Appleton wrote a poem in the same meter as the "Battle Hymn," entitled "Woman's Congress."

Behold a wondrous gath'ring of the women of the land!—
They come from fair Atlantic homes and far Pacific strand,
To aid with wit and wisdom life's best uses to command,
The world is marching on!

And as of old the wise man journey'd long and journey'd far,
(Tho' they on patient camel's-back and these by steam and car),
Yet like them, come our sisters now, at the beck'ning of a star,
Whose light is marching on!

And as they sought the Living Word in far-off Galilee,—
These seek a live Evangel and diviner liberty,—
To hasten on the day of grace—the year of Jubilee.
Whose dawn is marching on!

So here we pledge ourselves anew to work with might and main,
To help dispel the darkness that the world doth still enchain,—
And be worthy of the glory of the glad Millennial reign
Whose Lord is marching on![62]

A woman who desired to work for the millennium must support her own autonomy, for it was synonymous with a righteous society. And women's organizations would help to create that just world. Julia Ward Howe told the First Congress of Women: "Plant an Association like this in the sparse settlements of the wilderness, or in the moral jungle of great cities, or in the roughness of mining and agricultural districts, and I can tell you what will come up—a redeemed society."[63]

Since woman had a moral duty to help improve society, she should not waste time doing her housework. Efficiency was the key. In a paper entitled "The Organization of Household Labor," Anna C. Garlin advocated the "annihilation of the private kitchen and laundry. She urged the acceptance of private nurseries and simplified clothes-making.[64] Melusina Fay Peirce reported on food and laundry cooperative experiments in Cambridge, Massachusetts. Lucinda Chandler announced, "It is more convenient and more economical that one central establishment should do one kind of work for many homes than that each home should have its own isolated and expensive machinery."[65] She urged bringing hot food home from a restaurant, European style. "Better to fold the hands," Abby May said, "than do fancy work, that is, useless fancy work."[66]

Homemaking, all agreed, was a career, but housekeeping was not. The two were often confused, but Domestic Feminists insisted that creating a happy, virtuous haven was superior to mere washing and cooking. The Congresses worked to separate woman's housecleaning drudgery from the vital work of uplifting the morality of America. Here are the roots of the home economics movement which sought to free women from household drudgery, so that they could have time for moral pursuits.

The AAW also sought to liberate women from restrictive clothing. Clothing fashions, and their effect on woman's health, were frequently discussed as harmful to the spread of good works. Abba Woolson, of the New England Woman's Club, carried her ridicule of fashionable women to the New York Congress. Christian women are, she said, "a race of gasping, nervous and despairing women, who with their compressed ribs, torpid lungs, hobbling feet, and bilious stomach, evidently consider it their first duty to crucify the flesh and to render themselves, and all humanity belonging to them, as frail and uncomfortable as possible."[67] Chandler pointed out that fashionable clothing was unhealthy, and, in fact, could destroy motherhood. This alone ought to deter women from the senseless wardrobe of the fashion. "A woman dies at the birth of her first child, from the results of tight lacing; but her sister continues to draw her corset strings as before, in order to mold her shape according to the standard styled beautiful."[68] Julia Ward Howe complained that the money men spent on their wives', daughters', and spinster sisters' elaborate clothing was a poor substitute for woman's independence. "Our present habits of dress are so exorbitant that men, when they have given us more jewelry than they can afford, and more silk dresses than we can wear, providing for us expensive households, full of bad order and worse economy, think that we have had our share of such profits as their business can bring them."[69] Sensible fashion would improve health, motherhood, and finances, and would free women for public work.

Once women were freed of confining home duties and fashions, the AAW anticipated they could exert influence throughout all society. The field of education was especially attractive. Women were already dominating the teaching profession and they, after all, had special maternal insights into the needs of children that well-suited them to participate in school governance. "The school board may admit a bachelor who has no qualifications for managing school nurseries, while the mother who has perhaps had years of experience in these as teacher is ignored," Chandler complained.[70] The women criticized education at every level, particularly if it did not marshall women's energies. Topics examined included "Women's Work in School Boards," "The Place of Women in Public Schools," "Co-education of the Sexes," "Endowments to Women's Colleges," "Physical Education of Girls," "Defects in the Higher Education of Women," "High Schools and Home," "Children's Books," "Scholarships for Women," and the "Association of Collegiate Alumnae."

But women did not restrict their hopes to the field of education. The AAW members "proposed that women shall have the right to enter any and every occupation for which their tastes or talents shall fit them."[71] The association worked to prepare women for responsible positions which were opening daily in numerous fields. Speeches were heard on "What Practical Measures will Promote the Financial Independence of Women," "Women as Landholders in the West," "Photography for Women," and "Women's Work in the Pulpit." The recurring message was that women should no longer limit themselves to traditional domestic occupation.

> From Adam down, all men have said to all women: "House-keeping is your sphere. In that you are most admirable. Literature, art, science, these are all beyond you. Stay in your own sphere and we will worship you, we will adore you: therein you are angels. Out of it you are a misery and a detestation: if you go out of it we will abhor you, we will shun you, we will have none of you." And women like to please men, you know![72]

In reality, many women already worked of necessity and had found that the rigors of the male sphere were difficult to overcome for women bred as ladies. Such a woman was S. A. C. Bond, whose husband died and left her in charge of his watch and chronometer business. If she was to support herself and her young son, she had to learn many skills. Even though she at times regretted having to enter the market place—"I feel more strongly every day how enviable every woman is who can stay quietly at home, finding in the domestic circle an ample sphere for her highest and noblest energies"[73]—she nevertheless set an example to others. Her realistic reminder that the joys of labor had been exaggerated in the rush to take on new responsibilities was ignored.

Naturally, women with families could not pursue most of the careers suggested, for childbearing and raising limited their mobility. But, as a result, they now found themselves glorified instead of shunned or pitied. At the Fourth Congress, Miss E. D. Sewall spoke on "Homes for Unmarried Women." She rejected the notion that spinsters should board with their relatives. Instead, she suggested that women deserved their own house and garden area.[74]

Mary Livermore, too, defended single women. In a speech entitled "Superfluous Women" she lauded the "social failures" scorned by Henry James.

> They have been brave enough to elect to walk through life alone, when some man has asked them in marriage, whom they could not love; with white lips they have

said "no," while their hearts have said "yes," because duty demanded of them the sacrifice of their own happiness. Their lives have been stepping stones for the advancement of younger sisters.[75]

They have earned money to send brothers to college, they have helped aging parents and provided comfort for all, Livermore explained. She cited countless single women who had made great contributions to society, including fifteen centuries of Catholic nuns, Florence Nightingale, Dorothea Dix, Maria Mitchell, and painter Rosa Bonheur.

Education and career discussion did not prevent political discussion at the Congresses. After 1881 the AAW came to be dominated by Julia Ward Howe, one of the most noted and respectable members of the Boston-based moderate American Woman Suffrage Association. Despite Croly's early resistance to the inclusion of suffrage, Howe's hegemony signaled the demise of Sorosis's control over the organization and resulted in a more open sympathy for suffrage in AAW ranks. Harriet Hanson Robinson noted, "Since 1876, AAW has gradually drifted from the control of its founders and Massachusetts women now 'turn the crank' of the machinery of the association."[76]

Favorable response by the AAW to suffrage discussions hastened Croly's disassociation from the group. Although quick to lead her friends in Sorosis, to write on injustices against women, and to engage other women in carrying out her Domestic Feminist program, she was never comfortable in the limelight, giving speeches, or guiding the AAW from the top office. Howe cannot be said to have usurped the founder's power, for Croly only temporarily and reluctantly presided over any organization she founded. Howe was competent, willing to govern, and did not share the hesitancy others had brought to the post before her long reign. Still, the silence each maintained about the other, unusual in two such careful historians of the Woman Movement, suggests a gracious effort to hide a rivalry, if not an antagonism. Croly may well have been disgruntled when Howe succeeded in combining suffrage and Domestic Feminism in the AAW, after she had formed the organization as an alternative to suffrage. Howe probably thought Croly narrow-minded.

Actually, even prior to Howe's AAW presidency, suffrage interested many members and was cautiously discussed at the Congresses. At the First Congress, the topic "Woman's Place in Government" disguised two pro-suffrage papers by Mary F. Eastman and Isabella Beecher Hooker. The following year, the program included another speech on suffrage. These papers, of course, comprised a very small segment of a diverse program. Suffrage gained wider acceptance among AAW members after they had been attuned to injustice in education, careers, and household responsibilities, but the cause was never central to their program; it maintained a gentle presence and was clearly only one part of the AAW scheme.

In fact, suffrage was so soft-pedaled that Lucy Stone incorrectly assumed the topic had never been touched. "The Congress, I think, is doing its very best. It has made a great deal of progress. And there has been a great deal to contend with. They began, afraid to say the word suffrage, and in three years, they are ready to have a paper on that subject. Don't let us condemn, but give them time."[77]

When the AAW failed to endorse suffrage openly, the newspapers concluded that the association was eliminating suffrage from its program. At times, clubwomen saw the merit of doing just that. At the Congress held in Syracuse in 1875, suffrage was not mentioned. The AAW leaders, in order to attract wide audiences, felt they must move guardedly on the most explosive of women's rights issues. In 1881 in Buffalo, where many clergymen had forewarned congregations against the upcoming Congress, the AAW also proceeded cautiously. "Although I am a suffragist, I am not here to speak of that," said President Julia Ward Howe.[78] Even so, audiences supported suffrage. Two days later in Buffalo, when Mary F. Eastman announced that the vote for women would not be harmful, her listeners applauded her.[79] At the Congress held in Springfield in 1897, the last sessions showed "much woman suffrage sentiment."[80]

The AAW was more concerned with coupling suffrage with Domestic Feminism than with educating women in the necessity of suffrage alone. In 1891 one speaker called suffrage in Wyoming responsible for "better schools, better order, better protection to women, juster legal verdicts, less crime, fewer divorces."[81] Suffrage provided another way for Domestic Feminists to extend their morality to the corrupt world outside their sphere. "If woman in the home needs politics to broaden and strengthen her intellectual and moral perceptions, politics needs the home to quicken its conscience, to animate it with unselfish life, and to purify it from cruelty and grossness."[82]

This effort on the part of the AAW to subordinate suffrage to their Domestic Feminism philosophy undoubtedly helped the association win the respect of the press[83] in spite of initial public suspicion. In Buffalo in 1881, when most clergymen had preached against the association,[84] the women tried to assure the public that there was nothing to fear. The *Buffalo Express* announced: "The ladies express a hope that this city's clergy will attend the meetings of the Congress and participate in its deliberations, at least by their countenance and presence."[85] The AAW quelled fears and gained acceptance. "To some who knew nothing of us, we appeared in the light of disturbers of the public peace. Our friends, however, carried the day."[86] In St. John's, Canada, in 1896, the populace also had expressed uneasiness at women speaking in public, but "here, as elsewhere, there was a great change of feeling caused by the meeting of the Congress."[87]

Some communities positively heralded the Congresses, owing in part to the favorable image of its president. The *Springfield Republican* reported, "Of Mrs. Howe, nothing need be said. Whether viewed as a woman of refinement, a broad student of the world's progress, a scholar, a gracious and charming society woman, her life and history are known to all."[88] But all the women created a pleasing impression. "It was a very handsome audience," said the *Providence Journal*.[89] The *Buffalo Express* admired the smart, beautiful, well-dressed and ladylike AAW participants, never hinting that they possessed any aura of "strong-mindedness."

The *Buffalo Courier*, which had expressed doubts about the AAW before its arrival,[90] later complimented the women on their success: "Talented, earnest and cultured, the members have in the past few years won an undisputed place in the affections of the women of the country and in the esteem of all right-thinking men."[91] A *Chicago Tribune* editorial remarked on the high tone of the discussions[92] and even urged the community to adapt Julia Ward Howe's suggestion of starting a bank to be run by and for women. The *New York Herald* wrote, "These women of the Congress seem to be working more rationally for their sex and infinitely more successfully than the suffragists, who know only one thought—the ballot box."[93] The *Syracuse Daily Journal* agreed: "Heretofore many of the great assemblages of women in this country have had three distinct characteristics: acidity, vituperation and "give-me-that-ballot or die!" But it is not so in this Woman's Congress. . . . No, not force, but love is the motive power of these wives and mothers."[94]

Politicians soon jumped on the bandwagon and welcomed the Congress to their localities. For instance, the mayor of Providence, who was also the brother of a prominent local clubwoman, attended a session and "rejoiced that the Congress had been held there, and he paid a high tribute to the worth and power of women."[95] In every city where the Congresses were held, officials bestowed compliments on the organization.[96]

In spite of the AAW's ability in assuaging public fears, it was not as successful in instituting concrete reform programs as the New England Woman's Club had been. Although committees were formed to examine problems,[97] they merely served as clearinghouses where information could be collected on new women in science or journalism or other professions. The absence of headquarters, the annual gathering in a new city, and the lack of organization and political involvement by audiences made the establishment of concrete programs difficult. The AAW, like Sorosis, remained content to awaken women to injustices and possible solutions.

The chief success of the AAW was its influence in creating more socially active clubs. Julia Ward Howe boasted, "Many a good Women's Club has sprung from these, our meetings. And these clubs seem to me to fulfill the gracious prediction of the Jewish prophet, 'The desert and solitary places shall be glad of them, and the wilderness shall rejoice and blossom as a rose.' "[98] Alice Stone Blackwell concurred. "Wherever it met, it left behind it a trail of new women's clubs and other organizations then considered novel and dangerous!"[99] Mary Bagg of Syracuse supported their generalizations with the report that the following clubs began in Syracuse as a result of the Third Congress: Syracuse Botanical Club, Ladies' Social Art Club, Portfolio Art Club, Housekeepers' Club, Coffee Club (to study German), Leisure Hour, Bureau of Labor and Charities, and Our Friendly Inn, a temperance organization.[100]

In addition to actual clubs, the Congresses created an intangible feeling of sisterhood which inspired women to recognize and redress grievances against their sex. One Buffalo member spoke of the AAW as "a power for practical idealism... and the women who came under its vivifying influence were never the same again."[101] Other members talked of the same thing. "I know more than a score of frivolous women who felt themselves convicted and ashamed by the wholesome and searching words of the good women who spoke from the platform of our opera house."[102] "Results were deep rather than demonstrative. It is evident in many ways that the Congress quickened, in our State, the forward march of women."[103] One officer wrote:

> The general results of our existence are, I may briefly state, a wider realization by women of her own place in the social fabric, and of her innate powers as well as rights; it has served to waken many a listless, idle woman into some active study or occupation; it has connected false notions and underestimates of labor itself; for, when these noble, earnest women come upon the platform of a strange city, given over, as is all the world too much, to fashion and gossip–and assert that labor is holy, and all honest workers are to be respected, and all drones despised—their hearers are electrified and inspired with the determination to engage in some practical improvement for themselves or others. Its effect has been also to introduce women to each other from the extremes of our continent, to broaden and deepen our love and trust in each other, and our charity for all.[104]

Even though the AAW did not initiate concrete reforms, efforts were made to introduce to Congresses a sense of the importance of social action. In Providence, a few leading clubs reported on their work, thereby giving ideas and inspiration to others.[105] At the Seventh Congress, members made a successful effort to get women interested in working on the specific problems of putting women on state boards of education, managing insane asylums and reformatory institutions. It urged them also to learn legislation in order to remove unjust laws.[106] By 1891 the Congress was asking state vice-presidents to investigate the status of children and young people in public institutions.[107]

This latter project duplicated the efforts of the new General Federation of Women's Clubs, which formed in 1890. With the appearance of the General Federation, the AAW was no longer necessary, in part because it had done its work so well. Education and career barriers were crumbling daily through the efforts of the AAW members and the clubs inspired by the organization. Women now simply chose to go to work through individual clubs or the more publicly active General Federation, instead of through the AAW. The itinerant nature of the AAW reduced its effectiveness as cities developed their own women's rights groups. The AAW had to repeat cities and go farther south, west, and even to Canada, at great expense, to try to attract members.

Early intentions to keep membership exclusive were abandoned as the number of members declined. The AAW in 1888 sent souvenirs to women to interest them in joining.[108] In 1894, with unrealistic optimism, Julia Ward Howe corresponded with Ednah Dow Cheney about the preparation of a pamphlet designed to enlarge the membership, especially among young people.[109]

The last Congress was held in Springfield in 1897. Because it was poorly attended, there was talk about disbanding, but no decisions were made. Members appointed a committee of Howe, Cheney, Mitchell, Reverend Blackwell, and Chandler to consider producing a publication or reorganizing to meet biennially as the General Federation did.[110] Howe, reluctant to abandon the organization in which she had invested so much energy, wrote to Cheney,[111] "AAW stares me in the face. I feel perfectly unable to decide.... If you don't help me I'll bust." Even though Howe realized that the AAW could no longer actively compete with the General Federation, she felt that reflection on social problems was too valuable to abandon. "The quiet study of social problems may not make a great noise in the world, but without it, the world will not be greatly helped."[112] She was not alone. Harriet Townsend of Buffalo noted, " 'A sower of infinite seed was it.' When it was succeeded by the General Federation of Women's Clubs its work was not done and the harvest is still plentiful."[113] Indeed, the clubs it inspired transformed the lives of millions of American women. The women's culture club had become an institution in America.

# CHAPTER FOUR

# Literary Clubs

Women throughout the United States during the 1870s, 1880s, and 1890s began to found individual literary clubs, oftentimes directly inspired by Sorosis, the New England Woman's Club, and the Association for the Advancement of Women. They met to discuss papers that they themselves had researched and written on such subjects as Shakespeare's plays, Dante's *Inferno*, and Browning's poetry. Unlike their Sorosis predecessors, however, most of these clubwomen did not pursue the arts with career goals in mind. For the most part, they were older women who joined after their families had grown, and who believed their sensitivity as ladies lent itself to cultural concerns. Here was a serious subject they could study without abandoning their valued domestic traits.

The study of art and literature was not as closely allied to traditional concepts of ladydom as the study of home or child care might have been, but neither was it as radical as suffrage work. Its form and content was fairly rigid and limited to particular topics which, if not entirely within the bounds of orthodoxy, surely were not extremist. Each meeting of most clubs presented information on an annually chosen topic. The most popular subjects were the literature, mythology, or history of classical antiquity, the Bible, American or English literature or history, or the geography of a certain region or nation along with its art, music, literature, religion, politics, and history. These programs were diversified with musical performances, dramatic productions, and discussions of current events. Talk of socialism, the Czar, the Indian as a national problem, the tariff, and civil service was part of most programs. Thus, when club members boasted that they belonged to "universities for middle-aged women," they spoke in hyperbole for, in fact, they evaded the mental rigors imposed by a good college curriculum. Institutions of higher learning still demanded the study of Latin and Greek language and literature, the natural and physical sciences, mathematics, and with increasing frequency, modern languages with their literature in the original.[1] Colleges made increasing efforts to include music and art in the curriculum, but basically, clubwomen did not wish to catch up to their daughters. Members' primary efforts had been put into family life, and now they often sought an education that would not demand too much of them.

The format of one or two short papers, ten to twenty minutes in length, left little time for group discussion. Often, explosive issues related to politics and religion were specifically banned. This narrow format served to limit free-wheeling forums that would stimulate thought.

Consequently, topics related to the most avant-garde artistic movements or newest social thoughts were less frequently explored than more classical subjects. Little notice was taken of Freud or Darwin, impressionism, or, later, the Ashcan school of painting, or the naturalistic school of writers. Instead of exposing shocking or critical new views, optimistic members propagated their belief that late nineteenth-century America was the culmination of civilization. Such problems as immigration, poverty, or immorality only awaited firm guidance to be righted.

Finally, clubs' emphasis on cultural appreciation was essentially passive. Members were seldom prepared for the mastery of any skill which would enable them to undertake independent careers, although it happened occasionally. For all their talk of music, art, literature, history, philosophy, and even science, few clubs provided music lessons, sketching classes, French language exercises, or scientific experimentation. Clubs developed their programs for the acquisition of less tangible talents.

While they did not often produce scholars, career women, social critics, or avant-garde aesthetes, literary clubs still served as a first step for feminists determined to improve their status. The significance of the development of sufficient audacity to strive for self-improvement in an era that defined ladies as selfless agents devoted to the well-being of others cannot be underrated. Certainly it was noticed by male critics.

The effort to unify their study through yearly topics signifies a seriousness about their labors and an awareness of the danger of dilettantism. For all the weaknesses in their programs, clubwomen were not always slow to tackle the challenging issues of the day when they saw them as vital to their alternative vision of the rich life for both men and women. Socialism, Edward Bellamy's *Looking Backward*, and Ibsen's controversial plays were frequent subjects of club meetings.

A strong sense of sisterhood grew among these women, along with confidence, and skills in speaking, researching, and writing, which gave all a new sense of worth and enabled some members to move on to more political activity. Most importantly, the branching out by women into the cultural domain represents an important extension of Domestic Feminism. Utilizing society's notion of female sensitivity to defend entry into a new realm was a significant step for the autonomy of women and their flight from confinement in the home.

In order to understand how culture came to absorb the late nineteenth-century woman of America, it is necessary to recognize the extent of the

Woman Movement during the second half of the nineteenth century and how its demands were modified to suit the realities of life for married women with families. Although the post-Civil War suffragists were viewed by the populace as daring and radical, their influence was widely felt. Not only were suffrage demands well publicized, but the other inequities which hampered woman's growth began to receive more popular recognition. The need for women's colleges and careers, better wages and health care, more sensible clothing and home care, wider participation in the church and in temperance issues, was explored in pulpits, publications, and in government. After mid-century, as women's colleges proliferated and universities admitted more women, as women began to dominate the field of primary school teaching and to professionalize nursing, many Americans began to be aware of the restrictions upon opportunities for women.

Schools that educated women were exceedingly conscious of the Woman Movement all around them. They gained support from that movement and reinforced it by providing students with models of strong, single women who ignored fashion and harbored sympathy toward women's rights. The students were self-conscious about the Woman Movement that was questioning the role of women and challenging it on every front. In 1875 a prizewinning essay at the Buffalo Seminary, a high school for girls, insisted that woman "has an intellect equal to man's; why must she fold her talent in a napkin and lay it away." The author of the prizewinning essay in 1884 railed against history, when savage women "slaved at the plough" while husbands rested and feudal women were "petted dolls," "imprisoned by chivalry." She continued, "Be thankful that this age is growing more and more enlightened, and that you are regarded as equals of your husbands in intellect by all except a few lyrical philosophers."[2]

In such an atmosphere, young women dreamed of pioneering in new careers which were just beginning to open to them.[3] Some of them were able to do so by foregoing marriage. The Gold Rush and Civil War had resulted in a shortage of men in much of the Eastern seaboard, which to a certain degree alleviated pressures on women to marry. Many young women with no marriage prospects successfuly engaged in academic pursuits that led to careers.[4] Most students, however, did not escape the harsh gaze of those who categorized schools for women as part of the threatening Woman Movement. Critics were fearful that graduates would become freakish, "strong-minded" women with goals that would challenge the supremacy of the family. They feared that educated women would not marry or raise children. In reality, however, whether or not women remained in the academies, seminaries, and colleges long enough to receive degrees, and many of them did not, most also married. Mrs. George Wadsworth told the Buffalo Female Academy graduates of 1875 of her experience: "Twenty-two years ago, when I received my graduate's diploma, I thought myself just entering upon a career of letters. Like yourselves, dear young ladies, who stand to-day where I stood then, I was fully determined to devote myself to the higher walks of learning. My vanity even whispered of a 'coming book,' which might electrify you all—but *man* proposed."[5]

These former students spent their married lives in a restricted atmosphere in which insignificant routine and tedium went unrelieved. To be sure, many women had domestic servants to assist them in the ordering of their houses.[6] And great varieties of household conveniences came on the market, which perhaps brought additional assistance, but also increased the complexity of the housework and raised standards of cleanliness.[7] These conveniences meant that some women could enjoy concerts, visiting, whist, shopping, and church socials. But these diversions were few and far between compared with the responsibilities of supervising, training, and assisting domestic servants in cooking, cleaning, and shopping, entertaining the husband's associates, and child-raising. Nineteenth-century women also often had responsibility for nursing aging parents.[8] These necessary obligations muted the ambition of their schooldays. Housewifery was too time-consuming to allow for fulfillment of high aspirations and dreams.

As home responsibilities superseded all other activity, many women discovered how fully they had ignored themselves. Said a Buffalo Seminary Collegiate Department essay in 1875, "We see, daily, mothers whose lives are burdened with care, whose every hour is occupied in attending to the wants of others, and who yield up every pleasure and every selfish desire of their own, to minister to the pleasures and desires of their children, husbands, or friends." In the same year the Class of 1870 historian, Mrs. Spencer Clinton, wrote, "The lives of our classmates are uneventful, and, to the outside world, barren of result. We have not among us generals, judges, or senators. We are not distinguished upon the field, the bench or in the forum. The story of the life of one would seem to be the story of all."[9]

The woman in her forties, whose last child was born, who was experienced at but tired of child care, now had room and need in her life to renew the ambition of her past. "We were no longer in our first youth, our babies were out of our arms and their bringing up was past the nursery stage with its insistent claims while their future opened wide vistas, where we needed all the wisdom we could get."[10] In a society that valued a woman for her maternal duties, the woman finished with child-rearing had a void to fill. She was ready for a role that gave her self-esteem and importance in life. Rather than push her children into paths she may have regretted not taking, she could forge her own.

Thus, the diverse directions in which the persistent Woman Movement grew held varying messages for different women. To a growing minority who followed careers, at the expense of a family of their own, it provided inspiration in the face of job and social discrimination. To the married woman raising a family, the optimism of the Woman Movement was used in other ways. To these women, many of whom had enjoyed some higher education but sacrificed personal ambition for marriage and children, middle age was seen as a second opportunity to reevaluate their lives in literary clubs and learn skills to remake their own lives.

Single women also found a need for clubs, although they comprised a minority of the membership. The inspiration they received from the Woman

Movement did not eliminate the sense of isolation that enveloped them in a world that revered the woman for her childbearing capabilities. Since the single woman in nineteenth-century America usually lived with her relatives, she daily faced a norm which defined her as an outsider. If she had embarked on a career, she suffered job as well as social discrimination, both of which caused her to seek support from clubs. In addition, her lack of child-raising responsibilities meant she could join associations at an earlier age.

Women, then, found many reasons to join literary clubs. Whether married or single, they discovered that such factors as freedom from domestic duties, discontent with their lives under the influence of the growing Woman Movement, and the sense of isolation from husband and from other women engaged in the same household routine made associations for the study of culture attractive to them.

Woman's passage into secular club activity was facilitated through several means. As their antebellum counterparts had done, late nineteenth-century women were conditioned for club work through their church-related endeavors. Building on the model of lady as a pious and pure agent of goodness, these women affiliated with religious societies through which they could spend some of their vast energies. By 1893 in Rhode Island, there were at least fifty-eight such associations governed by women.[11] In Buffalo, women participated in many such organizations as rank and file members, even if they were not permitted to officiate.[12] *The Missionary Helper*, one of many magazines for women's benefaction, reveals wide activity and huge contributions by women in charity work of all kinds. The biographies of countless clubwomen as well as fiery suffragists reveal that this public work was a starting point for vast numbers of both groups.

Another factor assisting women in their willingness to join clubs was the increasing number of secular associations rapidly springing up throughout the country—patriotic organizations, fraternal orders, luxurious men's clubs. Maria Owen, founder of the Springfield Woman's Club in Massachusetts, declared, "Association is the watchword of the age—association for labor, for trade, for instruction, for entertainment, for advance of all kinds. Women naturally feel the impulse and are banding together for work."[13] Ellen Henrotin, a Chicago clubwoman who became president of the General Federation, spoke of clubs as part of that development. "It is a necessary step in the evolution toward higher social and educational conditions. It came, I believe, in answer to a demand for efficiency."[14]

In addition, Sorosis, the New England Woman's Club, and the Association for the Advancement of Women had influenced the founding of numerous other clubs. These early organizations enjoyed wide publicity, and many members made personal visits to potential clubwomen, teaching them how to establish clubs of their own. Women's increased exposure to the participants and work of established clubs inspired their emulation in greater and greater proportions. Acceptance of club work climbed with membership growth.

There are no reliable figures on the total number of women who joined literary clubs during the second half of the nineteenth century, but many thousands of women found refuge in the dozens of clubs that formed in almost every city, town, and village in the country. The active participation of many respectable women countered the opinion that the literary club was an aberration in American life. Meetings generally lasted about two hours and were held from one to four times a month, but only from September or October until May or June. So many clubwomen summered in vacation spots or were busy supervising their children on vacation from school that most clubs disbanded during public school holidays. Since Saturdays and Sundays were reserved for family, clubs generally met during the week either in the morning or afternoon. Rarely was a club meeting held in the evening. Not only were the children home then, but social norms dictated that a proper woman stay home at night. "To venture forth after nightfall without a husband (if you had one) was indeed a hazard in those days."[15]

The names of the clubs usually described meeting time or purpose. Frequent titles were "Friday Afternoon Club," "The Wednesday Morning Club," "Alternate Tuesdays Club," "The Fortnightly." Locale sometimes determined the organization's title as in "The Rhode Island Woman's Club," and "Chicago Sorosis," while the subject matter under study determined others— "The Shakespeare Club," "The Browning Society," "Literary Delvers." Sometimes, however, origins of the names are less obvious. "Ardirhebiah" signified the initials of the founders in Providence, Rhode Island; "Ka-na-te-nah Club" in Syracuse is an Indian name; the "81" Club of Kansas City, Missouri, was founded in 1881; and "The McRae" was named for English professor Emma Mont McRae.[16]

The clubwomen met in each other's homes if their numbers were fewer than ten or twelve. If larger, they met in public meeting rooms, in church parlors, or, if they were financially able, in clubhouses they funded themselves. Women who valued their reputations, and most of them did, were limited to these meetings places since their virtue was suspect if they frequented public restaurants. Some organizations desired to remain small and intimate, limiting their size to twenty women. Others, like the Rhode Island Woman's Club, which started with five women in 1876, grew to ninety-seven the following year and had constant inquiries from potential members. In 1889 they established a limit of two hundred. In 1892 they raised it to two hundred fifty and still had a waiting list.

It is difficult to make steadfast generalizations about the composition of literary clubs because the large number of clubs attracted such a variety of members. In Providence alone, in the late nineteenth century, the following clubs are known to have existed: Women's Educational and Industrial Union; Sarah E. Doyle; Fortnightly; Read, Mark and Learn; Four-Leaf Clover Club; Saturday Club; Ardirhebiah; Providence Mother's Club; Rhode Island Woman's Club; Embreaso; Vincent Club CLSC; Catholic Woman's Club; Rhode Island Sorosis; Providence Social Club. But not all of these left records. No doubt there were other clubs, especially short-lived ones, whose records are now also lost. Printed records are also unreliable. Membership lists, when they are available, misspell names, exclude new members, and retain those who had actually withdrawn.

A study of extant membership lists and other club documents, however, reveals some general trends in membership. Most clubwomen were intensely loyal. Great numbers of women joined a club and stayed in it year after year. A member often interested her sisters, daughters, and sisters-in-law in joining. As a rule, clubwomen were mature since most joined after their children were grown. The Tuesday Morning Club of Elmira reported they "never admitted a lady under the age of 50."[17] The Rhode Island Woman's Club estimated that its average member was fifty years of age.[18] The smiling faces in club photographs reveal gray-haired, matronly women, with wrinkled faces. The fact that only occasionally did a club boast a great range of ages underlines the homogeneity of most memberships. The memorials and eulogies to newly deceased members, common in club programs, testify to the maturity of club membership.

Clubs were generally composed of women who shared a common background of some sort. Some were associations of alumnae of a high school, college,or professional school.[19] Some women shared a birthplace,[20] while others shared religion. The Literary Club of the Church of the Messiah in Buffalo was originally composed of Universalist women, though they eventually admitted outsiders if there were no Universalists on the waiting lists. Some women merely shared a neighborhood, like the Walnut Street Club of Elmira. Others shared a profession.[21] Some clubs were limited to mothers. The Mother's Club of Cambridge, Massachusetts, represents a literary club in which members studied child-rearing techniques in addition to literature and defended both as enriching the home.[22] Predominantly, however, occupations of husbands, or economic status, determined the composition of a club. The members of the Woman's Club of Orono, Maine, for example, were largely wives of professors at the state university there.

Consequently, in most communities, there was a social hierarchy of clubs which reflected class, status, and ethnic differences. Members of the most prestigious organizations valued their aristocratic credentials. "The Friends," a Buffalo club, boasted that "the club numbers three direct descendants of Roger Williams, two descendants of signers of the Declaration, a member of the Holland Society, descendants of commissioned officers in the French War, and one-half of the members are Daughters of the American Revolution."[23] In such clubs, membership was restricted, in part because of meeting places and goals for discussion, but also because elitism enhanced prestige for the original members. New candidates often had to be proposed by two or more members to an executive board, which could blackball the nominees. Careful screening of prospective members invariably resulted in membership lists that were overwhelmingly Yankee. Rarely in the elite clubs were women of Central or Eastern European or Mediterranean descent included among the membership. Only an occasional Jewish name was seen.

These selective organizations, even those founded by northern abolitionists, excluded black women, who would form their own clubs and federations at the turn of the century. Even American-born women of Irish or German descent were seldom admitted.[24]

The hierarchy of clubs in Providence, Rhode Island, was typical. Membership in no other club in Providence carried such widely acknowledged status as that in the Rhode Island Woman's Club. Professional women and wives of influential husbands were predominant. Many members' spouses were listed in the elite Blue Book of the City.[25] Although the organization had some room for the wives of small businessmen, an artist, and an occasional bookkeeper, clerk, or cashier, the city directories reveal that most women were married to owners of manufacturing companies, bankers, lawyers, clergymen, and engineers.

Most of the professional women who joined the Rhode Island Woman's Club were single, although a few, like suffragist and writer[26] Fanny Purdy Palmer, were married. One of the club's founders and a dominating presence throughout club life in nineteenth-century Rhode Island was public school teacher and suffragist, Sarah E. Doyle, who attracted many teachers to the club. But other single career women also joined. Physician Martha H. Mowry, a suffragist who also originated health programs for Providence clubwomen, and the assistant librarian of the Providence Atheneum both belonged. The club also welcomed single women who were not employed, but who boarded with relatives and were supported by them.

The next most exclusive group was the Providence Ardirhebiah Club, whose membership was also made up of wives of influential men—dentists, lawyers, presidents of manufacturing companies, the head of the Public Works Department at City Hall. One woman was herself the Society Editor of the *Tribune*, and another was president of the Young Woman's Christian Temperance Union.[27] But this organization remained small. The members were content to work without fanfare, not seeking a widespread reputation for itself as the Rhode Island Woman's Club did.

Beneath Ardirhebiah in the Providence hierarchy were several clubs made up of wives from the prosperous middle classes. These clubs included fewer wives of professionals and owners of commercial establishments, but more wives of clerks, teachers, grocers, general managers, and bookkeepers.[28] Still lower on the hierarchy of clubs were those of non-Yankee women—the clubs of Irish women, for example, or the settlement clubs of working-class women.

Financial resources of the clubs varied as widely as the clubs themselves. Budgets, generally, were small. Despite the fact that many members had affluent husbands, the clubwomen did not control the family purse strings. Dues, even for prestigious clubs, were seldom exorbitant, ranging from fifty cents to ten dollars per year, with a two to five dollar initiation fee. Unusual, indeed, was the Buffalo Twentieth Century Club's entrance fee of five hundred dollars.[29] Tiny clubs like the Walnut Street Club in Elmira, whose members met in homes and did not pay rent or buy refreshments, charged five cents per month in 1898. Some clubs fined members twenty-five cents for lateness or absence. Clubs rarely indulged in the fund-raising bazaars typical of charity organizations. They instead created hundred-dollar life memberships or welcomed donations by generous members or interested parties. Some clubs earned interest on those funds they managed to collect. In Springfield, an admission was charged for club plays. The Rhode Island Woman's Club, in 1878, opened Elizabeth Stuart Phelps's speech on George Eliot to the public. "Our enterprise was the source of genuine and refined pleasure to many outside our immediate circle. It was a rare intellectual and spiritual treat, and was delivered in a manner most fascinating. It brought a substantial sum into the treasury, which was not the least pleasing feature of the affair."[30]

For the most part, literary clubs did not need a great deal of money. Expenses were modest—at the most, printed programs, reports, ballots, and perhaps rent, flowers, postage, and refreshments. Members paid for their own badges. The lack of money bothered only those members of the most ambitious clubs who desired a clubhouse. "It is humiliating to know that clubs younger than ours, with fewer members, own buildings which give a dignity to their standing, which the Rhode Island Woman's Club fails to possess."[31] These clubwomen sold ten-dollar shares to raise the fifty thousand dollars to build a clubhouse and paid dividends from the rents they collected from other clubs which met there.

Not all clubs depended upon older homemakers for the bulk of their membership. The Providence Mothers' Club attracted unusually large numbers of young, busy women who sought to gain information on child care. But literary improvement was also a substantial part of its program. Here, however, members were not required to give their own papers. Time limitations imposed by small children meant that guest speakers were invited to come to the club.

Another unusual club in Providence was the Four-Leaf Clover Club. Three-quarters of its membership were single.[32] Unlike most clubs, the members met in the evening since many were employed. The women were clerks, telephone operators, music teachers, elocution teachers, public school teachers, stenographers, manicurists, bookkeepers, and dressmakers. The minority of married women had husbands who were foremen, clerks, and bank tellers. It is significant that women who were teachers, the most prestigious job open to women at the time, associated with wives of foremen in the Four-Leaf Clover Club. Income acted as the leveler. For women, class status was a complex matter, partly reflecting their own position, and partly reflecting that of the man in their lives.

Most clubs, which were dominated by married women, apparently failed to meet the needs of single professional women. Although married women respected the single women's desirable skills and regular income, teachers' special status-consciousness and personal needs drove them, in particular, to congregate in clubs of their own. In 1894, when the Sarah E. Doyle Club for teachers formed, most Providence women's clubs experienced a drop in membership of single women. The withdrawal of professional women from general clubs gave them an opportunity to collaborate to correct occupational abuses, but it also meant that the chance for women of all backgrounds to associate and acknowledge their common problems was now diminished. Nevertheless, lack of interaction among clubwomen of different backgrounds did not blunt their determination to gain self-improvement. Members of all backgrounds shared an interest in enjoying new exposure to ideas that had recently seemed well beyond their province.

Unlike their Sorosis and New England Woman's Club predecessors, many women did not meet for self-improvement without guilt. "We are for the most part busy women oppressed by the routine of our daily lives," one clubwoman noted defensively. She admitted women had little time for the study they craved, but that was because the "treadmill" of their lives almost "killed within them the hope of progress."[33] Despite the admission that their lives needed development, still women questioned, "How much time can we, in justice to ourselves and our families, give to outside matters?"[34]

But these doubts did not prevent women from meeting in literary clubs in great numbers. A few, but not the majority, defended the activity by stressing its compatibility with domesticity. At the Rhode Island Woman's Club, for instance, the organization's pin was described as "a pair of scales, having in one a distaff and in the other a book, palette, and a musical instrument. As the scales are perfectly balanced it typified the principle that the club together with the home tend to make the perfectly developed woman."[35] Others were less cautious and made no effort to justify club work for its domestic utility. "To some of us," said Mrs. Reuben Kellogg of Sorosis in Elmira, New York, "it has at times afforded our only relaxation from daily routine outside of our church life."[36]

Clubwomen of Rhode Island and elsewhere used their clubs to build a Domestic Feminism from which they launched their critique of American society. They began to acquire the speaking, organizational, and leadership skills that enabled them to develop and express their ideas. An examination of the details of typical literary organizations is revealing, for every aspect of the clubs pointed to women's growth and reveals both the strength and limitations of their feminism.

Cliques and elitism were a genuine part of women's clubs in the 1870s and 1880s, and the use of clubs for class consolidation and upward mobility was real. The groups nevertheless gave participants important skills that would enable them to grow out of their self-consciousness and isolation. In measuring the ways in which the literary club aided women, the sisterhood engendered by the clubs is especially important. Regardless of the degree of snobbery women experienced in a particular organization, there was a joy in breaking out of the isolation of the household to share news and companionship with women like themselves.

Although the partaking of refreshments by clubwomen has been considered frivolous, it actually served a useful purpose. A Chicago club history explained, "Many of us mute, inglorious Miltons who had not the courage to speak our minds before several hundred in formidable array, expressed our humble opinions freely over the teacups."[37] Newspaper accounts of meetings of the Buffalo Graduate Association barely mention the topics discussed and instead spend a paragraph describing the type of refreshments, the name of the women who poured the tea, the color scheme of the tablecloth and flowers.[38] In such familiar domestic details and setting, women took hesitant steps beyond domestic concerns toward more ambitious club work.

The social interaction was necessary preparation before formal club work could advance. Women "not only had not the experience which would make them exact thinkers and accurate in the presentation of facts, but they lacked the self-possession to do so before an audience,"[39] said one clubwoman. Buffalo clubwomen were satisfied with the preparation from social intercourse. "Conversations have proved an excellent school for extemporaneous speaking. Women no longer lose their heads where they find their feet."[40]

The task of freeing women from inhibitions about speaking publicly was not an easy one. For generations, women had been taught that silence in public was a virtue. Before entering into the usual club procedure of hearing formal papers written by members, many clubs went from informal teas through a transitional phase of inviting outside speakers to the meeting. These speakers not only set an example for timid women, they also delivered strong messages of feminism to the members. Feminist Charlotte Perkins Gilman was in such demand that she was able to support herself by speaking at clubs.[41] Antoinette Brown Blackwell, Helen Campbell, and Mount Holyoke College president Mary Woolley continually stirred clubwomen to consider the possibilities of dress reform, cooperative housekeeping, women as architects and ministers and photographers, women as guardians of the public health, and the merits of women as educators. These feminists raised consciousness about the clubwoman's responsibility and ability to change the world.[42]

Yet club leaders knew they would never develop the talent of their own members if they relied on these special women. They had to force themselves, however painful, to learn to speak publicly. The Springfield Woman's Club resolved not to invite any speakers so the members would have to learn by doing. The Literary Club of the Church of the Messiah in Buffalo boasted that it relied less and less on outside speakers as the members grew more skilled in presenting papers. The Rhode Island Woman's Club limited itself to one outside speaker per month, hoping to reach the day when no outsiders would be necessary.[43]

One way to combat timidity regarding public speaking was to hold topical sessions, as the Rhode Island Woman's Club did. "Timid persons learned to discuss questions before a few, and, in time gained self-possession, which enabled them to do the same before the club."[44] The Literary Club of the Church of the Messiah in Buffalo also tried conversations based on experience. "Although many members obeyed St. Paul's injunction and kept silence in public, the conversations were a help. Gradually the ladies were induced to talk and the earnestness of thought expressed showed how interested women are in all practical questions."[45]

Clubwomen needed more than confidence in order to present papers in public. They also needed skills in the preparation of the papers they would read. Researching and writing a paper was a new and frightening task to many women. Even those who may have begun to master those skills as school girls now found they had deteriorated. Most communities had no libraries where members could grow familiar with research tools. The earliest clubwomen scoured each other's homes for books. In New York State, they were able to gain help from the Albany State Library, which also sent New York books to grateful clubwomen in Maine. As a result, one of the first projects clubwomen embarked upon was the founding of public libraries. In communities where libraries had already been established, clubs published lists of specific references at the library and the name of the librarian who would acquaint them with the topic of the year. Women planned their general themes and specific topics one full year ahead and painstakingly prepared the papers. "Never before had I spent so much labor in the preparation of anything,"[46] said one woman.

For every outsider's criticism of "second-hand wisdom," and "ency-clopedic rehearsals,"[47] there were those who said the quality of the work was high. The Springfield women found that the quality of the papers raised their husbands' estimation of them. "When the paper is finished and he finds it a most creditable production, showing undreamed of power and needing none of his embellishments; when he begins with only half-concealed pride to tell of this and finds seventy more men with similar discoveries to relate, it is plain that woman has begun to win a new kind of respect from those who never realized before how much of condescension there was in their regard for the other sex."[48] Some authors were so successful that they sent their papers to other clubs, and some even became club lecturers. In Harriet Hanson Robinson's diary, she confided, "Papers were read by several ladies and all were good. We have developed a great deal of talent in Old and New. And some have learned to speak and write well who never thought they could before."[49] One Buffalo clubwoman wrote of the early years of her club:

> Such a thing as a discussion of the papers by the general membership of the club was absolutely unheard of, and indeed no one could then have expected that without the interposition of a miracle, the frightened and unready women of that time, who, clinging to a chair for support, and with eyes chained to the manuscript, uttered in husky tones their halting thoughts, could ever be transformed into the really skilled debators that some have become. In fact the transformation has been brought about by a miracle, the miracle of ten years persistent practice.[50]

For a few hours each month the study of culture took precedence over motherhood. Clubmembers devised ingenious means for moving toward the mastery of their subject matter. "Sewing was forbidden except between Thanksgiving and Christmas," says the 1894 minutes of the Wednesday

Morning Club of Elmira. Home duties were not to intrude on meetings most of the year. Meetings frequently started with a roll call in which members answered with a quotation from Shakespeare's works. Many clubs tried to correct their errors by self-consciously appointing a critic who could criticize them, but this was rarely successful. One Buffalo woman later admitted, "Ladies had not learned to give and take in those days. Although conscious of manifold errors and imperfections, they were extremely sensitive and did not care to be told their mistakes. The office was not a success and was soon abolished."[51] Among the "Friends" of Buffalo, the critic was even more demanding, insisting "on a drill on pronunciation and the use of words, at each meeting."[52]

Women may have shied from criticism of their grammar, but they did not fail to learn to organize committees, plan and execute club programs, use Parliamentary procedure, study general themes from several perspectives, and chair meetings, often by using a rotating chair so everyone would gain experience. Clubmembers gained a little knowledge, some selfishness, and self-confidence, attributes that had always been available to most men. Carrie Chapman Catt wisely said, "Club women are like Kansas corn. You can see and hear them grow."[53]

Although these attributes were vital to the development of the nineteenth-century woman, a more important result of club life was that women learned to support other women. Charlotte Perkins Gilman captured this when she observed, "Club women learn more than to improve the mind; they learn to love each other." Other American clubwomen agreed.[54]

Not surprisingly, men were not welcome at these assemblages. The male presence intimidated women and hampered them from acquiring the public speaking skills they desired. In Buffalo, a group which congregated in a church parlor could not refuse to admit the church pastor. But the women chafed under his scrutiny; he challenged the views expressed and effectively silenced most of the membership.[55] While most clubs emphatically barred male membership, many permitted male speakers, generally pastors, to lecture to their members. Still, there were efforts to reduce even these male contributions. Women in the Rhode Island Woman's Club bragged in 1890 that men had appeared before them only twice that year.[56] Most clubs tried to limit male participation to a single annual open house.

The distance between their husbands' world and their own fostered a bond of sympathy among women, and this bond began to appear in the papers they presented. Again and again, the topics dealt not only with the arts, but with women's place in the arts and, finally, women's place in society. Clubwomen gave papers on such subjects as "Catherine the Great," "The New Woman," "John Stuart Mill," "Woman's Share in Russian Nihilism," "Margaret Fuller," "Women's Work in the Sanitary Commission," "New York State Laws Affecting Women," "Legal Status for Women," "Women's Suffrage," "Women's Work in Agriculture," "Influence of Women in Revolutionary Days." All these were discussed in various clubs in the early years with great frequency. The point of view was not always defiant, but was generally critical. A paper entitled "Women in History," given by a Syracuse clubwoman, was typical.

> A celebrated teacher of History once said to me, "When women do anything worthy of record, they will get due recognition," and I wondered if he had had a mother.... What has history been in the past? Men's story of men's triumphs and trials; his victories and defeats.... It has not been considered by the ordinary historian...that woman's work, sufferings, achievements, were worth recognizing and recording.[57]

At first this pride and solidarity among women brought little organized action on behalf of their sex. In their homes and neighborhoods, clubwomen expressed enthusiasm for the clubs that encouraged social interaction, exposure to books, ideas, and community problems that deserved attention, and optimism about their ability to solve those problems, but they stressed establishment of women's college scholarships and clubhouse funds. They did not sponsor diverse programs for women or for their communities until the General Federation of Women's Clubs in the 1890s pressured them to do so by spreading encouragement for initiating municipal reforms.

Suffragists and temperance advocates saw literary clubs, however, as an important training ground for their causes. Both issues were discussed, although they never dominated culture concerns. Suffragists knew clubs could educate women to the need for woman suffrage,[58] but they also knew their active proselytizing scared off potential supporters. "The more prominent suffragists wish to keep in the background as much as possible," Elizabeth Churchill wrote to Ednah Cheney regarding the origin of women's clubs in Providence in the face of great indifference.[59] Yet the presence of suffragists in clubs meant the concept of the franchise could be introduced with some subtlety to those who had not been exposed to its supporters before. Plenty of intitially wary clubwomen learned to endorse the vote through this route.

Men, on the other hand, saw the literary club as an incubator for trouble. Many men were hostile to club work because they felt that it challenged woman's traditional place in society, and because they feared that the self-centeredness literary clubs encouraged would result in women's abandonment of home duties. The Rhode Island Woman's Club, which husbands nicknamed the Society for the Prevention of Home Industry, recorded, "The idea seems widespread and almost ineradicable that we are an organization for the promotion of women's rights, so called."[60] Some men blamed women's clubs for the decrease in America's output of home-made pies.[61]

Some men simply hoped the phenomenon would blow over quickly. One man predicted, "It would not last long, this club business, the woman will soon get tired."[62] Still other men tolerated clubs as long as they noticed no change in domestic arrangements. One woman observed, "Their only interest in the organization was that we should be home in time to prepare supper. If we were, they were perfectly satisfied."[63]

Some criticism of clubs jabbed at the quality of the learning experience. Clubwomen themselves admitted, "There is still truth in the satirical remark that the subject of conversation at our teas is 'first Shelley, then Charley, then Mary Ann.' "[64] Martha E. D. White, familiar with club life, was scathing in her fictional picture of club members.[65] She recorded a conversation between a zealous, scatterbrained club member and a more sensible woman who has not attended the meeting because she has been able to keep herself occupied at home. The flighty member cannot remember the content of the lecture, demonstrates insincerity about reading further on the topic, and seems most interested in spending her money on clothes and her attention on social engagements.

Literary clubs, then, were criticized for their members' failure to study as intensively as they might have. Sometimes, this attack was well-founded. Pettiness, social climbing, and cliquishness were unattractive elements that at times were evident in club life. And, unlike the radical suffragists, clubwomen never challenged the notion that they were ladies with special qualities. While this ideology gradually assured huge numbers that clubs and motherhood were compatible, the failure to eradicate a reliance on ladydom ultimately limited the success of clubs for the suffragist's objectives. As the social stigma of clubs diminished, encouraging more and more women to use ladydom to justify assertion of their own demands for improved status and increased autonomy, ladydom grew stronger.

Yet for all the deficiencies, clubs developed in women a sisterhood which extended beyond the membership to all women, a respect for women's sphere, and a critique of male values in addition to expanding their intellectual aspirations. In the face of ridicule and censure, women learned that silence was no longer the virtue it once had been. Instead of feeling intimidated by large groups or impolite for asking questions, women found it smarter to probe, first about problems in the arts, and then about the problems of women in society. Gradually, they were moved to act on their own behalf, in the form of establishing scholarships and clubhouses and later through grander programs. Club life succeeded at reaching and assisting a large body of American womanhood to grow, by altering their expectations of both their social functions and their ability to carry out change.

## CHAPTER FIVE

# Women's Educational and Industrial Unions of Boston and Buffalo

While literary clubs were growing throughout the country, a new phenomenon was beginning in Boston. The Women's Educational and Industrial Union (WEIU) was formed in 1877, developing a program of services and opportunities for women which most literary clubs would later adopt. Two major differences distinguished the WEIU philosophy from that of clubs which preceded it—a broader concept of cross-class sisterhood and a second phase of Domestic Feminism, which became known as Municipal House-keeping. The former was evident in club leaders' insistence that in terms of oppression, non-employed women shared much with wage-earning women, particularly a need for economic independence through honest work.

Although there were many Americans in the late nineteenth century who recoiled at workers' strikes, public demonstrations, unionization efforts, and violent confrontations with police, many Boston women of the WEIU were not intimidated. They saw the widespread poverty of working-class people and tried to deal with it in their club. The fact that the WEIU then escaped the biting criticisms aimed at earlier organizations was not because the press and public were more tolerant of club ambitions, but because they had initially viewed the WEIU as a body which would assist the poor of Boston in a philanthropic manner. In this, the public was not far wrong. The word "union" in the club name thus embodied two meanings: an attempted cross-class sorority, but also a reference to earlier, respectable, philanthropic and charity organizations of women.

The second phase of operations, not unrelated to an awareness of inequities between people of different social strata, renewed Jane Cunningham Croly's 1869 proposal that women exert their moral sensibility toward the perfection of all society. This goal took on two important dimensions in the WEIU. First, members sought to create new careers for women, not merely to urge the entrance of women into male-dominated professions, but to establish occupations which would enable women to utilize their special moral qualities. Secondly, and applicable to many more nonemployed clientele of clubs, the WEIU institutionalized the concept of Municipal Housekeeping.[1] This, like the form of Domestic Feminism practiced in literary clubs, was built on the premise that women possessed special moral qualities which ought to be applied outside the home. Not satisfied with the association between women and the arts, members turned to civic reform. They insisted that the community was the extension of the home and that women must apply their special sensibilities to its problems. One writer explained, "Woman has a special function in developing the welfare of humanity which man cannot perform. This function consists in her power to make, of any place in which she may happen to live, a *home* for all those who come there. Women must now learn to make of their cities great community homes for all the people."[2]

Clubwomen had to defend their new participation in public affairs after it became clear that their activity was not identical to early church-related benevolence. Many journalists expressed displeasure at this work. As a few of their counterparts had done before, WEIU members insisted this diversion would not harm, but assist them in their homemaking functions. The Buffalo WEIU president explained that the public sphere also held lessons women could use.

> The advice is often given by the narrow-minded that home is the only place for the development of a true womanhood.... We are glad that such opinions are fast loosing [sic] ground and hope that a truer sentiment will soon prevail, that even the most favored one must sometimes go outside her home to gather the wisdom which shall fit her to rightly govern the kingdom of her own household.[3]

Another defense resembled an argument used to allow women to become involved in the arts; men had no time for community problems, just as they had none for the acquisition of culture. "Women must do the studying, the investigating, the detail work, for which men have not time, and leave them to do the executing. The time has come when men and women stand side by side and together work for the social, civil, and intellectual uplift of humanity."[4]

A more important reason why women should concern themselves with civic problems was not publicly stated. Such work was a vehicle for women's heretofore forbidden participation in the public sphere. Yet, as the social analysis and experimental programs initiated by the WEIU made the organization indispensable to social services in the many cities in which it operated, the club programs also gave women new prominence in the public sphere. Other American cities besides Boston needed innovative approaches for dealing with urban problems, and the leadership tapped eager clubwomen for solutions. The Boston plan was rapidly transmitted to many other cities, including Buffalo, foreshadowing the rapidity and uniformity with which the General Federation of Women's Clubs would share its programs with every American community in which there were clubs.

Boston's WEIU was founded by Harriet Clisby, a London-born physician. When she was seven, her father, a corn merchant, moved the family to Australia. At the age of twenty-nine, she was running a community house for young women in Adelaide and editing the world's first shorthand magazine. Inspired by a book by feminist physician Dr. Elizabeth Blackwell, Clisby returned to London in 1862, at the age of thirty-one, to become a doctor. After being denied admission to the English medical schools because of her sex, she immigrated to the United States where conditions were more favorable. Clisby studied in New York with the feminist Dr. Clemence Lozier, president of the New York Medical College and Hospital for Women.

Whether it was Clisby's frustration in the effort to obtain her own education, sympathy with Dr. Lozier's feminist ideas, or the realization that women suffered from ignorance and lack of control over their own bodies, she grew active in the nineteenth-century Woman Movement. In New York City, Clisby lived in a house for professional working women established by Reverend Henry Ward Beecher and was the president of the Working Woman's Association founded by its residents under the guidance of Susan B. Anthony.

After Clisby graduated from medical school in 1865, she went to Boston and practiced medicine there for twenty years. In 1873 she began a regular Sunday afternoon religious meeting for a few female friends. Although its purpose was ostensibly to discuss "ethical, moral and spiritual questions," the women who gathered explored their own problems as well. As early as November 1875, Clisby seemed to be striving for a women's organization. She invited Ednah Dow Cheney, the originator of the New England Woman's Club Horticultural School plan, to her Sunday meeting, saying, "Our body is but small yet appreciative and I do trust we may rank you among our true helpers. To carry on effectually such a movement as this promises to be, requires aid and sympathy from loving and wise hearts. If you can I know you will assist us."[5] Clisby was already planning the organization that would "aid, strengthen and elevate women by drawing them into a bond of unity." She wrote, "I believe in this necessity of organization and mutual cooperation among women, for what might we not do as women for women if we were banded together as men band themselves together for mutual helpfulness."[6]

Clisby saw potential and broad appeal in an organization designed for the cooperation of all women. She hoped that the sharing of experiences would enrich the lives of all women.

> How can we reach the unknown woman, the lonely, the misunderstood, the cruelly treated, the sick and indigent woman, any women who want us, and whom we want, because they want us?...Let there be no distinction felt. It is right that differences exist, for we need differences, but the possibilities of the highest spiritual growth lie in the harmonic blending of all varieties of human life to the end that each may give and receive for the good of each and the whole.[7]

Clisby officially formed the Boston WEIU in May 1877, when forty-two women responded to her call. The membership roster did not merely expand rapidly; it exploded. After one year, the WEIU surpassed the New England Woman's Club in size with four hundred members, and held expectations for even further enlargement.

> This seems when looking at its commencement, like an almost fabulous growth, but looking forward to the immense work which lies before us, hardly yet conceived, it is only the little shoots of the oak, springing from the willing, fertile soil which promises as its trunk strengthens and branches spread, to give protection in all directions to Women.[8]

Indeed, ten years later it had twelve hundred members and by 1915, membership had reached forty-five hundred.

Among those who joined were many members of the New England Woman's Club, whose previous experience of actualizing concrete programs for women was vital to the rapid development of the WEIU.[9] The New England Woman's Club members had earlier expressed interest in working-class sisters, but their efforts to acquaint themselves with problems of wage-earners had not been very successful. They had founded a Friendly Evening Association to provide comfortable club rooms for working women, but the program was not well attended. In 1869 the New England Woman's Club had conducted a study of 20,828 Boston needlewomen, and cited hard work, abominable factory conditions, and the seasonal nature of the employment as factors prompting girls to flirt with ruination in dance halls and theaters. One solution proposed was to encourage affluent women to stop sewing for pin-money and for a feeling of independence, since they glutted the market and drove down the wages.[10]

The New England Woman's Club members were joined in the WEIU by other Boston reformers such as Annie Fields, wife of the publisher, Mary Garrison, author Sarah Orne Jewett, Mount Holyoke College president Mary E. Woolley, and reformer Kate Tannatt Woods. Many of the members' names appeared in the Blue Book of Boston,[11] and some of the rich women made large contributions to WEIU club work.[12] Yet less affluent members, by paying the one-dollar annual membership fee, were also comfortable in joining the WEIU. The leading members' connections with the commercial elite enabled them to obtain advice about investing WEIU capital in railroads which yielded dividends. The 1905 budget records impressive receipts of $18,450, although expenditures of $23,094 required supplementary donations.[13]

For all the members there was appeal in the programs that resembled those of the New England Woman's Club—classes, receptions for celebrities, social entertainments, and club rooms with a library and reading room.[14] Yet the original attraction of the WEIU was not its similarity with its predecessors but its singular focus on morality. The Moral and Spiritual Development Committee, the outgrowth of Clisby's original meetings, continued to meet on Sunday afternoons under the auspices of the WEIU. It attracted women of all faiths and continued to serve more as a forum for discussion of woman's potential moral power rather than as a strict religious group. Speeches were given on such topics as "Shall Women Keep Silence in the Church?" "Temperance," and "Are We Not Our Brother's Keeper?"

This committee declined in popularity even though music was added to the program in 1891 in a futile attempt to attract members. In 1892 it folded. The demise of the committee was not evidence that women were abandoning their moral responsibilities. On the contrary, the entire WEIU program had become so closely associated with good works that a special committee of spiritual development was redundant. In addition, the club secretary explained, "There are so many opportunities for women to meet and exercise themselves, and it is so common a thing for them to speak freely, even in mixed audiences, that special meetings for women only, for the free interchange of thought are apparently no longer important."[15]

The great numbers who joined the club were not only attracted by the newspaper ads and word of mouth. Preachers announced the existence of the WEIU from the pulpit. The ministry sanctioned such WEIU projects as the Befriending Committee, which was designed to aid unfortunate women, often "gentlewomen in reduced circumstances,"[16] and thus assured those fearful of "strong-mindedness" that WEIU claims to sisterhood would be tempered by old-time charity. The work of the Befriending Committee combined customary philanthropic projects like visiting the sick, holding charity drives, and collecting clothing with more creative offerings—including helping women into hospitals, securing them a week of board on a quiet farm, finding them homes in the country, raising money for the Sea Island Tornado damage in 1894, establishing a boarding house agency, and cooperating with other Boston organizations to install police matrons in the jails.[17]

In the WEIU, direct benevolent activity coexisted with less traditional programs. Clisby created the WEIU so women could break away from the "immense imprisonment of life which was stifling them."[18] She believed that women's limitations were due to their lack of educational opportunity and urged that women acquire new marketable skills. This project was more clearly developed by Abby Morton Diaz, a founder of the WEIU who became temporary president when Clisby fell ill in 1878. Serving as president from 1881 until 1892 and as vice-president from 1892 until 1902, she helped shape the WEIU into both the adventurous and reactionary organization it became.

The woman who pushed the WEIU to become a "Ministry of Service" and inspired other clubs to do the same had a background similar to that of many club leaders before her. Diaz's heritage was American blue blood.[19] She was introduced to reform work early in life. When she was twelve, her Unitarian father took her to hear the preaching of Theodore Parker, and she became a dedicated member of the Juvenile Anti-Slavery Society in Plymouth. After the family tried life at Brook Farm for a short time, she stayed to teach the kindergarten from 1842–1847. There she met Manual A. Diaz from Havana and married him in 1845. They had three sons, but the marriage apparently failed and she was forced to support herself and two surviving sons.

In a variety of occupations, Diaz developed sympathy for all working women. She taught at a juvenile singing school and at public and private schools, went into practical nursing, and ran a dancing school. She worked as a summer housekeeper and cook at a summer resort[20] and brought needlework to women sewing at home for factories. Finally, she tried writing. Her first story, "Pink and Blue," was published anonymously in the *Atlantic Monthly*, May 1861. Even though she was not proud of her work, calling it "nothing but poverty-cake,"[21] she went on to publish numerous magazine articles and children's and women's books.[22]

Writing did not absorb all her energy. In 1888 she joined the First Nationalist Club of Boston, established by followers of Edward Bellamy. She was a speaker at the Free Religious Association and became interested in Christian Science. By 1896, however, she had rejected all religious involvement. She told the press that she did not go to church[23] but was indisputably as moral as any devout churchgoer. Her philosophy augmented the attractive charity element of church programs and thus made the more progressive aspects of the WEIU palatable to critics who might have considered them too radical.

Like Croly, Diaz was no revolutionary. They both insisted that domesticity was woman's major asset, not a liability. Diaz boasted that although she was a confirmed "strong-minded woman"[24] and suffragist she still could sew, do housework, and care for the sick.[25] These experiences, plus the moral superiority that was nurtured in the home in which these tasks were performed, entitled her to criticize and redefine woman's role in society. Diaz subscribed to much of the ladydom ideology, but she managed to take it further in the direction of woman's public participation than Croly had done.

Men played a far more prominent part in Diaz's explanation of the origins of women's oppression than they had done in Croly's. Diaz counted men reprehensible for dictating to morally superior women their course of behavior. "It is this poor innocent weakling, man, on whose account one half of humanity has been remanded into obscurity, and for whom a whole continent, so to speak, labors to remove liquor temptations; it is he, even he, who assumes to be the guide and ruler of women."[26] She saw male domination as a distortion of natural autonomy. Endorsing the concept of separate spheres for men and women, she insisted, "If a pine-tree should try to tell an oak-tree how to be an oak, or a rose to tell a lily how to be a lily, it could only do harm; and so it is when men try to teach women how to be womanly."[27]

Having spotlighted man as central to woman's underdevelopment, Diaz stressed woman's moral obligation to elevate him. "Woman should rate herself high and make herself worth the rating, and then demand of man the highest qualifications...demand freedom from sensuality, demand the same standard for man as for woman; and all this not only in regard to marriage, but to his general standing in society." She felt that women tolerated wild ways in men and accepted "damaged goods," for the security of marriage, which she called a "private charity." Women, Diaz said, "marry without love for it; they marry fools for it; they marry knaves for it; they lead lives of shame for it." Marriage to an alcoholic, for example, was prostitution which women endured for lack of marketable skills.[28]

According to Diaz's plan, women must work for equality to achieve independence. She urged women, as Croly had, to free themselves from domestic drudgery by abandoning unnecessary projects such as fancy sewing. Woman should provide simple food and dress, making "the present race of husbands aware that their wives are being killed, or crazed, with hard work and care." She argued that excessive domesticity could hurt the family. A tired woman, Diaz insisted, should not make her husband a cake. If he was a loving husband, he would rather be with a healthy companion than eating cake alone. Too often, marriage resembled a stint in a workhouse, a sentence "to hard labor for life." Indeed, if men did not take heed, they would suffer, for the unhealthful mental and physical repression women endured could spread to the children. Her sons, and his, after all, were influenced by "the condition, pre-natal and post-natal of the mothers. So the ignorance in which woman is kept by man reacts on man."[29] Pure motherhood without intellectual stimulation could be harmful. "Love without enlightenment is a strong, a terrible strong force, working at random, marring where it could make, killing where it would cure, destroying where it would save."[30]

Diaz argued that once women rid themselves of time-consuming and fruitless domestic labors, they must seize economic independence. Only with a job and a personal income could women be free of man's rule, free to insist on chaste husbands, free to raise upstanding children in a more wholesome, less hypocritical environment. "When women are more independent, and labor for them is honorable, they will not be so willing to take up with unworthy husbands and the men will have to make themselves worth marrying. Marriages if fewer would be truer, and of these truer marriages will be born better children, and here will be a gain to the community."[31]

Diaz saw, as Croly did not, that women who were not employed were just as dependent on untrustworthy husbands, brothers, and fathers as were working-class women and that a cross-class alliance of women could help to change that shared dependency. She did not advocate the abolition of social classes to create this coalition, however. Her solution was rather more modest—an effort among rich women to set an example worthy of emulation by poor women. Instead of indulging in idle luxury, tempting working girls to scrimp on proper food and shelter in order to emulate the elaborate costumes of "their betters,"[32] more comfortable women ought to consider the benefits of work. "Rich young women cheated themselves by not working for money.... A great many smart men never would have amounted to much if they had spent their time making tidies, painting a little, playing on the piano a little, and putting on their good clothes, out calling on each other."[33] Diaz was so insistent in her plea for responsible behavior on the part of affluent women that she offended clubwomen in Springfield, Massachusetts, who wrote:

> Her ideas were most radical in regard to the development of character and the relation of the rich to the poor. She said there was a great need of missionaries to Christianize the Christians. Some of the speaker's statements aroused an indignant feeling among those who believed themselves advanced in modern processes of solving difficult religious, social, and civic problems.[34]

In practice, few clubwomen would defy class custom and take on occupations. They enjoyed an economically and socially privileged viewpoint, enhanced by the superiority that ladydom and culture study provided. Clubmembers' perspective enabled them to do no more than sympathize with the need for jobs for other women and to help create those jobs through the WEIU. When the limited programs proved unsuccessful, they turned instead to the Municipal Housekeeping which increased their own influence in the public sphere.

The WEIU constitution stated as its object, "to increase fellowship among women, in order to promote the best practical methods for securing their educational, industrial, and social advancement." Earlier clubs stressed educational and social efforts, but did not consider industriousness. One practical method WEIU members promoted, and one which took much of the clubs' efforts, was producing special services and work opportunities for women. The early experiments included a store, a lunchroom, a health clinic, investigations of city problems, a job bureau, and legal aid work. Together these provided a multitude of services to ease women's lives and a concrete approach to devising new job opportunities for women willing to work. The WEIU also provided a variety of voluntary projects in the area of Municipal Housekeeping. Employment, both paid and unpaid, was sacred to the WEIU for its relationship to the moral improvement of an unjust society.

The store the WEIU opened demonstrated their hopes of creating employment for a diverse segment of the female population. The WEIU called itself "The Mother of Exchanges," for it provided a salesroom or exchange where housebound women could make an income by selling their homemade handicrafts and baked goods.[35] Limited space in the store led to a controversy over whether any woman should be permitted to use sales space that could be used by the neediest women. The WEIU maintained that the income of a husband had nothing to do with his wife and that wives of rich men were as entitled to earn their own money as wives of the poor.

The WEIU prided itself on the merchandise it sold and won a reputation for selling superior products. Members inspected participating women's kitchens for cleanliness and absence of alcoholic ingredients before they sold the pickles, preserves, jellies, broths, creams, mince pies, ices, candy, and desserts. The operation started modestly but soon expanded. Sales amounting to $21.56 in 1878 rose to $53,183 in 1905, eighty percent of the latter coming from sale of food.[36]

Soon the WEIU branched out into establishing lunchrooms. The Providence Street Lunch Room provided women with cheap, nutritious food in a clean and quiet atmosphere. Another lunchroom was then established on Boylston Street. In 1903 a special WEIU members' lunchroom was added and two years later, an afternoon tea and supper room.

Here was a service intended for both rich and poor women, although not for the same purposes; primarily, it served leisured women who found it difficult to find a respectable place to eat downtown while they shopped. It also gave some wage-earning women the chance to earn money as cooks. It permitted Simmons College students the opportunity to learn to make menus, fix and serve food, market, and operate storerooms, as they prepared for future careers in food management. In 1900 WEIU lunchrooms served almost forty-five-thousand dinners and gained profits that supported less lucrative projects. The trainees received ample experience, the cooks received a living wage, and all women had a safe place to eat in downtown Boston.

Women's health was a vital concern to the WEIU since ill-health harmed both leisured and working-class women. Providing women with good food was one way to ensure their health and strength and make them fit for labor. But a more effective means was to help women overcome their ignorance of bodily functions and techniques of proper care. The work of the Hygiene Committee, run by Dr. Clisby and Dr. Arvilla B. Haynes, was designed to overcome this ignorance. The two physicians provided free lectures, two or three times a week, to any woman who was interested on such topics as prevention of disease, eyes, blood circulation, nutrition and assimilation, and the brain. A hygiene room was open all day to provide free advice and health care for poor women. But WEIU reports indicate that few women used its services, and the committee turned its attention to sanitary and industrial conditions. WEIU volunteers investigated pollution caused by industrial smoke, collaborated with the Twentieth Century Club and the Woman's Equal Suffrage Committee on street cleaning, and cooperated in 1904 on a joint committee of the Massachusetts State Federation of Women's Clubs on bettering the conditions of women and children in shops and factories.[37] Lack of contact with individual working-class women in the medical clinic pushed the WEIU to a wider, more public avenue of correctable abuses. It pioneered in Municipal Housekeeping, which the General Federation of Women's Clubs would undertake in the last decade of the nineteenth century.

The WEIU acknowledged that good nutrition and health were imperative in women who needed to work, but these were only the first steps in employing women. And the WEIU was anxious, above all, to find jobs for women. In 1877, satisfied there were sufficient numbers of agencies for domestic workers, the WEIU established a job registry for Higher Employment, or non-working-class women. The registry committee soon secured the names of two hundred women, "many of them of retirement, some of culture, asking for work."[38] Success was marginal. The WEIU placed only six women, perhaps, as they claimed, because jobs for ladies who sought dignified occupations appeared scarce and because the WEIU work was not known to the public.[39]

The WEIU also turned its attention to working-class women's needs. By 1885 it was clear that domestics were sorely exploited by irresponsible employers. A scarcity of domestics was felt by clubwomen as more and more potential servants turned to factory work. With some element of self-interest involved, the WEIU began to investigate, with the Massachusetts Bureau of Statistics of Labor, the possibilities of attracting women from factories and shops to the field of domestic service. The WEIU investigated the hours of labor and the conditions of domestic service. Their published findings showed that shorter hours, adequate wages, and allowing the employee to sleep out would increase the numbers of women interested in domestic service. This led the WEIU to provide a sample contract ensuring fairness for both employer and employee. Their second job bureau, more successful than the first, registered 15,700 applicants (both employers and employees) by 1908.

Once women were hired, however, their troubles were not over. A forerunner of modern Legal Aid Societies, the WEIU's Protective Committee provided assistance to women with employment-related grievances. In January 1879 the WEIU secured the services of lawyers, some of them female, who would provide free advice to women who brought their complaints to the WEIU offices.[40] In 1880 alone, one hundred forty complaints recovered $724.42. In twenty-five years and thirty-five-hundred cases, $16,000 was collected.[41] In most cases, unskilled working women were able to collect wages unfairly withheld. For example, one Harvard student was made to pay his laundress seven dollars. But sometimes leisured women collected. A dress-maker, for instance, owed her client $5.83.[42] The service, then, provided experience for some women lawyers and redressed financial grievances of a few leisured women, but it basically attempted to help working-class women collect small amounts of money due them.

The Protective Committee, foreshadowing the work of the National Consumers' League, also assisted saleswomen. The WEIU noted, "We form a Society for the Prevention of Cruelty to Animals, we form one for the Prevention of Cruelty to Children, and shall we forget the needless torture of women who must stand all day whether there is work to do or not."[43]

In 1891 a new WEIU president streamlined the practical, work-oriented nature of the organization and committed it further in the direction of Municipal Housekeeping. Mrs. Mary Morton Kehew, a professional reformer, reorganized club programs but retained Diaz's philosophy. With roots in seventeenth-century New England, daughter of a wealthy Boston merchant/banker, and granddaughter of a Massachusetts governor, she enjoyed a "private" school education and foreign travel. In 1880 she married a Boston oil merchant. They had no children. Kehew's practical work in the WEIU prepared her to be a Trustee of Simmons College and to become active in many other practical projects. Kehew worked for the College Settlements Association, Denison House, Tyler Street Day Nursery, the Milk and Baby Hygiene Association, the American Park and Outdoor Association, the School Voter's League, the Civil Service Reform Association, and state commissions on industrial education and child labor. She was also president of the National Women's Trade Union League. Kehew brought Mary Kenney O'Sullivan, a Hull House worker and American Federation of Labor organizer to Boston, and they founded a Union for Industrial Progress to foster trade unionism among women bookbinders, laundry workers, tobacco workers, and garment-trade workers.[44]

Kehew was a supporter of the growing trend toward efficiency in voluntary organizations, and in 1905 she replaced the volunteers of the WEIU staff with one hundred and twenty paid workers. She claimed that the complexities of WEIU work demanded reliance on the service of experts. One such expert was Susan Kingsbury, a Ph.D. in American colonial history, who taught at Vassar and pioneered in social research. Kingsbury came to Boston in 1905 to investigate the relation of children to industries for the Massachusetts Commission on Industrial and Technical Education. She taught economics at Simmons College, and in 1907 became the Director of Research of the WEIU. There she devised a systematic study of social fact-finding and gave five-hundred-dollar awards to woman graduate students initiating field work. Before she was lured to Bryn Mawr College in 1915, she took on the responsibility of the early Sanitary and Industrial Committee[45] through the WEIU and published several important studies regarding women and labor.[46] When these studies were cosponsored by the Massachusetts State Bureau of Statistics, Municipal Housekeeping gained new respectability. A legislative committee used the findings as the basis for Massachusetts regulation of installment buying, sale of milk, old age pensions, factory inspections, factory sanitation, minimum wages, protection for seekers of small loans, and prohibiting the return of women to work before a four-week rest after childbirth. Women's sensitivity to community problems had brought new concern for age-old questions.

Kehew's administration pushed the WEIU into adding innovative and practical classes for developing marketable skills. Dressmaking and millinery courses, instituted in 1895, turned out three hundred forty-two pupils the following year. The School of Salesmanship started in 1905 to train women for jobs in department stores. The training promised them higher starting wages and guaranteed them a job.[47] A School of Housekeeping grew out of the Domestic Service Bureau in 1897. It provided three months of separate classroom training for employers and employees in cooking, laundry work, and care of kitchen, dining room, parlor, and chamber. Employers made up the majority of the fifty-five pupils who graduated in two years. Soon a professional class for college graduates was opened to train women for home economics leadership positions. The topics they studied included house sanitation, chemistry of foods, home economics, home society, house architecture, elementary chemistry, cooking, housework, marketing, and household buying. In 1902 the program was absorbed by Simmons College.

The problems and advantages of the domestic science project represented, in microcosm, those of the Boston WEIU. The dual attempt to teach servants their work and to professionalize housekeeping is indicative of the WEIU vision of assisting both groups of women without breaking down rigid class distinctions. At the same time, the WEIU's most effective work was related to woman's traditional occupation as homemaker. Home economics has been misrepresented as a field urging contentment with the drudgery of housework, woman's traditional occupation. Such a reading fails to recognize the Domestic Feminism underlying the home economics movement's use of woman's traditional sphere to create new careers and public influence for women. Dieticians and home economists used science to elevate woman's work to a profession. These women were not succumbing to a life of housecleaning, but were wedding acceptable domestic talents with the desire for salary, recognition, careers, and skills by which society's problems could be solved. So too, the WEIU is misunderstood if one looks only as far as the charity program. The key to this organization was its sophistication in using women's special traits to provide them with an entrance into public realms.

Ellen Richards, who had begun her career as a chemist, was active in the Association of Collegiate Alumnae, and had pushed the Massachusetts Institute of Technology to open a women's laboratory for the instruction of women in science, was a significant personality in establishing the field of home economics.[48] Richards did some of her most important work in collaboration with the WEIU. She taught chemistry of food at the WEIU School of Housekeeping and helped outline related lab courses until, in 1902, it became part of the Simmons College Department of Home Economics. In addition, she established the New England Kitchen where the WEIU provided lunches for the Boston School Committee. By 1912 the WEIU served ninety-five-hundred school lunches daily. By 1944 eighteen-thousand were served.

Her work in home economics, like the general programs of the WEIU, easily attracted supporters, for all believed women had domestic abilities. This united conservatives with progressives, broke no traditions, but opened new areas through which women could infiltrate the public sphere. Home economics classes, like the WEIU itself, did less for the domestic servants trained there than they did for those who sought to professionalize domestic science. Yet in providing skills in domestic science, the WEIU achieved more than the multitude of clubwomen who created replicas of their own literary meetings for working girls.

If the WEIU made only limited headway in spreading opportunities, skills, and jobs to greater numbers of employable women, the club efforts must rank among the more realistic approaches for nineteenth-century women to deal with the oppression of the less affluent women. Countless other clubwomen naively supposed that cultural uplift would satisfy their laboring sisters. Florence Lockwood felt that uplift would help them "bear more joyfully the burden of life amid difficulties and temptations which would daunt the bravest and the strongest."[49] Club members organized working girls' clubs in mill towns and in big cities, and provided pleasant and wholesome rooms for the girls' entertainment, classes, and libraries. Foul language and cardplaying were outlawed. Dues and a charge for refreshments were collected to teach the girls appreciation of club benefits.[50]

Clubwomen engaged in setting up such clubs included Sorosis members Mrs. Mary Terhune, E. D. Clymer, and Rebecca F. Morse. They were worlds apart from wage-earning women. They truly felt that girls would learn good behavior from seeing ladies as models. The organizers were sometimes condescending, although one leisured lady warned women not to "underestimate the intelligence of the girls, particularly in practical matters, in which it is apt to be far greater than our own."[51] She also urged women not to "belittle our advantages," for "the very leisure and knowledge we are able to put at their disposal comes from this difference of conditions." Instead of being ashamed of having servants, wearing evening dresses, and going to the opera, all should realize these things were "comforts won for us by our husbands' or fathers' intelligence and labor."[52] The WEIU treatment of working girls, that is, providing skills for economic independence, was an advance over the attempt to establish literary clubs for wage-earners, but it fell far short of Diaz's dreams for a cross-class sisterhood.

Nevertheless, Diaz was certain her plan could be successful if it was established on a countrywide basis. She was anxious to create WEIUs everywhere.

> May the time soon come, where shall be a national and international system of such Unions, all under the same name, uniting women throughout the country and the world for mutual interchange of ideas and a general cooperation and becoming each in itself a centre of enlightenment, a social centre and a welcoming place for all women.[53]

The second of several WEIUs[54] was established in Buffalo, and reveals how readily American clubwomen could utilize the plans initiated by skilled reformers. The Buffalo branch was a self-conscious reestablishment of the original plan, although Buffalo lacked the innovative visionaries common to Boston. The women of Buffalo were philanthropically oriented, and they created programs for working women without Diaz's expectations of learning from them. Uninterested in developing cross-class sisterhood or in devising new careers to suit women's talents, they put their energies directly into teaching job skills to poor women and expanding Municipal Housekeeping for themselves. Their work demonstrates how attractive and useful the latter concept could become to millions of American Domestic Feminists.

The Boston WEIU program was copied, nearly in entirety, in Buffalo. Buffalo's Union used the same constitution, bylaws, and purpose, that is, "educational, industrial and social advancement for women." It met in spacious quarters in downtown Buffalo near the homes of wealthy members.[55] Classes in practical subjects like typing, stenography, and bookkeeping were provided for the working girl. An employment bureau was established. For the homemaker, there were programs in china painting, lectures on art, and monthly "coteries" on Thursday afternoons, where clubwomen delivered papers on a variety of topics for the edification of the membership. Young women had a suborganization of their own, the Girls' Union Circle.

The Protective Committee, staffed by some of the most prominent lawyers in Buffalo who often were husbands of Union members, recovered thirty-five-thousand dollars in wages for cheated seamstresses and domestics from 1884 until 1916. A "Noon Rest" provided a safe, clean, and inexpensive lunch for women downtown. An Exchange and Bake Shop sold women's homemade goods. The Mary C. Ripley Memorial Library opened at the clubrooms with five hundred volumes and many periodicals which all women could use. There were talks on hygiene and a domestic training school. Although the Buffalo Union had no religious meetings or investigations of labor problems such as the Boston organization did, the members did attempt to deal with the particular problems of Buffalo women.

The most prominent figure in the Buffalo WEIU was Harriet Austin Townsend, who presided over the Union through much of its life. Born of a Quaker mother and lawyer father who exposed her to liberal ideas including women's suffrage, she had attended the Buffalo Seminary for Girls. At the age of twenty-two, she married George Townsend, who was a wealthy real estate broker prominent in the affairs of the community.[56] Harriet, too, was community-minded. She represented the Church of the Messiah as corporate manager at a home for unwed mothers. She was the founder of the Literary Club of the Church of the Messiah, and this association took her to numerous women's conventions where she met the important leaders of the Woman Movement and became their link to Buffalo women. While she thought the franchise would be valuable to women, she did not work for suffrage, believing just laws for women did not depend entirely on the ballot.[57]

In January and February of 1884, the Literary Club of the Church of the Messiah, under Townsend's presidency, invited Abby Morton Diaz to give four Household Talks. One of these included a description of the Boston WEIU[58] which excited the women about the possibilities of establishing a union in Buffalo. Over thirty of the Literary Club of the Church of the Messiah women would hold leadership positions at the Buffalo Union.

Early Union supporters had backgrounds in social responsibility and philanthropic efforts in addition to participation in culture clubs. Through their husbands, many Union women were acquainted with the work of Buffalo's Charity Organization Society (COS). The COS was an organization founded in Buffalo in 1877 in an effort to apply business efficiency to charity by creating a centralized social service center to avoid duplication of services to the worthy poor. It promised to save the city money and to cure poverty through penny banks, a day nursery, sanitary inspections, a wood yard, inexpensive classes, a medical dispensary, and an accident hospital. Dominated by the elite males of Buffalo, the COS saw itself as a nondenominational, nonpolitical organization. In an attempt to stamp out dependency, dishonesty, and laziness among paupers, the COS reserved assistance for those exhibiting strong moral qualities. Regarding its creche, or day nursery, the COS asserted, "None but the children of married working mothers can secure the excellent care of the creche; thus are encouraged self-dependence and self-respect, two important factors in the elevation and betterment of the poor and struggling."[59] Unregenerate unwed mothers had to look elsewhere for child care services.

Women were excluded from membership at the COS. Their services could be volunteered as "Friendly Visitors" when their churches subscribed to the COS. Otherwise, they were isolated from this form of community action until 1889 when the creche attendance declined and COS's male members invited them to become special advisers to salvage the nursery. Finally, in 1892, women were permitted membership in the COS itself, but their names did not appear on the list of officers. Perhaps it was the absolute male control over the COS that caused Buffalo women to assert themselves in their own organization, the Union.

Diaz accepted the invitation of the Literary Club of the Church of the Messiah and spoke on 2 February 1884 at the COS's Fitch Institute. It was COS member Mr. J. N. Larned who made a motion that "There should be organized in Buffalo a Woman's Union,"[60] in response to Diaz's description of the Boston organization. Three days later, women prominent in a variety of clubs throughout the city responded to the COS invitation to meet with Harriet Townsend to establish a Union. By March, the new organization held its first meeting at the Fitch Institute, and it was attended by Buffalo women as well as Julia Ward Howe, Abby May, Frances Willard, and other celebrated AAW members who were in town for a mid-year meeting.

Like Boston's WEIU, the Buffalo Union attracted a wide membership which paid dues of one dollar per year. The Union began with sixty, grew to over seven hundred in a year, to eight hundred thirty-eight in two years, and by 1894, when the city's population was three hundred thousand, the Union had one thousand members. Two hundred of these were active as officers on thirteen different committees. In the early years, generous donations, such as Mrs. S. W. R. Watson's five-thousand-dollar gift and Mrs. Esther Glenny's ten-thousand-dollar gift, provided support for special projects. As was customary for many clubs, the furnishings of the headquarters were donated by department stores in search of good will. Like the lawyers on the Protective Committee, store owners were often husbands of members and may have felt obligated to support their wives' endeavors.[61]

The mayor's wife; the wives of state Supreme Court justices, the city auditor and the New York State Attorney General; the wives, daughters, widows, and spinster sisters of Buffalo lawyers, physicians, newspaper editors, bank presidents and vice-presidents and directors, trustees of hospitals and children's aid societies, builders and department store owners all belonged to this Union. The president of the Buffalo Natural Gas Fuel Company, the owner of the New York Car Wheel Works, the owners of flour mills, surgical instrument manufacturers, rubber boot manufacturers, the vice-chancellor of the University of Buffalo, the president of the Buffalo Historical Society, and the founder of the Nichols School all had wives who participated in the work of the Buffalo Union.

Not only were the wives of those listed in Buffalo's Blue Book active in the Union, but wives of those on the way up also joined. Wives of high school principals, bookkeepers, druggists, and foremen formulated policy as committee heads. Although Yankee names predominated in the membership, the Buffalo Union boasted that it was nonsectarian. A few Catholic Irish and Polish names appear on their lists, as do the names of some Jewish families. In addition, men held associate memberships, without full voting privileges.

As was the case in Boston, reaction to the forming of the Buffalo WEIU was generally favorable. A majority of the public assumed it would be another woman's philanthropic agency, this time specializing in the needs of poor women. This connection with established church-related charities insured a great deal of support. While the Buffalo Union was able to assist a wider constituency than any church-supported organization, the founders also expected the Union to foster a wide sisterhood. "Women accustomed to meet only those of their own church and circle in society have become selfish and narrow. Women must know each other better if society is to be elevated."[62]

Even though the Union was nonsectarian, Townsend called on God again and again to grace its work. "All realize that we cannot hope for a permanent success without the approval of the Giver of all Good."[63] And later, "The WEIU has cause for deep gratitude to Divine Providence, and its friends may realize today to the fullest extent the many blessings which have fallen to its lot."[64] Townsend was a master at using religious language to defend woman's new work:

> We no longer listen to the selfish moralist who cries, "Let woman stay at home, her only safe haven; if she steps outside its sacred precincts, she loses all womanly sweetness and dignity." The gospel of common sense has been proclaimed that this world is only one great home, the human race one universal brotherhood, that no one can live to himself alone and only as we help to bear our share of the common burden shall we reap the reward.[65]

Indeed, much of the members' charity work was truly unassuming and traditional, just as Townsend had painted it. The club provided food and clothing for thirty families during the winter of 1893–1894. They sent a dozen working girls for one- or two-week vacations in the countryside. Nine members attended the funeral of a friendless Swedish girl and sent a lock of her hair to her mother in Sweden.

The wide array of charitable efforts smacked of condescension and social control. A kitchen garden was established, based on the principles of Emily Huntington. Her program consisted of teaching housework to immigrant girls, aged seven to fourteen, by allowing them to "play" with toy dishes, mops, and miniature furniture.[66] In actuality, the girls learned how to become good domestic servants for clubwomen or at least how to bring Yankee standards of cleanliness into their own homes.

Echoing Diaz's feelings about the superiority of the wealthy, Union members saw the association of rich people with poor as beneficial. They paternalistically insisted that the "value of the ability to fill the position of cook in respectable families, where something more precious than mere 'wages' are given, namely, protection and a good home,"[67] benefited the poor. Domestic work in "good homes" was encouraged.

Other examples of condescension abound. Regarding a field trip of the children to South Park Conservatory, the members felt "not an unpleasant incident marred the day, and the custodian complimented them upon their good behavior. Without the Kitchen Garden these same children might have done wanton injury to the property, to say nothing of being less appreciative of what they saw."[68] Another club report boasted that the triumph of a concert by a singing class of Italian children was not the music, but the incentive which the concert provided to sew mandatory costumes, and "the lowering of the voices, and the exercise of self-control in these restless children."[69]

Despite the patronization evident in these services, some critics considered them dangerous to the status quo. Mrs. Townsend defended the actions of the Union as morally correct.

> One ignorant of the Union work has recently asserted that the tendency of our association is bad, as it serves to make the working girl dissatisfied with her lot in life; in giving equal opportunities to all women the Union is in accord with Mrs. John Stuart Mill, who says: "The proper sphere of all human beings is the largest and highest they are able to attain to."[70]

The programs designed by Union members for poor women reflected their own acceptance of class divisions and distorted perceptions of working-class women's needs. Rather than expecting that an exchange could take place whereby both groups of women might benefit, Union clubwomen felt the learning process should occur only for working-class women. Content to teach their housekeeping techniques to the worthy poor, the Buffalo Union operated with no more success than the Boston WEIU in tapping the possibilities for mutual growth and improvement.

Club life did more to awaken Buffalo's leisured women to the potential influence of their own moral and domestic traits than it did to cooperate with the poor. One said, "It is true that we cannot help others without helping ourselves. One of our most enthusiastic workers, herself a happy wife and mother, lately remarked, 'I joined the "Union" as an active member, desiring to help the less fortunate, but I find that in spite of all my good intentions for others I have received the greatest benefit myself.'"[71] Members received more satisfaction from the sense of growth achieved in testing and winning influence in the community than from assisting the poor. Buffalo women became most successful at criticizing woman's place in society and then acting to improve it. As in the literary clubs, members delivered papers on women in the American Revolution, in antislavery and in higher education. Opportunities for nine-teenth-century women were discussed, as was the issue of dress reform. Leading members of the Buffalo Bar presented a series of law lectures on women and property, inheritance, dower, and guardianship of children. A display case in the clubhouse exhibited the handiwork of women through the world. Feminist Julia Ward Howe spoke when she came to town for a midwinter meeting of the Association for the Advancement of Women.

The Buffalo women acted on the inequalities that troubled them. The club urged the city charter be altered to replace the word *man* with *citizen*.[72] They opened a gymnasium for women, insisting tht "the girl has the same right to a strong, sound body as the boy."[73] In 1887 they succeeded in their three-year campaign, in cooperation with the Women's Christian Temperance Union, Young Men's Christian Association, Home for the Friendless and Ingleside Home, to place a police matron in the First Police Station. In 1890 two additional matrons were hired. That same year, they met success in their campaign to place women physicians on all state institutions where women were housed. Members lobbied until two women were appointed to the Board of Managers of the State Hospital for the Insane at Buffalo. In 1892 they counted themselves responsible for the placement of a woman on the Buffalo Board of School Examiners. They also secured a place for a jail matron. In 1893 the Union lobbied in Albany to make husband and wife equal guardians of children. In 1904 they urged enforcement of alimony payments. In 1909–1910 they worked for an increase in the salary of police matrons and urged that they become members of the force, thus enabling them to receive pensions.

All this participation of women in city affairs was palatable to the public because it focused on municipal improvement, rather than on women's rights. In fact, gains for women were obscured in the glow of the club's wider civic work. Energy directed toward women's advancement by leaders in Sorosis, New England Woman's Club, and the Boston WEIU did not dissipate in Buffalo because it was coupled with wider civic reform.

In Buffalo, the core of Municipal Housekeeping activity grew from the Civic Club, which was a Union committee "formed to interest and inform women in matters relating to municipal affairs, to show how they might assist in the good government of our city, and to foster all movements within the circle of its influence which have for their ends the improvement of any phase of our city life."[74] The committee's motto was "Information before Reformation," but it tackled the organization of school boards, care of streets (lighting and cleaning), outdoor relief (as distinct from workhouses), and the establishment of parks. Members then petitioned the mayor to create a Bureau of Forestry (which would develop a systematic plan for beautification of the city streets). They worked to suppress objectionable posters and advertisements. They helped to found a school for truants. They purchased smokeless coal to improve the environment.[75] Their charity work, employment bureau, and instruction in marketable skills were all part of a program to make the city of Buffalo a congenial place to live.

Yet impressive as the flurry of activity was, in it were the seeds of the destruction of feminism in the movement. Gradually, the traditional "do-good" nature of women's work enveloped her efforts to help herself. When

Buffalo's Union folded in 1916 from lack of financial support, it was no longer needed. It had achieved its goals and lacked new ones to replace them. Its projects had become part of the city life. The public schools provided evening classes, the Young Men's Christian Association had an employment bureau for women. There were clean restaurants which admitted women. Other gymnasiums and physical culture classes were available throughout the city. The Union forgot that it had begun to help women. When its immediate Municipal Housekeeping projects were accomplished or absorbed by the government, it thought its work was done. At any rate, once eager and generous donors were no longer plentiful, so the Union had to close. It failed to realize that its support had diminished as its commitment to women had diminished. In a final gesture which symbolized the dual interests of the Union, it managed to elicit from the University of Buffalo a promise to maintain three scholarships for women in perpetuity, but it gave its clubhouse to the school and thus began the University's Department of Liberal Arts.[76]

None of the WEIUs have survived, with the exception of the healthy original in Boston. Even there, Diaz's hopes for cooperation among all classes of women never caught on. If working-class women could teach the dignity of wage labor and middle-class women the utility of developing a lady's moral superiority, the clubwomen's interests did not permit them to shape forums for the exchange of such lessons. The minimal effect of the classes, clinics, job bureaus, lunchrooms, and exchanges developed by the Boston organization and transported to other locales like Buffalo pushed WEIU members to reach out instead to Municipal Housekeeping. Here they were successful in winning prominence for themselves in the area of civic reform. The only relationship maintained between clubwomen and working-class women was indirect and one-sided, the advocacy by clubwomen of municipal reforms to be beneficial for the city's poor. Municipal Housekeeping, growing out of the WEIU failure to develop cross-class cooperation, was the culmination of the Domestic Feminists' praise of a lady's sensitivity and the hunger to gain public influence. This was widely adopted by literary clubs throughout America under the General Federation of Women's Clubs.

CHAPTER SIX

# Federation

In 1890 Jane Cunningham Croly resurrected a modified version of her 1869 plan to bring the values of woman's sphere to bear upon the problems of American society. She initiated the formation of the General Federation of Women's Clubs, which would bring literary clubs together in a national association. Once formed, however, the General Federation diverted clubs from their cultural programs, accelerating the drive toward Municipal Housekeeping which had already begun, notably in the Women's Educational and Industrial Unions. Federation became the vehicle through which clubs were led to consider ways in which woman's special sensitivity could be applied to the problems of the community. Clubwomen's solutions, an impressive array of social services and legislative reforms, became a permanent part of what Americans expected from their governments. In the process, of course, women attained a new and vital influence upon American life, of a type which had been denied them when the club movement burgeoned in mid-century.

Croly believed that the General Federation could tap great strength. Once clubs united for mutual support and to avoid duplication of effort, clubwomen's collective response to problems would carry weight with legislators. Investigation of civic problems and pressure to correct them would be conducted efficiently by a centralized, national alliance. The Association for the Advancement of Women had already created a strong network of club leaders, and countless clubs had growing memberships.

Two other large and successful women's organizations demonstrated that such an association was possible for literary clubs. The Women's Christian Temperance Union had mushroomed since its formation in 1873, and Croly borrowed many of the techniques of that impressive "army of women" for her federation. She utilized the basic structure of a central organization built hierarchically on local branches that carried out the policy of leaders through different departments.

The other successful group was the National Council of Women, a new national association sponsored by suffragists for women's groups of all kinds. It originated in 1888, in celebration of the fortieth anniversary of the Seneca Falls Convention, when the National Woman Suffrage Association called a meeting of fifty-three women's organizations in Washington, D. C. The eighty speakers who extolled women's achievements of the past forty years prompted those attending to create both a National Council of Women and an International Council of Women, uniting suffrage, temperance, and other women's organizations.[1] Although Elizabeth Cady Stanton conceived the idea of such a conference as early as 1882,[2] her original plan was to unite only suffrage organizations from all over the world. In January 1887, over Stanton's objections, the National Woman Suffrage Association had decided not to limit the conference to suffragists, but to invite "women workers along all lines of social, intellectual, moral or civic progress and reform...whether they be advocates of the ballot or opposed to women's suffrage."[3] The NWSA members apparently hoped that the Council would rouse all participants to become active suffragists. In practice, the National Woman Suffrage Association's generous invitation to all types of women's associations resulted in the National Council of Women failing to aid the cause of suffrage. When the Council was formed, its constitution did not include a firm commitment to the franchise.

> We, women of the United States, sincerely believing that the best good of our homes and nations will be advanced by our own greater unity of thought, sympathy and purpose, and that an organized movement of women will best conserve the highest good of the family and the State, do hereby band ourselves together in a confederation of workers committed to the overthrow of all forms of ignorance and injustice, and to the application of the Golden Rule to society, custom, and law.[4]

The only literary club invited to the founding meeting of the National Council was Sorosis. Croly used this opportunity to assert Sorosis's dominance. She announced that Sorosis valued its leadership in the national literary club movement, even though the present national organization, the Association for the Advancement of Women, was controlled by Julia Ward Howe of the New England Woman's Club. Croly also boasted of Sorosis's influence in forming the AAW.[5] The New England Woman's Club, which had expected to be invited to the 1888 International Council of Women,[6] was upset at being overlooked and its members began to talk of starting their own union of women's literary clubs.[7]

Frances Willard, a prominent figure in the National Council, apologized to the New England Woman's Club publicly at the 1888 convention: "When it was decided to invite Sorosis, we thought it was the oldest club, but the New England Club vies with Sorosis in having been organized a little earlier; but no matter who was first, somebody must be first, and I have noticed that when any movement comes into the world it springs up in a dozen places at the same time."[8] But members of the New England Woman's Club remained disgruntled. The minutes of a NEWC meeting included this report: "This assumption on the part of Sorosis of priority in age and apparently of superior importance and influence was discussed at some length. Our own club was thought to represent the general character and purposes of the women's clubs throughout the country more accurately than Sorosis."[9] Nonetheless, dominance of the New England Woman's Club over the clubwomen's national association was about to cease. Sorosis would soon replace it as initiator of a new national organization of clubwomen.

Less than a year after the International Council of Women met in December 1888, Croly proposed to Sorosis that it hold a convention of literary clubs in honor of Sorosis's twenty-first birthday, at which it would initiate a General Federation of Women's Clubs.[10] On 18–20 May 1889, Sorosis launched its drive to unite all literary clubs. Sixty-one clubs sent delegates to Sorosis's anniversary.[11] A committee was selected to draft a constitution to present the following year. An important member of the Committee, Julia Ward Howe, dropped out when the embittered members of the New England Woman's Club decided not to join Croly's federation. In 23–25 April 1890, without NEWC assistance, the General Federation of Women's Clubs was created in New York City to "bring into communication with each other the various women's clubs throughout the world, in order that they may compare methods of work and become mutually helpful."[12]

The General Federation soon acquired a fashionable, societylike reputation because many of its leaders were newsworthy, wealthy women. Phoebe Hearst of San Francisco was the first treasurer of the organization. An active clubwoman and wife of a United States Senator and mining magnate, she was the mother of William Randolph Hearst, founder of the Hearst chain of newspapers. While she was active in building a women's gymnasium and getting a woman named to the Board of Trustees of the University of California at Berkeley, she was also well known for her parties. A later president of the federation, Ellen Henrotin, the wife of an influential Chicago banker, worked for reform in her club, but also socialized with the moneyed interests of Chicago and gave glittering social affairs.[13] Many other delegates from literary clubs enjoyed local or national prominence as wives or daughters of noted political or commercial figures.

Every two years, the General Federation, with member clubs throughout the United States and in many other countries,[14] sent representatives to a convention held for several days in a different American city.[15] These Biennials took on the tone of a social ball, and newspapers sometimes devoted the society pages to descriptions of the fashions the clubwomen wore. One newspaper reported elaborate gowns, "cream brocaded satin, black grenadine, black silk with transparent yoke and diamonds, black lace over silk, sage green satin with garniture of duchess lace, pink panne velvet, black silk net with a brilliant touch of scarlet at the corsage, black crepe de chine, rich black silk with French point lace and rubies, black silk and diamonds." One Maine representative to the Philadelphia Biennial in 1894 reported, "The women were gowned to the Queen's taste. The president of the club was one blaze of diamonds...."[16] Although disciples of dress reform were also present, sensible attire generally was sacrificed for luxurious display.

Host clubs and clubwomen gave elaborate receptions for visitors. Lavish entertainment was such a large part of these gatherings that the Mississippi delegation decided not to host the 1912 Biennial when the servant girls of their state went on strike. With no domestic help, rich women were forced to close their big houses and move to hotels where they could not entertain as they were accustomed to do at home.[17] The possibility of restricted hospitality caused such alarm that Mississippi women chose to abnegate social duties rather than settle for a modest welcome.

While the General Federation was forming nationally and even internationally, state and local federations were being modeled after it. In Portland, Maine, Mrs. Eunice Nichols Frye, founder of the Traveler Club, suggested that the fifty Portland Clubs meet together two or three times a year. Several clubs responded to her suggestion and in April 1890 formed a Woman's Literary Union. After attending a General Federation Council Meeting in 1891, Frye returned to form the first state federation, the Maine Federation of Women's Clubs, in September 1892. Numerous other state federations followed.[18] The purpose of the state federations, like the General Federation, was to permit the many clubs to collaborate, cooperate, avoid duplication of efforts, and, increasingly, to coordinate civic projects. The constitution of the Vermont Federation was similar to most in declaring that its object was "to bring together women's clubs of the state for mutual help, social union, united action on measures conducive to the public welfare."[19]

At first, formation of state and regional federations made the leaders of the General Federation very uneasy. They feared that their potential national membership would be stolen by the local federations.[20] Their fears proved groundless, however, for although the Maine Federation and the Utah Federation which followed it did not join the General Federation, the third federation, Iowa, did. Eventually, all state federations automatically affiliated with the General Federation.

The growth pattern in New York State was fairly typical. In 1895, the first annual convention of the New York Federation was held in Brooklyn, and ninety-nine clubs joined. The organization grew rapidly, with a total of one hundred eighty-five clubs the following year. In 1897 there were two-hundred member clubs representing twenty-five thousand women. Still, it was estimated that in New York there were one hundred thirty additional, unfederated clubs. No doubt this figure is modest since it more than likely excluded great numbers of clubs which were short-lived, unrenowned, limited of means, or desirous of autonomy.

In western New York, an independent regional federation of twenty clubs was formed when it was denied admission to the state federation in 1897 because one of its member clubs was a suffrage organization. The New York State Federation did not, at that time, wish to be tainted with radicalism, fearing the loss of potential members. The General Federation had urged federations at the state level to follow its policy of avoiding all discussion of religion and politics.

The two New York federations were united in 1912 when Marjorie Shuler of Buffalo, president of the separate Western New York Federation, was also elected president of the state organization. She merged the seventy-one Western New York clubs (or twenty thousand women) with the New York State Federation. Leaders of the state federation no longer feared the impact on their members of a suffrage organization in the ranks. Shuler also brought in the Buffalo City Federation with fourteen thousand women, increasing the total to four hundred thirty-two clubs and two hundred eighty-one thousand women. By 1914 there were three hundred thousand women in the New York Federation.[21]

All federations, anxious to accelerate the impulse to reform, welcomed many clubs that were not strictly literary clubs and were already engaged in emphasizing civic projects. In 1902 a study was made of the two hundred and five New York clubs which then belonged to the state federation. Over one hundred twenty of them were literary or educational in purpose. But twenty-five were department clubs, with literary work substantially supplemented by committees dealing with a variety of civic topics. There were nineteen alumnae associations, six law, medical, and civic clubs, two specific reform clubs, one of business women, one for politics, many urging hospitals and homes for invalids, a health protective association, household economics clubs, mothers' clubs, needlework guilds, and the Women's Educational and Industrial Union network in Buffalo, Rochester, and Syracuse. These organizations, initially, were more apt to support civic reforms than were the literary clubs.

In the long run, these state and regional federations strengthened the General Federation at the expense of local autonomy. The enormous federation network facilitated the transmission of national policy to local and state federations and, from there, to all clubwomen.[22] Through local annual conventions, General Federation officers recruited workers, learned of viable projects, and sent representatives to speak on federation-wide programs to unify the work of all clubs. In addition, thousands of women heard their national leaders at the General Federation Biennials.[23] Both the annual and biennial conventions enabled the clubs to stay in close communication. Officers from the General Federation spoke at state and regional conventions with great frequency. At their own expense, the General Federation and state presidents traveled great distances to attend meetings of clubs and federations and to communicate policy on programs.

Close coordination was achieved in other ways as well. A General Federation Committee on Reciprocity answered questions and collected information on clubs. In 1906 an official Bureau of Information was established in Portsmouth, New Hampshire by Mary I. Wood, an active clubwoman and participant in a wide range of women's activities.[24] The bureau supplied local clubs with papers, books, and information, and collected club materials for the General Federation. State federations set up similar bureaus. They often supplied papers to clubs, for the custom of preparing papers was falling off rapidly. In an environment where they increasingly were able to speak up, clubwomen were abandoning earlier self-improvement techniques in order to invest their energies in public reforms.[25]

In addition, periodicals kept clubwomen informed of General Federation policy and the work of other clubs. Immediately after the formation of the General Federation, Croly began to edit *Woman's Cycle*.[26] This magazine and its successors were not fashion magazines but exuded optimism about the expanding role of women. They included news of pioneer women doctors, lawyers, and entrepreneurs, book, art, and music reviews, and announcements about club work.

The reports of those who attended Sorosis's 1889 convention indicate that many clubs were already beginning to investigate and attack problems in their communities, rather than focusing on literary culture. Library and school work, scholarships, and many other programs were initiated at the local level. Both state and national federations consciously accelerated this process by pushing clubs away from culture and toward community reform. They hoped to build on women's developing self-confidence to spread the influence of woman's special sphere, and thus spread their philosophy of Municipal Housekeeping. Croly began to boost reform work, explaining that it was a necessary step after literary study.

> The eagerness with which the women's clubs all over the country have taken up history, literature and art studies, striving to make up for the absence of opportunity and the absorption in household cares of their young womanhood, has in it something almost pathetic. But this ground will soon have been covered. Is there not room in the clubs for out-look committees, whose business it should be to investigate township affairs, educational, sanitary, reformatory, and on lines of improvement, and report what is being done, might be done, or needs to be done, for decency and order in the jails, in the schools, in the streets, in the planting of trees, in the disposition of refuse, and in the provision for light which is the best protection for life and property.[27]

Alice Winter Ames, author of *The Business of Being a Club Woman*, explained that literary clubs had prepared women for reform. "The period of the old-fashioned culture club was one of incubation. Women had to turn in on themselves and learn to know each other before they dared or knew how to turn outward.... Human culture is a preparation of ourselves to become productive."[28]

In order to understand the rapid change from emphasis on culture to reform which accompanied federation, it is important to realize that a new generation of clubwomen had grown up since 1869. The world had changed greatly in the years between the Civil War and the turn of the century, and women's place in it had altered considerably, thanks, in great measure, to the work of the federations' forebears. One of the most important changes for women had been the opening of large numbers of coeducational and women's colleges, universities, and professional schools. Public libraries, university extension programs, night schools and chautauquas, and less expensive printing techniques had made knowledge easier to acquire. Women now dominated the professions of teaching and librarianship. They were more visible outside the home; women were now secretaries, clerks, and typists. Large numbers worked in factories, department stores, and settlement houses. They rode public transportation, ate in public restaurants, stayed in hotels, and even rode bicycles. Women's views were taken more seriously. World's fair organizers included women's pavilions in their plans, and communities gave serious attention to women's concerns regarding prostitution and alcoholism. Increasingly, there were public concessions to women's moral superiority; women gained the vote in school, municipal, and even state elections, in deference to their special ability to identify and combat sin.

These changes produced a new woman. She was more confident and aggressive because she had alternative channels through which she could express her energies and talents. The New Woman was equal to the society which provided her with greater and greater opportunities. Such a woman did not have to undergo the painful lessons in self-assertion in the ways that her mother and grandmother had in culture clubs. Women, in other words, had less need for literary study now. Social and intellectual needs were met in school, jobs, in the world at large. For the New Woman, the old brand of literary club was obsolete.

These traits were not limited to the vivacious young women of the turn of the century. The women who reached middle age during the founding of the General Federation and the state federations also yearned to participate in new avenues open to women. These women had joined literary clubs during the 1870s and 1880s because they were dissatisfied with home life and yearned for some outlet for their energies other than domesticity. Now they wanted to do even more, to exert some influence on the world around them. Civic reform promised alternatives to such women who responded by supporting the General Federation, which promoted the new program of public work. "We prefer Doing to Dante, Being to Browning.... We've soaked in literary effort long enough; today nothing but an orgy of philanthropy will satisfy us."[29] One spokeswoman explained,

> Women were no longer content to pass unsightly dump heaps of refuse matter on their way to a club meeting where they might listen to a lecture upon Dante. The lack of harmony between a delightful Browning program within doors and unsanitary, unsafe and unwholesome odors and sights without, was beginning to be apparent to the entire membership.[30]

Actually, culture never entirely disappeared from federation conventions. Musical programs provided entertainment between speeches,[31] and women continued to make side trips to museums. Occasional papers and pamphlets on art, the Bible, literature, and poetry continued to be presented. The importance of culture in club life, however, gradually diminished as Croly's plan to seize more power for women gained adherents. In 1905, for example, the Maine

Federation had to make a special point of retaining a place for literature and art on its programs.

Culture-defenders were now expected to justify their work. They increasingly depended upon the conservative justification that culture enriched not only the clubwoman but also her home because it enabled her to uplift her husband and children. Culture now had to be useful.[32] In Vermont, it was said of the literature classes that they "may become not merely a source of self-culture and enjoyment, but, far more important, critic classes, from whose meetings may be disseminated a spirit of literary rightness through home and school and social avenues."[33]

The transition from culture to reform, as could be expected, was first made in those public institutions most closely related to culture—the libraries and the schools. Clubwomen at the local level had always emphasized the importance of books. Once they satisfied their own love for information, they were eager to supply others with books and magazines. One of the earliest projects sponsored by the federations in response to the work of local clubs was the establishment of traveling libraries to provide communities with wholesome literature. Their progress was impressive. They created makeshift libraries in schools, churches, stores, town halls, hospitals, prisons, asylums, and lumber camps and provided a vast range of materials.[34]

In Maine, the state federation, accelerating the work of local clubs throughout the country, succeeded in convincing the state legislature in 1899 to appropriate fifteen hundred dollars for traveling libraries. It also managed to put its own representative, Mrs. Kate C. Estabrooke of Orono, on the Board of Library Commissioners, along with a Bowdoin College librarian, a professor from Colby College, and another from Bates College. When the state wanted libraries to charge ten cents per volume to send a book out, the Maine Federation, fearful that the cost would discourage readers, agreed to pay the bill.[35]

As early as 1896, ninety percent of the federated clubs in Vermont were securing space for library rooms, giving and buying books, and providing the impetus for the building of libraries.[36] The Vermont Federation began its first traveling library program in 1900, donating books and money to communities that needed them. At the New York State Federation Convention in Buffalo in 1901, the literary sessions dealt not with Tennyson or Browning, but with organizing libraries. "How to Start Small Libraries," "How to Stimulate Interest in Local Libraries," "Should Public Library Boards Include Women?" were among the topics explored.[37]

The Rhode Island Federation began its library activity in 1903. It collected funds, books, and provided repair and cleaning of children's books as part of its program. By 1907 the federation secured some state aid. By 1911, when the federation had established one hundred and nine libraries of seven thousand volumes with a circulation of seventeen thousand, the state of Rhode Island took over the entire program.[38]

The American Library Association reportedly credited women's clubs with the responsibility for initiating seventy-five percent of the public libraries in existence in the United States in 1933.[39] The library profession was grateful. James H. Canfield, Librarian of Columbia University and husband of clubwoman Flavia Canfield, a founder of twenty-six clubs in Columbus, Ohio, told the 1908 General Federation assembly: "I know of no one power, no one influence, which has accomplished more for education in this country than the organization known as women's clubs."[40]

With an organized national federation to advise clubwomen on how to implement their concern for school children, they soon expanded their efforts from establishing school libraries to other educational directions. In 1896, at the Third Biennial of the General Federation held in Louisville, Kentucky, a resolution was passed urging clubs to investigate all aspects of education in their communities, from kindergartens to universities.[41] Women were urged to inspect the schools and enlist the aid of school boards, newspapers and legislators to campaign for a complete transformation of the schoolhouse from its physical appearance to the curriculum taught inside. Clubwomen criticized school conditions and demanded better heat, light, ventilation, drinking water, drainage, seats, and desks, along with fresh paint and pictures on the walls. They agitated for the abolition of the communal drinking cup. They supported and sometimes initiated the bills that created free kindergartens. Playgrounds for all children were supported rigorously. The clubwomen urged vacation schools, manual training, art and music training, social hygiene (sexual purity), scientific temperance, "schools for the defectives and even for the delinquents."[42] They demanded medical inspections for school children, hot lunches, women on school boards, savings banks to encourage thrift, and the study of local history.[43] Many clubs of the federations, in the scramble to elevate education, provided scholarships for girls to go to college.[44] In 1910 they invited William H. Allen, Director of the New York Bureau of Municipal Research, to come to the Cincinnati Biennial, telling the women exactly how to inspect, what to look for, who to contact for the correction of particular abuses.[45]

Not all women moved easily from culture to reform, reflecting a gap between the Federation and club goals. Rhode Island's Ardirhebiah tried civics but quickly returned to culture. A General Federation speaker, Mrs. J. L. Washburn, reported in despair, "A large proportion of our membership is indifferent to the serious problems over which our committees are struggling... 'indifferent as to the work for general education, philanthropy and reform under-taken by the Federation.' "[46]

Several Buffalo literary clubs dutifully discussed the General Federation's annual official projects (Practical Sociology, Practical Sanitation, Twentieth-century Problems, Practical Art), but were not large or interested enough to assume any concrete city investigations.[47] The Highland Park Literary Club in Buffalo did not even list the federation's special yearly topic, although members did have current events discussions regularly. Rhode Island State Federation of Women's Clubs Literature Committee was grateful for noninterference from civic-minded members: "Your patience and toleration of it [the Literature Committee] seems to exist without sufficient excuse."[48] The Saturday Club of Rhode Island was more hostile, its minutes revealing that "the serene enjoyment of our social hour was disturbed by the nervous activity of the federation committees."[49] Later, the club "declined" to contribute to the General Federation endowment. However, when the meeting of the New York State Federation of Women's Clubs at Binghamton in 1905 sponsored a paper that argued for a cultural curriculum rather than a utilitarian program,[50] the audience was unsympathetic. The bulk of the federation had already sided with practicality at the expense of culture.

Eventually, outright hostility broke out in New York State between the advocates of culture versus those of reform, over the establishment of a State Industrial School for Girls. The idea had been surfacing at conventions and behind the scenes at State Federation board meetings between 1898 and 1905. The federation decided to assume the school project because state legislators were unresponsive to requests for aid since various city public schools had begun to teach industrial education. To raise money for the project, the federation sponsored resplendent festivals in New York City's Metropolitan Opera House and the Waldorf-Astoria, which netted thousands of dollars. The small culture clubs in the state, however, resisted the efforts to establish a school at federation expense. Above all, literary club members refused to pay for a school that they felt would serve as a showplace for reform-minded women in large clubs. Even though the 1903 convention voted to place such a school in rural Amsterdam (perhaps intentionally nestled equidistant from New York and Buffalo, where there were large clubs which were strongholds of reform support, yet also in a rural factory area), the 1904 convention voted to abandon the project and distribute the festival funds elsewhere. In 1905 the New York State Federation gave money to help run a school similar to the Syracuse Women's Educational and Industrial Union, where such a project was already underway.[51]

The victory of the culture supporters, however, was only temporary. Although reformers never again tried to propose a physical plant to show off women's civic work in New York State, they dominated the conventions and overwhelmed the culture forces with their interests. Civic pursuits eventually won public approval, but in the process of persuading clubwomen to pursue the program, many reformers tried to discredit the importance of earlier cultural efforts. Ultimately, reform work won over. The General Federation, under the presidency of Ellen Henrotin, embarked on total reform effort.

Municipal Housekeeping, it seemed, could be applied to any issue, and clubwomen were creative at finding and solving problems in American life. The textbooks would have us believe that Upton Sinclair's novel, *The Jungle*, was solely responsible for the passage of a Pure Food and Drug Law, or that conservation was a one-man campaign of President Theodore Roosevelt. In fact, these measures, and others like them, were supported by the hundreds of thousands of active clubwomen who made it their business to transform America and the notion of what a responsible government should provide.[52]

Clubwomen consulted specialists before embarking on reforms. M. Carey Thomas, president of Bryn Mawr College, spoke on "Educated Women in the Twentieth Century." Beatrice Webb talked on the English working class. Senator Albert J. Beveridge of Indiana talked on national legislation on child labor. Florence Kelley chaired the Industrial Committee of the General Federation. Maud Nathan spoke on the National Consumers' League. In 1910 the New York State Federation asked Jacob Gimbel of the New York City department store to come to Ithaca to explain his treatment of workers. He sent a representative who assured the clubwomen:

> We also give them music. We have piano recitals. We have the only department store in America where five hundred employees leave their work from 8:30 to 10 in the morning and go to these recitals. We have our own talent, our own orchestra, a violin club, a mandolin club, basketball teams, and baseball teams in the summer.[53]

Thinking she was absorbed with the arts, he misjudged the new clubwoman, who sought to examine abuses in business.

Henrotin established committees to investigate problems and develop solutions. Some of the committees were cultural (literature, music, art). Others were mechanical, keeping the work of the federation going (finance, clubhouse, reciprocity, and information, club extension, press, printing, nominating, constitution). The scope and inventiveness of federation club work was extensive. Among the committees which undertook public reforms were legislation, public health, conservation or forestry, household economics, pure food, civil service, civics, industrial problems, and child labor.[54]

The Civil Service Committee urged the end of loyalty to political party. It provided information on Civil Service Examinations and offered school prizes on Civil Service topics. The Conservation or Forestry Committee supervised the planting of trees. To protect birds of plumage, it protested women wearing feathers on their hats.[55] Arbor Day celebrations were encouraged, the Audubon society was supported, and there were successful efforts to preserve the Palisades, Mesa Verde, the pine forests of the West, and the Redwoods of California.[56]

The Industrial and Child Labor Committee urged amendment of factory laws. They supported the establishment of the Children's Bureau in Washington, D. C. In Rhode Island, 2,375 women petitioned the department stores to close at 9:00 P.M. on Saturdays and for the four nights preceding Christmas so delivery boys and salesgirls could get home.[57]

The Civics Committee stood for the abolition of roadside advertisements that defaced the countryside.[58] They supported attractive community measures such as the planting of gardens and public parks. There were campaigns against expectorating in public. They urged better ventilation of streetcars, and steps on the cars for embarking passengers. They sponsored restrooms, drinking fountains, public benches, streelights, sewage and garbage collection.

Public Health Committees, in an effort to end tuberculosis, worked for the end of the common drinking cup and set up tuberculosis camps, sanatoriums, clinics, and hospitals.[59] They urged hiring district nurses, cleaning textbooks to prevent the spread of disease, and the appointment of state bacteriologists. In Maine, in 1898, children were paid ten cents for a hundred collected nests or cocoons of troublesome caterpillars. In Buffalo, all the school children were supplied with fly swatters.

Moral judgments played a large part in these committees' work. Members attacked white slavery, dances like the "tango" and "hesitation," and suggestive stories in magazines. They also supported censorship of moving pictures.[60] Rhode Island's Sarah E. Doyle Club endorsed President Taft's request for fifty thousand dollars to convict and punish all engaged in white slave traffic.[61]

The General Federation and its supportive state and regional federations frequently collaborated with other associations for municipal reform. The General Federation agreed with the Association of Collegiate Alumnae (later the American Association of University Women) on many educational matters. It cooperated with the DAR on the problems of historic preservation. Like the WCTU, the federation was concerned about temperance, lack of sexual purity, the low age of consent for girls, and white slavery. It supported the Women's Trade Union League in improving labor laws affecting women and children. There were ties with the National Household Economics Association,[62] the National Civic Federation, and National Educational Association.[63]

Federation leaders were themselves active in those other associations. General Federation President Henrotin, who actively took part in woman's suffrage and peace efforts, was president of the National Women's Trade Union League, and vice-president of the Woman's Branch of the Congress Auxiliary of the Columbian Exposition in Chicago in 1893.[64] Suffragist and General Federation President Sarah Platt Decker was active in politics.[65] Eva Perry Moore, of Missouri, another General Federation president, also served as president of the Association of Collegiate Alumnae and later, in 1915, as president of the National Council of Women.

This vast compendium of civic projects in which federation clubwomen were engaged had pushed literary activities further and further into the background. Both realms of work, however, shared a common feminist motive—a desire to move women out of traditional roles and into decision-making positions, both for the advantage of women and for society at large. In civic reform, clubwomen finally attained the goals for which they had worked in literary clubs; they made an impact on society by bringing changes to their communities in a flurry of activity we now label the "Progressive" impulse.

Historians have supplied many explanations for the wave of civic reforms that occurred at the turn of the century. Hofstadter saw status-anxiety among professional men, outdistanced by new businessmen, leading to the assertion of middle-class power. Wiebe calls Progressivism a search for order in an age disrupted by industrialization, urbanization, and immigration. Weinstein and Kolko suggest a capitalists' program to reshape America in a way that would enhance their own profits. To these explanations must be added the reality of feminism. Women's determination to make a mark on their world was surely a source of Progressive activity. Attesting to the feminist origins of Progressive reforms, women's concern for social services and civic improvements on the part of the government preceded the Progressive era by decades.

All this public activity by women disconcerted many powerful men. In 1905 Grover Cleveland had second thoughts about the twenty-five dollars he had donated to the Buffalo Women's Educational and Industrial Union twenty-one years before. As Municipal Housekeeping mushroomed, he complained, "There are woman's clubs whose objects and intents are not only harmful, but harmful in a way that directly menaces the integrity of our homes."[66] The ex-President feared that the club was undermining motherhood. Edward Bok, editor of the *Ladies Home Journal*, was also wary of the new club work. It must, he said, be "put into its rightful place." The clubwoman was tolerable "provided she joins merely one [club] and does not place its interests, in importance, before the higher duties of the home."[67]

Clubwomen were angered by this criticism. General Federation President Decker told the New York State Federation, "When there is a decrease in the birth rate, or a lack of news in the papers, the clubwomen are blamed. But, friends, this is only the raging of the heathen. Let them keep on talking and we will keep on working."[68] But at the same time, they were also sensitive to it. In response, these new clubwomen once again conservatively invoked their love of domesticity, but to a far greater extent than had been necessary when members were primarily engaged in cultural activities. They now relied on their home duties and devotion to protect themselves from criticism of the new public work that absorbed them. William Grant Brown, husband of the woman who had been the first president of the General Federation and the president of the New York State Federation, defended his wife's activities. "Mrs. Brown never neglects me. She may be president of the New York State Federation and on dozens of committees, but that doesn't mean that she hasn't time to mend my socks and sew on my buttons, and she never lets me out in a shirt with a hole in it."[69]

*The President of Quex*, a novel by clubwoman Helen Winslow, conveyed the same message. Home, she wrote, is the "greatest word in the English language." "No club is big enough or interesting enough to make up to the real genuine woman for the home. It's an auxiliary and a training-school. That's all." "I begin to see now...where a woman may be doing wrong in giving herself too freely to club work. If the woman has a family who needs her, if she has children, or a husband, or any one dependent upon her for comfort or inspiration or support, she cannot afford to devote herself too generously to causes."[70]

In order to continue to expand power in a public way, women had to enlarge the notion of what was proper activity for ladies. To do this, they invoked the idea of Municipal Housekeeping by insisting that "women's function, like charity, begins at home and then, like charity, goes everywhere."[71]

Woman's special qualities were utilized to justify her new public work. Members' belief in their public work, "when their nature fits them to do the work better than a man can do it,"[72] was stronger than ever. Ella Dietz Clymer, the Sorosis president who welcomed the first Biennial to New York in 1890, said of federation, "It will stand related to clubs throughout the land and eventually throughout the world, as a great mother to her children, inspiring and controlling, by the forces of wisdom and love, pledging ourselves to work for a common cause, the cause of womanhood throughout the land."[73]

God was invoked again, this time to support women's civic reform work. At the Ninth Biennial in Boston, Mary E. Woolley conducted a vesper service in which she gave a speech entitled "Paul's Message to the Modern World."

> You have been worshipping just as thoroughly during these past meetings in efforts toward the betterment of humanity, in efforts toward civic righteousness, toward the saving of children from ignorance and suffering, toward helping women in better conditions for earning their own living, toward the preserving of the nation's forests—in all these ways you have been worshipping just as truly as you are here tonight.[74]

New Hampshire club members defended Municipal Housekeeping by insisting that the good work women did outside the home would eventually improve domestic life. "The increase of ideal homes must mean the decrease of many of the evils which we club women are trying to correct, such as illiteracy, intemperance, divorce, child labor, juvenile criminals, feeble minded children, tuberculosis, and many others, in fact, the millennium awaits only the perfect home."[75] Clubwoman Helen Winslow endorsed moderate club work for home improvement: "The club exists for the happiness of the whole family. When that ceases, the club's reason for existence will cease. So long as we are thus considerate, never allowing our club life to absorb the attention that belongs to our home life."[76]

Women began to win some endorsements as well. The Binghamton mayor spoke before the New York State Federation in 1905 and praised their work, which was growing more civic-minded every day. The *Milwaukee Daily News* expressed the idea that "it is Milwaukee's good fortune to entertain the representatives to the fifth biennial convention of the General Federation of Women's Clubs," and went on to praise particular programs.[77] In May 1908 President Sarah P. Decker was the only woman invited by Roosevelt to the White House to discuss conservation.[78]

Even though federation women stressed the importance of home and family, they did not abandon their original commitment to women's advancement. Reform was an important aspect of this commitment, and women viewed their work for the public as efforts to help themselves. One woman sent a letter to Croly:

> No other woman writer in this country has taught women so truly to know themselves or thrown such light upon the woman problem; our "progressive" times having made the "woman question" as much a problem to many women as to men. I am encouraged by those who have known you personally, to frankly tell you what a helping hand you have extended to me, how much you have stirred and quickened my life, until I, too, feel that I must gird on the armor of usefulness, and as a beginning send in my mite to aid your work, knowing that it cannot live unless women who realize its value "lend a hand."[79]

Women retained a sense of pride in their sphere and remained firm in the realization that their talents were significant and in their contention that their values should be spread to all of society. At the 1894 meeting of the Maine Federation it was resolved, "that the members of the thirty-six clubs of which the organization known as the Maine State Federation of Women's Clubs is composed declare it to be their conviction that the standard of morality and purity by which their own sex is judged is equally binding upon men and that a deviation from the accepted standard which debars the one from social and public life should debar the other also."[80] Federations granted scholarships for women, provided forums, papers on careers for women, and approved studies on "Women of the Renaissance" and "Chinese Women." Lecturers in New York State offered to speak to clubs on "Women of the Anti-Slavery Movement," "Heroes and Heroines of the American Revolution," and "Some Mothers of the Revolution." In Rhode Island there was a drive to erect a statue of Anne Hutchinson. The New York Federation assisted in a national plan to build a Susan B. Anthony Memorial Building at the University of Rochester. There was continued pressure by the clubs on governments to hire police matrons and put woman physicians in state facilities. The New York Federation Education Committee investigated the treatment of women in education by surveying each club about education in its area. Club members favored out-of-doors exercise for girls instead of cultural music lessons and thus abandoned the notion of women's special affinity for music by advocating that girls do what boys do.

Toward the end of the century, a new kind of feminism began to emerge alongside pride in woman's culture. It resulted from the increasing integration of women into the male domain of schools, professions, and public affairs. The traditional nineteenth-century feminist concept that woman's sphere was as important as man's began to fade as women had access to the male world. Now club members saw that women and men both had developed valuable characteristics and the ideal was to merge them. In Berlin and Plymouth, New Hampshire, girls as well as boys were taught carpentry.[81] There was insistence that men share family responsibilities instead of leaving them to the wife. Women now wanted "a man who, beside earning his share of the living, will expect to do as much as the mother does toward making the home a lovely place in which to live; who will take an intelligent interest in the education of the children and, by example and works, foster spiritual life in the child."[82] This was an important concept to be gleaned from a new society in which the distinctions between men's and women's spheres were blurring. Men in some cases were responsive. Ohio's Governor Judson Harmon said in 1910, "I don't believe that a man who cannot take care of his own children and enjoy it once in a while is worth very much."[83] The federation, however, still devoted most of its attention to propagating woman's sphere and its possibilities for altering the world, rather than working to blend those spheres. When emphasis on separated spheres was superseded by equality between the sexes among feminists at large, the former remained dominant in General Federation ideology and continues to do so into our own era.

Some women in the clubs, of course, never became advocates of women's advancement. *The Northern*, the magazine of the Vermont Federation, spoke with uneasiness of the "everhaunting fear which the average woman has of being called by such terms as 'strongminded woman' or 'advocate of equal rights.'"[84] Such women found it easy, therefore, to carry on General Federation projects in the name of Service. For these members, the same activities that were for Croly the culmination of her feminism were a return to woman's traditional ideal of selflessness. Their lack of perspective on the impressive achievement inherent in public reform by clubwomen led an early supporter of the New England Woman's Club, Dr. Marie Zakrzewska, to note in 1899:"New life and spirit has entered the N. E. W. Club. Prospects are good for its continuance and we shall have to get accustomed to a new activity. The many new members are of entirely different type, excellent but without tradition."[85]

In addition to the uneven degree of feminism produced by federation, it also may have hampered the political development of its membership regarding the issues of racism and suffragism. In order to achieve the widest appeal, the General Federation took stances opposing the admission of black women and the passage of woman suffrage legislation.

Clubs had always had limited sympathy for black and working-class women. Sorosis had decided early in its history to deny admission to blacks. The New England Woman's Club had admitted Josephine Ruffin[86] but had also hired a newly freed slave as the clubhouse domestic worker rather than permit her to join. As the clubs' efforts became more public, their discriminatory practices became more obvious. The process of federation nationalized and spread this racism.

Racism in the General Federation came to the forefront in 1900 when Boston's New Era Club, the black club established by Josephine Ruffin in 1894, applied for and won membership in the Federation. Ruffin planned to attend the Biennial in Milwaukee as a representative of three organizations—the New Era Club, the Massachusetts Federation, and the New England Woman's Press Club. The officers of the General Federation, especially President Rebecca Douglas Lowe of Georgia, became quite concerned when it was realized that they had unknowingly admitted this club with black membership. As she had done with many others, she had admitted the New Era Club without securing ratification from the Board of Directors. This technicality enabled her to return to the New Era Club the dues it had paid the General Federation and to ask the black club to return its certificate of membership, supposedly because the rules of ratification had been ignored.

This action precipitated a heated, albeit unofficial debate,[87] which usurped all other federation news in the newspapers. The Massachusetts delegation and the delegations from Wisconsin, Illinois, Pennsylvania, Utah, and Missouri wanted Ruffin to be seated as a representative of the New Era Club.[88] Southern clubs, however, along with some Northern sympathizers, objected to the admission of black clubs into the federation. A decision was postponed for two years, until the Los Angeles Biennial. Ruffin was told in Milwaukee that she could be seated as a representative of the Massachusetts Federation and the New England Woman's Press Club, but not the New Era Club. On principle, she refused.[89] In anger over the General Federation's decision, two Massachusetts clubs—the Middlesex Club and the Brighthelmstone Club—withdrew from the federation.[90]

The Ruffin incident generated much discussion of black membership in the clubs and federations in anticipation of the Los Angeles Biennial. Massachusetts clubs devised a plan opposing the stipulation that "white club" be added to the bylaws on admission. Instead, state federations would control the admission of clubs to the General Federation. This would allow the Massachusetts Federation to bring the New Era Club and its black members into the federation, while permitting southern federations to bar "colored clubs" in their states from the federation. Georgia clubs favored denial of admission to all black women's clubs, leaving the final screening of applications not to state federations but to the General Federation.

A compromise was reached at a special conference in February 1902, only a few months before the Biennial. The Wednesday Club of St. Louis, Missouri, proposed that the state federations review membership for the General Federation, as Massachusetts wished, while permitting the southern states, which rejected state federation autonomy, to rely on the General Federation membership committee and Board of Directors to eliminate black applicants for membership:[91] "Clubs containing colored women shall be eligible to the General Federation in those states and territories in which they are eligible to membership in their state or territorial federation, and that where these organizations do not exist, race eligibility shall be declared by a three-fifths vote of the clubs."[92] In Los Angeles, in 1902, the compromise was passed without any confrontation. The clubwomen were grateful for the absence of much fuss over this delicate matter.

> Much praise is due to the good taste of the delegates from Massachusetts. They withdrew the obnoxious amendments which had been such a bugbear to those states holding different views—and those states also made concession. The

colored clubs were virtually barred out by the Amendment which was carried by a large majority—making it necessary for each club desiring admissions to have the unanimous vote of the Board of Directors. The term "colored clubs" was never mentioned, and no race speeches were made—only one woman broke the decorous proceedings and crossed the "color line"—a Mrs. Gallagher of Ohio.[93]

Federation women also held unsympathetic attitudes toward the white working class. Snobbery and social control often appeared as themes in federation work.

> It has been said that the mission of the Anglo-Saxon race is to give to the world the idea of service—that as the Greeks gave Reason, the Hebrew, righteousness, it falls to us to so use this equipment, that we shall be enable [sic] to wisely serve our fellowmen. At the head of our General Federation is one who has shown that she has grasped this idea.[94]

Although cooperating with the Women's Trade Union League, Consumers' League, and other organizations working to aid the working class, clubwomen were frequently chastised for turning a deaf ear to the problems of the poor. Mrs. Rheta Child Dorr, author of a bestselling book about the vote, *What Eight Million Women Want*, urged that clubs support factory strikes and unionization. "The club women of Troy have never interested themselves in these thousands of girls to the extent of even forming reading circles among them and then they wonder why the girls should not be able to fit themselves for something better."[95] Mrs. Raymond Robins, who chaired the industrial committee of the Illinois State Federation and the National Women's Trade Union League, stated that membership in the General Federation was so elitist that not one of the six million working-class women was represented at the Boston Biennial.[96]

Club work often reflected nativist attitudes toward immigrants. The New York State Federation's Civic Committee proposed that music clubs give free concerts in the poorer parts of the cities for ethical uplift, but suggested that a small fee would make the programs more desirable and solicit more interest. Another New York member asserted that there were no strikes in a German neighborhood because the music in the homes of these working people diverted them from labor problems.[97] In Buffalo, there was a "general feeling that every effort should be made to counteract the tendency to lawlessness and violence so full of danger to the country at large." The Education Committee report encouraged education as a way to "develop all class of children into law-abiding citizens. Self-restraint, simplicity, obedience, consideration for others, reverence for law."[98] Miss Kate Holliday Claghorn spoke quite openly on "Social Conscience and the Immigrant Population" in 1902 at the New York State Federation:

> The foreign population in this country is a fixed fact, to be reckoned with by use; we cannot rid ourselves of it. The main thing we want to accomplish, of course, is to transform an alien element into one harmonious with other parts of the social whole, to "assimilate" the foreigner, as the phrase goes, and make an American of him.[99]

Suggestions of anti-Catholicism were also heard. In 1902, when Mrs. Louise Van Loon Lynch of Syracuse failed to win the New York State Federation presidency, she declared to the press that she lost because she was a Roman Catholic.[100]

Club conservatism was not limited to nativism and racism. The General Federation and most state federations remained quiet on woman suffrage, a question which had been explosive when the club movement began in the 1860s, but was now growing more acceptable.

Suffrage had never been a primary objective of club women. Such overt political participation was incompatible with their more cautious approach to obtaining influence through invocation of women's traditional domestic qualities. Although some clubwomen had subscribed to both strategies[101] in hope that the strengths of one would overcome the limitations of the other, suffrage had taken a back seat to Domestic Feminism in the state, regional, and national federations. Accordingly, a concerted effort by suffragists was necessary to win the General Federation's endorsement of women's right to vote.[102]

The suffragists who had long populated the clubs and federations now began to voice their convictions and urge that suffrage debates come to the floor of clubs and federation conventions.[103] In 1906 the Industrial Advisory Committee of the General Federation urged endorsement of woman suffrage on the grounds that the American Federation of Labor had already done so.[104] The Rhode Island delegation tabled the proposal, but New Hampshire complied. When Carrie Chapman Catt asked the General Federation for cooperation the following year,[105] a massive campaign for club support ensued.

During the 1908 Boston Biennial, suffrage work was openly discussed. The Boston Equal Suffrage Association for Good Government and the Brooklyn Equal Suffrage Association invited convention delegates to a dramatization of Elizabeth Robins's suffragist novel, *The Convert*. The New England Woman's Suffrage Association and the Maine Woman's Suffrage Association competed with the Maine Association Opposed to Furthering Extension of Suffrage to Women in inviting delegates to open houses. The 1910 Biennial in Cincinnati included the suffrage issue on the program.[106] Ex-president Sarah Decker openly spoke of the clubwomen who were converts to suffrage when they saw the reforms that could not be effected without it. A survey was taken and more than half the delegates favored suffrage. Three hundred twenty delegates attended a suffrage dinner, and twice as many were turned away. One thousand women attended the after-dinner suffrage reception.

Meanwhile, within the clubs, suffrage was gaining support. The Sarah E. Doyle Club voted to support suffrage in October 1910, and presented a play, "How the Vote was Won." The following year, the Buffalo Graduates Association debated suffrage and the affirmative side won, although the group adjourned to listen to a speech by an anti.

There was considerable support among membership to push suffrage at the 1912 Biennial.[107] At the convention, delegate Mrs. W. W. Bain of Houston, Texas, told newspaper reporters: "If the federation does not endorse women's suffrage at this convention, there are thousands of women in Texas who will ask this delegation why.... Inasmuch as this is a women's convention, it seems to me that the question of suffrage, the livest of any issue in which the women of the country are concerned, should be acted upon."[108] Other Southern women, however, were fearful that black women's votes would outnumber white women's. Mrs. Philip C. P. Barnes of Louisville, Kentucky, explained, "The colored population in the South, which in some of the States exceeds the white voting population, has given us trouble that you people of the North cannot even guess. If to this we add the illiterate vote of the colored women of the South, what is to become of the white race in the South?"[109]

Other conventioneers advocated patience on the suffrage issue, asking, "Why go on record on a thing most of us believe in anyhow, and offend the Southern clubs which have just come to us, and will learn what we know if we give them time?" She went on optimistically. "Suffrage will get into the federation. Never think it won't. It's well into it now—all but the declaration."[110] Another Southern delegate threatened secession. But the North maintained pressure of its own. In New York State in 1912, after years of association with suffragists, the New York Federation voted on a suffrage resolution.

> Whereas women are, for economic reasons, entering more widely into industrial and public activities, and Whereas thoughtful women realize that indirect influence is a slow and wasteful process for securing the protection of dependent children, justice for the wage earning woman, and the elimination of dangerous social conditions, and Whereas balloting is a more effective and dignified method than begging therefore, Be it Resolved that the New York State Federation of Women's Clubs endorse the submission of a Constitutional Amendment to the people of this State granting the ballot to women.[111]

Although federation failed to pass the preamble, they did pass the main resolution, becoming a model for the General Federation. Some New York members, however, objected to their apolitical organization entering the realm of politics. Sara A. Palmer resigned from the federation, even though she was prosuffrage, because she believed that the federation should not be a partisan body.[112]

By 1914 most clubwomen were convinced that suffrage could do no more harm to the family and homelife they valued than did club work. Mrs. J. T. Cowan of Utah told a Chicago reporter, "I've voted most of my life. First, for school officials in Montana, and now for everything in Utah. And let me tell you right here that my husband hasn't run away, and my children are perfectly fine and well looked after."[113] Far from hindering their efforts, clubwomen were convinced that the vote would help them apply Domestic Feminism. Frances Willard, years before, had said the ballot was needed for home protection,[114] and now Belle de Rivera, of the New York State Federation, echoed her.

> Wherever woman goes, there goes the home. When a woman sends her child to school, her home enters the school. When her child goes to the factory, her

home goes there. A woman is never dissociated from her home. Women are punished if they offend against the laws of the country, their voices should be heard in the making of those laws.[115]

Clubwomen had persuaded themselves and society that home values belonged in the world. Suffrage could speed that now-respectable goal. A Sorosis club member clearly demonstrated this affinity in a poem she presented to the club:

The Woman of the Future
If I read the stars aright
Will love her club at Breakfast
But she'll love her home at night....

The Woman of the Future
Will cast an honest vote;
She'll seize the erring lobbyist
By a metaphoric throat;
She'll dust the halls of Congress
And she'll sweep the civic stair;
And ventilate the corridor
With some unpolluted air.[116]

By the time convention delegates descended on Chicago in 1914, the groundwork had been laid for federation endorsement of suffrage. The conservatives of the 1912 Biennial were silent and newspapers hardly mentioned antis.[117] Many state groups lobbied for a federation suffrage endorsement. Illinois suffragists in particular were hoping that federation action would affect the Illinois Supreme Court's decision on the constitutionality of the state suffrage law.

On the morning of 13 June 1914, the question of suffrage was brought before the thousands of delegates in the Auditorium Theatre in Chicago, who represented one million seven hundred thousand American clubwomen.

Whereas, the question of political equality of men and women is today a vital problem under discussion throughout the civilized world; there be it Resolved, that the General Federation of Women's Clubs give the cause of political equality its moral support by recording its earnest belief in the principle of political equality regardless of sex.[118]

When President Anna J. H. Pennybacker called for the vote, the huge wave of ayes overwhelmed the twelve nays, which came, not from the Southern delegations, but from Rhode Island and Delaware. The women stood, wildly cheering and crying. The newspapers described their applause as "deafening." Suddenly, amidst the pandemonium, the women broke into song. Julia Ward Howe's "The Battle Hymn of the Republic" had come to symbolize their freedom, and now they spontaneously sang it together to celebrate their joy. Howe had died four years earlier, but her dream of autonomy for women now had tangible promise, both in the impressive numbers of confident, intelligent women who had convened in Chicago to deal with important civic reforms and in the suffrage endorsement they had just made. A woman from Indiana caught the attention of the President. "Madame President, may I offer a motion for three cheers for the emancipation of women as voted by this federation?"[119] This the chair denied, and ten thousand delegates, suppressing further demonstrations, resumed club business, once again proper ladies.

Although federated clubwomen were late in endorsing suffrage, to chastise them for reluctant feminism is to fail to understand that clubwomen had developed their own response to woman's restricted place in the home. Early feminists in Sorosis and the New England Woman's Club were every bit as aware of the obstacles to women's growth as the suffragists. They did not reject the myth of woman as guardian of the home, but used it to their advantage. In the Association for the Advancement of Women, the early clubwomen conscientiously worked to instill in others their own pride in woman's work and woman's worth. The programs conducted in literary clubs throughout America evidenced their success. In these clubs, women had the opportunity to grow in ways that had been closed to them elsewhere. In the club format—an elected president calling a meeting to order using parliamentary procedure, the reading of the minutes and committee reports, the paper of the day, perhaps followed by comments and music, a current events discussion and tea—Domestic Feminism developed.

Self-pride and self-confidence were only the first step in a two-part program. Using woman's sphere as a base from which to build influence, the General Federation's reform activity, like the Women's Educational and Industrial Unions before it, successfully carried out club pioneers' dream of applying woman's best qualities to the public sphere, gaining recognition of her worth and power as well. By 1914 men were no longer frightened that civic work by clubwomen meant the demise of marriage, family, and the home.[120] The Domestic Feminists had protected themselves carefully, and were completely successful in encompassing Municipal Housekeeping into the lady's role. The *Chicago Record-Herald* conceded in 1914, "Woman has conquered everything, has taken her rightful place in society, and behold, she is ready! Who will talk now about her narrow sphere, about the kitchen and the nursery? Woman has educated herself. She stands ready for duty—serene, confident, conscious of power and anxious to serve."[121]

One clubwoman, attending the 1914 Biennial, reminisced about the changes she had witnessed in attitudes toward the clubwoman in the last twenty-two years. "Men boast now that their wives are club women. It means something quite different now from what it meant then, in the general mind. A club woman used to mean then, to the average man, a woman who was away from her home a great deal and neglected her family for her club." She recalled "the change in the general attitude of woman when she comes into contact with outside life. It used to be apologetic. Women don't feel that way any more, and men do not expect it of them."[122] Clubwomen had attained public power and were now welcomed for it.

Clubwomen shared with suffragists the dream of making an impact on the world and both were ultimately successful. Domestic Feminists were less overt in their challenge to woman's traditional place, but the results helped women in significant ways. The clubwomen of 1914 knew that their goals had been achieved in the General Federation of Women's Clubs. Club work was perhaps best summed up by an old woman who rose to speak on the convention floor:

> I came here to listen. I never expected to speak. I never made a speech in my life... but I want to say that for the first time in my life I have heard women speak up and tell what they themselves want and it has done my soul good.... I mean to speak up more from now on. You women have lighted a fire in me that won't go out.[123]

# Conclusion

Significant changes occurred in the woman's club movement between the years 1868 and 1914, but almost nothing of our contemporary stereotypes of clubwomen are useful for interpreting any of the club history. We have misjudged such realities as the maturity of the members and the formality of parliamentary procedure to be synonymous with excessive propriety and undying conservatism. Such conclusions are so distorted as to render unrecognizable the association between literary clubs and the nineteenth-century Woman Movement. The clubs were not estranged from feminism. In their vitality and ingeniousness at stretching convention through the manipulation of the lady's supposedly natural traits, clubs became a significant part of the women's rights campaign.

The brand of feminism to which clubwomen subscribed was not a startling and innovative ideology manufactured by a corps of clever visionaries. It was a natural outgrowth of the efforts of countless women of the early nineteenth century to embody the spreading ideal of ladydom. In their attempts to achieve moral and domestic perfection, women ventured into schools and benevolent organizations which extended new influence on the male-dominated public sphere. The search for the ideal necessitated its vicissitude. This incongruity escaped nineteenth-century women. If their characteristics were sacred to the quality of homelife, surely they were essential for the betterment of the wicked world. The deification of the home resulted in the demand for women's particular talents in the society surrounding the home.

Domestic Feminism, or the extension of woman's domestically nurtured traits into the public sphere, became politicized in 1868, when Jane Croly founded Sorosis in New York City for career women and the New England Woman's Club was developed by reformers in Boston. The members of both organizations were self-conscious about nurturing a pride in the lady's supposedly special morality and domesticity. With this, in New York and Boston was developed the significant and appealing concept which served to unify the club movement throughout the nineteenth and early twentieth centuries—a dual commitment to extending woman's influence and to improving the world by employing women's superior sensibilities. The direction of this plan altered over the years, but its basic goals never changed.

The early clubwomen, sensitive to sexism through pioneer participation in careers and reforms, hoped to create similar clubs throughout the United States through the Association for the Advancement of Women, which they founded in 1873. Members were able to gain followers because Domestic Feminism provided a logical extension of the "ideal lady's" qualities. Women who were fearful of the radicalism of suffrage, who wept with patriotic feeling at the sounds of the "Battle Hymn of the Republic," who scorned Carrie Nation's violence and Susan B. Anthony's arrest, who swore by motherhood and home, found in Domestic Feminism attractive possibilities for wider influence. In addition, many suffragists found the clubs' Domestic Feminism compatible with their brand of women's rights.

The rank-and-file clubwomen, usually white, often affluent, and native-born Americans, generally did not share the backgrounds of the Sorosis careerists and the Boston reformers, however, and the clubs in such states as New York, Ohio, Massachusetts, Rhode Island, New Hampshire, Vermont, and Maine transformed the movement in an unexpected way. Few of the many literary clubs founded in the 1870s and 1880s were bold enough to emulate the New England Woman's Club Horticultural School, dress reform store, and school suffrage campaign. Neither did they flirt with the possibilities of assisting working women, as Sorosis did for a time. Instead, most clubs stressed personal growth and development from the viewpoint of social and intellectual improvement. Clubs provided an exchange among women and an opportunity to refine the educations they had begun as schoolgirls, but had abandoned for marriage and family.

Although these early clubs were less active than Sorosis and the New England Woman's Club, they gave women much that was valuable. They provided a meeting place for women, allowing them to know each other, to develop pride in their strengths, to grow sensitive to sexism, and to become aware of the possibilities for abolishing inequities through Domestic Feminism. In addition, club life taught women the speaking and organizing skills which they later applied to civic reform. Finally, clubs enabled women to become so closely associated with culture that they expropriated the previously male world of literature and the arts as their own, feeling they possessed a special humanistic sensitivity which provided an alternative to the acquisitive and competitive goals of men in an industrializing America.

Artistic sensibility, however, would not be able to check the faults that accompanied America's growth. The country was expanding in every direction in the late nineteenth century and if clubwomen were to have any impact on this world, they could not turn their backs on it. When Abby Morton Diaz, at the Boston Women's Educational and Industrial Union, worked to subdue clubwomen's nativism and to formulate a cross-class sisterhood around the common need for economic independence, the rank and file undermined her plan. Their privileged social status prevented them from creating influential and genuinely helpful and cooperative programs. They refashioned Diaz's synthesis of woman's and society's problems into the concept of Municipal Housekeeping, which justified women's right to correct social problems through the relationship of public work to domestic work.

The creation of the General Federation of Women's Clubs in 1890, and the state and regional federations which followed it, formalized the right of women to turn their attention to civic work. The new clubwoman of the 1890s was far more ready to tackle public problems than her mother and grandmother had been, due in large part to the success of the Woman Movement in creating jobs and schools for her. Culture study and growth of confidence became less relevant as clubwomen discovered, in bringing their beloved libraries and art programs to the public, that collectively they could bear considerable influence upon any issue they deemed important.

Under the label of Municipal Housekeeping, the General Federation of Women's Clubs and the state and regional federations emulated the Women's Educational and Industrial Union and established woman's influence upon the public sphere on a wide scale. Public problems (such as conservation and sewage), family problems (child labor and juvenile courts), working-class problems (minimum wages and factory abuses), and women's rights (police matrons, scholarships, and coeducation) coexisted on club platforms and won women new respect. The late endorsement of woman suffrage in 1914 testified not to an estrangement from feminism, but to their commitment to integrating women into the public sphere using traits nurtured in the domestic sphere. The vast compendium of clubwomen's programs which were absorbed by government attests to clubwomen's creativity in both improving the public sphere and making themselves prominent within it.

In their failure to challenge the concept of ladydom or the myth of woman's instinctive domestic and moral traits, clubwomen's Domestic Feminism called for more moderate goals than the suffragists did. Yet its very moderation made it attractive to millions of women who were able to enrich the quality of their own lives while transforming the worlds of culture and reform. Certainly, clubwomen of the late nineteenth and early twentieth centuries were so successful at extending woman's sphere into the public realm by building on the concept of separate spheres, that they did not respond to the emerging demand for equality between the sexes. Yet they rendered obsolete the notion that "woman's place is in the home," and thereby made a significant contribution to women's struggle for autonomy.

# Notes

## Introduction

1. Barbara Welter was a pioneer in describing ladydom as "the cult of true womanhood," or passivity, piety, purity and domesticity in "The Cult of True Womanhood: 1820–1860," *American Quarterly*, 18 (Summer 1966): 151–174.

2. *A Girl's Life Eighty Years Ago. Selections from the Letters of Mrs. Eliza Southgate Bowne* (New York: Scribner's, 1887). Thomas A. Woody, *History of Women's Education in the United States: Volume I* (New York: Science Press, 1929), p. 96.

3. Mrs. John Sandford, *Woman in Her Social and Domestic Character* (from the Fifth London Edition) (Boston: Otis, Broaders, 1838).

4. For suggestions as to why this moral characteristic came to be located in women, see William R. Taylor, *Cavalier and Yankee* (New York: Harper, 1961) and Glenda Riley, "Origins of the Argument for Improved Female Education," *History of Education Quarterly* (Winter 1969).

5. Reverend F. D. Fulton, *Woman as God Made Her: The True Woman* (Boston: Lee and Shepard, 1869), pp. 39–40.

6. Reverend Hubbard Winslow, *Woman as She Should Be* (Boston: Otis, Broaders, 1838), p. 9–16.

7. Fulton, pp. 41–42.

8. Winslow, p. 9.

9. Alexander H. Sands, "Intellectual Culture of Women," *Southern Literary Messenger*, 28 (May 1859): 329.

10. Sandford, p. 10.

11. See Carroll Smith-Rosenberg, "The Female World of Love and Ritual," *Signs*, I (Autumn 1975): 1–30. See also William R. Taylor and Christopher Lasch, "Two Kindred Spirits: Sorority and Family in New England, 1839–1846," *New England Quarterly*, 36 (1963).

12. Among the sources on suffrage available are: H. H. Robinson, *Massachusetts in the Woman Suffrage Movement* (Boston: Roberts Brothers, 1881); I. H. Irwin, *Angels and Amazons* (Garden City: Doubleday, Doran, 1933); Eleanor Flexner, *Century of Struggle* (Cambridge: Harvard University Press, 1975); Elizabeth Cady Stanton, *Eighty Years and More: Reminiscences, 1815–1897* (New York: Schocken, 1971); Ellen DuBois, "The Radicalism of the Woman Suffrage Movement: Notes Toward the Reconstruction of Nineteenth Century Feminism" *Feminist Studies*, 3 (Fall 1975): 63–71; Elizabeth Cady Stanton et al., *History of Woman Suffrage*, 3 vols. (Rochester: Susan B. Anthony, 1881–1886); Carrie Chapman Catt et al., *Woman Suffrage and Politics* (Seattle: University of Washington Press, 1970; reprint of

1923 edition); Abigail Scott Duniway, *Pathbreaking* (New York: Schocken, 1971); Aileen S. Kraditor, *Ideas of the Woman Suffrage Movement, 1890–1920* (Garden City: Doubleday, 1971); Ellen DuBois, *Feminism and Suffrage* (Ithaca: Cornell University Press, 1978).

13. Barbara Welter describes a dazzling array of vehicles for transmitting the ideal in *Dimity Convictions: The American Woman in the Nineteenth Century* (Athens: Ohio University Press, 1976).

14. Aileen S. Kraditor, ed., *Up from the Pedestal: Selected Writings in the History of American Feminism* (New York: Quadrangle, 1968), p. 9.

15. Kraditor, *Ideas of the Woman Suffrage Movement*; DuBois, "The Radicalism of the Woman Suffrage Movement"; Flexner, *Century of Struggle*; Ross Evans Paulson, *Women's Suffrage and Prohibition* (Glenview, Ill.: Scott, Foresman, 1973); Joseph R. Gusfield, *Symbolic Crusade* (Urbana: University of Illinois Press, 1972); Janet Giele, "Social Change in the Feminine Role: A Comparison of Woman Suffrage and Woman's Temperance, 1870–1920" (Ph.D. diss., Radcliffe, 1961); Mary Earhart, *Frances Willard: From Prayers to Politics* (Chicago: University of Chicago Press, 1944); Nancy Schrom Dye, "Creating a Feminist Alliance: Sisterhood and Class Conflict in the New York Women's Trade Union League," *Feminist Studies*, 2 (1975); Gerda Lerner, *Black Woman in White America* (New York: Vintage, 1973); *The Grimke Sisters of South Carolina* (New York: Schocken, 1973); Ellen DuBois, "Struggling into Existence: The Feminism of Sarah and Angelina Grimke" (New England Free Press, 1970); Mari Jo Buhle, "Women and the Socialist Party, 1901–1914," *Radical America* (February 1970); James Keneally, "Women and the Trade Unions, 1870–1920: The Quandary of the Reformer," *Labor History*, 14 (1973): 42–55; Robin Jacoby, "The Women's Trade Union League and American Feminism," *Feminist Studies*, 3 (Fall 1975).

Andrew Sinclair, in *The Emancipation of the American Woman* (New York: Harper and Row, 1965), mentions that women's clubs had an impressive membership, but he attributes no significance to this. Page Smith, in his chapter of *Daughters of the Promised Land* (Boston: Little, Brown, 1970) entitled "Women's Clubs," says not a word about culture clubs. William L. O'Neill thinks of self-improvement clubs as mere support for the Progressive impulse in *Everyone Was Brave: The Rise and Fall of Feminism* (New York: Quadrangle, 1969). He damns the clubs as reactionary organizations which propagated the domestic and maternal mystique. Eleanor Flexner, who has documented varied segments of the women's rights movement in *Century of Struggle* has devoted barely a paragraph (p. 180), and an uninsightful one, to this movement. Gerda Lerner in *The Woman in American History* (Menlo Park, Cal.: Addison-Wesley, 1971) recognizes that women's clubs satisfied women's needs for self-importance and sociability. She dwells on the racism at the expense of any other aspect of the organization. Those who briefly mention the reform aspect of the clubs are Lois Banner, *Women in Modern America* (New York: Harcourt Brace Jovanovich, 1974); Edith Hoshino Altbach, *Women in America* (Lexington, Mass.: D. C. Heath, 1974); and Mary P. Ryan, *Womanhood in America* (New York: Franklin Watts, 1965). June Sochen's two-volume *Herstory* (New York: Alfred Publishing Co., 1974) omits any mention of clubs. She speaks of the General Federation in *Movers and Shakers* (New York: Quadrangle, 1973), calling it one of the major women's organizations, but she dismisses the notion that it is feminist in any way. William H. Chafe, *The American Woman* (New York: Oxford University Press, 1972) speaks of the reforms, too, but only Anne Firor Scott, *the Southern Lady* (Chicago: University of Chicago Press, 1970), pp. 150–163 gives a close and sympathetic account of clubs and provides a sense of their importance to Southern women.

16. Daniel Scott Smith coined the term Domestic Feminism in "Family Limitation, Sexual Control, and Domestic Feminism in Victorian America," in *Clio's Consciousness Raised*, Mary Hartman and Lois W. Banner, eds. (New York: Harper and Row, 1974), pp. 119–136.

17. Linda Gordon, "Voluntary Motherhood: The Beginnings of Feminist Birth Control Ideas in the United States," in *Clio's Consciousness Raised*, Ibid., pp. 54–71, or Gordon's *Woman's Body, Woman's Right: A Social History of Birth Control in America* (New York: Grossman, 1976).

18. Carroll Smith-Rosenberg, "Beauty, the Beast, and the Militant Woman: A Case Study in Sex Roles and Social Stress in Jacksonian America," *American Quarterly*, 23 (1971).

19. Nancy F. Cott, *The Bonds of Womanhood: "Woman's Sphere" in New England, 1780–1835* (New Haven: Yale University Press, 1977), p. 125.

## Chapter One

1. Whitney Cross, *The Burned-Over District: The Social and Intellectual History of Enthusiastic Religion in Western New York, 1800–1850* (New York: Harper and Row, 1950). Barbara Welter, "The Feminization of American Religion, 1800–1860," in *Clio's Consciousness Raised*, Mary Hartman and Lois W. Banner, eds. (New York: Harper and Row, 1974), pp. 137–157. Keith Melder, "Ladies Bountiful: Organized Women's Benevolence in Early Nineteenth Century America," *New York History*, 48 (July 1967): 231–254. Nancy F. Cott, "Young Women in the Second Great Awakening in New England," *Feminist Studies*, 3 (Fall 1975): 15–29.

2. New England alone had 445 auxiliaries of the American Female Moral Reform Society in 1839. See Carroll Smith-Rosenberg, *Religion and the Rise of the American City* (Ithaca: Cornell University Press, 1971), pp. 100, 107.

3. On Beecher, see Kathryn Kish Sklar, *Catherine Beecher* (New Haven: Yale University Press, 1973). On Mary Lyon, see Fidelia Fisk, *Recollections of Mary Lyon* (Boston: American Tract Society, 1866); Marion F. Lansing, ed., *Mary Lyon Through Her Letters* (Boston: Books, Inc., 1937); and Beth Bradford, *Life of Mary Lyon* (Boston: Houghton Mifflin Company, 1910). On Willard, see Alma Lutz, *Emma Willard: Pioneer Educator of American Women* (Boston: Beacon Press, 1964).

4. Lyon to Hannah White, 1 August 1834, *Mary Lyon Through Her Letters*, p. 222. Catherine Beecher verified this at the AAW speech on Endowments for Women's Colleges, Sklar, Catherine Beecher, p.158, "The Mount Holyoke plan never aimed to instruct in woman's profession, the family work being done by those at home, and chiefly as a measure of economy."

5. Keith Melder, "Mask of Oppression: The Female Seminary Movement in the United States," *New York History*, 55 (July 1974): 261–279.

6. Hartford was attended by writer Fanny Fern. Elizabeth Cady Stanton went to Troy Female Seminary. Mount Holyoke educated poet Emily Dickinson, suffragists Lucy Stone, Abby Kelley, and Olympia Brown, and educator of black women, Myrtilla Miner (Mary Elizabeth Massey, *Bonnet Brigades: American Women and the Civil War* [New York: Knopf, 1966], p. 1).

7. C. C. Smith, "Self-Culture of Women," *Christian Examiner*, 51 (September 1851): 186.

8. Reverend Hubbard Winslow, *Woman as She Should Be* (Boston: Otis, Broaders, 1838), pp. 30, 76–77.

9. F. W. Halsey, *Women Authors of Our Day in Their Homes* (New York: James Pott, 1903), p. 215.

10. Flexner, *Century of Struggle*, pp. 115–116.

11. *New York Tribune*, 4 November 1928; *Medical Pocket Quarterly*, June 1930 and April 1931.

12. E. C. Lee, *Biographical Cyclopedia of American Women*, (New York: Franklin W. Lee Publishing Company, 1925) 2:295.

13. Susan M. Hartmann, "The Paradox of Women's Progress 1820–1920," in *Forums in History* (St. Charles, Missouri: Forum Press, 1974), p. 6.

14. Anna Howard Shaw, *Story of a Pioneer* (New York: Harper and Row, 1915), pp. 75–78.

15. Caroline L. Hunt, *The Life of Ellen H. Richards* (Boston: Whitcomb and Barrows, 1912), pp. 90–91, regarding 1870–1871.

16. Helen Grayone, "Women in Literature," in Annie Nathan Meyer, ed., *Woman's Work in America* (New York: Henry Holt and Co., 1891; reprint, Arno Press, 1972).

17. Abolitionist and suffragist author Lydia Maria Child wrote *The Frugal Housewife* in 1829, which went through thirty-five editions, and her *Mother's Book* in 1831. Jennie June Croly, founder of Sorosis, started her career with *Jennie June's American Cookery Book* in 1866. Sorosis member Mary Virginia Hawes Terhune, writing under the pseudonym Marion Harland, turned to *Common Sense in the Household* (1871), *The Dinner Year Book* (1878), and twenty-three other volumes on housekeeping after the success of her early novels. She and Croly wrote newspaper columns on these topics as well.

18. Maria Cummins' *The Lamplighter*, published in 1854, sold forty thousand copies in two months, seventy thousand in the first year. (Edward T. James et al., *Notable American Women, 1607-1950* [Cambridge: Harvard University Press, 1971], p. 415.) Fanny Fern's *Ruth Hall*, also published in 1854, sold fifty thousand in eight months. Her *Fern Leaves from Fanny's Portfolio*, a collection of magazine and newspaper articles, sold seventy thousand in 1853, a second series sold twenty thousand, and a juvenile edition brought total United States sales to 132,000 and 48,000 abroad. (James D. Hart, *The Popular Book: A History of America's Literary Taste* [Berkeley: University of California Press, 1961], p. 94).

19. Hart, p. 14. For further information on Fanny Fern and her numerous books, see James et al., *Notable American Women*; Ann D. Wood, "The 'Scribbling Women' and Fanny Fern: Why Women Wrote," *American Quarterly*, 23 (Spring 1971): 3–24; Elizabeth Bancroft Schlesinger, "Fanny Fern: Our Grandmother's Mentor," *New York Historical Society Quarterly*, 38 (1954): 500–519; Florence Bannard Adams, "Fanny Fern or a Pair of Flaming Shoes," (West Trenton, N.J.: Hermitage Press, 1966).

20. *Folly as It Flies*, 67, cited in E. B. Schlesinger, "Fanny Fern," p. 515.

21. *Life and Beauties of Fanny Fern*, p. 138, cited in E. B. Schlesinger, "Fanny Fern," p. 514.

22. *Fern Leaves from Fanny's Port-folio* (Auburn: Derby and Miller, 1853), p. 379.

23. *Ginger Snaps* (New York: Carleton, 1870), p. 40.

24. E. B. Schlesinger, p. 508, cites *Folly as it Flies*, p. 61.

25. *Fern Leaves*.

26. Elizabeth Buffum Chace and Lucy Buffum Lowell, *Two Quaker Sisters* (New York: Liveright Publishing Corporation, 1937), p. 31.

27. Mary I. Wood records some on pp. 350–352 in *History of the General Federation of Women's Clubs* (New York: Norwood Press, 1912). See also H. M. Winslow, "Story of Women's Club Movement," *New England Magazine*, 38, July 1908, p. 556; and Louis B. Wright, *Culture on the Moving Frontier* (New York: Harper and Brothers, 1955).

28. Winslow, "Story of the Woman's Club Movement," *New England Magazine*, July 1908, 38 (1908): 552.

29. Henry Baldwin, "An Old-Time Sorosis," *Atlantic Monthly*, 74 (December 1894): 748–752.

30. Sherry Brown and Debra Goldman, "A Study of the Buffalo Chapter of the United States Sanitary Commission During the Civil War" (paper, State University of New York at Buffalo Archives, 1975); George M. Frederickson, *The Inner Civil War: Northern Intellectuals and Crisis of the Union* (New York: Harper and Row, 1968); Anne L. Austin, *The Woolsey Sisters of New York, 1860–1900* (Philadelphia: American Philosophical Society, 1971).

31. Mary A. Livermore, "Women and the State," in Annie Nathan Meyer, ed., *Woman's Work in America* (New York: Henry Holt, 1891; reprint, Arno Press, 1972); Mary A. Livermore, *My Story of the War* (Hartford: A. D. Worthington and Company, 1889); and "Massachusetts Women in the Civil War," in Thomas Wentworth Higginson, *Massachusetts in the Army and Navy During the War of 1861–65*, vol. 2 (Boston: Wright and Potter, 1865).

## Chapter Two

1. Edward T. James et al., *Notable American Women, 1607–1950*, vol. 1 (Cambridge: Harvard University Press, 1971), pp. 409–411.

2.   Her first regular column was in the *New York Sunday Times and Noah's Weekly Messenger*. By 1857 she was writing under her pen name for the *New York Herald* and was syndicated in New Orleans, Richmond, Baltimore, and Louisville newspapers. Among the papers she wrote for were the *Delta* and the *Picayune* in New Orleans, the *Enquirer* in Richmond, the *Louisville Journal*, and the *San Francisco Chronicle*. See Elizabeth Schlesinger, "The Nineteenth Century Woman's Dilemma and Jennie June," *New York History*, 42 (October 1961): 365–379 and Henry Ladd Smith, "The Beauteous Jennie June: Pioneer Woman Journalist," *Journalism Quarterly*, 40 (Spring 1963): 169–174.

3.   M. James Bolquerin, "An Investigation of the Contributions of David, June [sic] and Herbert Croly to American Life—with Emphasis on the Influence of the Father on the Son" (M.A. thesis, University of Missouri, July 1948). Bolquerin cited clipping from *Rockford Republican* 3 May 1868.

4.   Bolquerin cited clipping in Rockford Public Library, 25 December 1901.

5.   For instance, she wrote for the *Weekly Times* in New York. She began to write for the *Chicago Times* and several other New York papers, including the *Daily Graphic* from 1872 until 1878, the *Messenger*, and the *Democratic Review*.

6.   Croly tried to revive *Godey's Magazine* from 1887–1889 and edited three periodicals of the General Federation of Women's Clubs. The magazines were the *Woman's Cycle* (1889), the *Home-Maker* (1890–1893), and the *New Cycle* (1893–1896).

7.   Charles Forcey, *The Crossroads of Liberalism: Croly, Weyl, Lippmann and the Progressive Era, 1900–1925* (New York: Oxford University Press, 1961), pp. 13–14. Forcey, in his biographical account of her son, Herbert, views Jane's work schedule as child neglect, responsible for Herbert's extreme shyness.

8.   *Demorest's Illlustrated Monthly Magazine and Mme. Demorest's Mirror of Fashions*. "Physical Life of Women," August 1872, p. 236.

9.   *Demorest's*, "Talks with Girls," January 1879, p. 13.

10.   Ibid., pp. 13–14.

11.   *Demorest's*, "Talks with Girls," September 1878, p. 471.

12.   *Demorest's*, "Physical Life of Women," February 1872, p. 43.

13.   *Demorest's*, "Physical Life of Women," May 1872, p. 140.

14.   Ibid., p.

15.   *Demorest's*, "Physical Life of Women," December 1872, p. 365.

16.   *Demorest's*, "Physical Life of Women," February 1872, p. 43.

17.   Ellen C. DuBois, "The Radicalism of the Woman Suffrage Movement," *Feminist Studies*, 3 (Fall 1975): 63–71.

18.   Mrs. Jane Cunningham Croly, *Sorosis, Its Origin and History* (New York: Press of J.J. Little, 1886), pp. 5–6. The event took place on 19 April 1868, and two hundred of the most important journalists in America attended. Greeley presided. No mention was made of the woman problem in the *New York Times*, *New York World*, or *New York Tribune* accounts of the event.

19.   See Karen J. Blair, "The Clubwoman as Feminist: The Woman's Culture Club Movement in the United States, 1868–1914" (Ph.D. diss., SUNY/Buffalo, 1976), Chapter 2 for biographies of Sorosis and NEWC members.

20.   Hester M. Poole, *History of Sorosis*, 25th anniversary, Sorosis papers, Smith College Library, p. 25.

21.   Sorosis minutes, 18 May 1868.

22.   For instance, during 1889, when the membership was 145, 60 to 86 members attended the social meetings, while the business meetings averaged only 42.

23.   Croly, *The Revolution*, New York, 7 October 1869, p. 214.

24.   The *New York World* chortled "Sorosis Succumbs," explaining that Sorosis had aspired to a sexual segregation, but was unable to maintain it (19 April 1869, p. 4). The newspaper was more honest in an editorial on 28 April 1869, p. 4. There it was admitted that the

women had not weakened but had given the men a taste of their own medicine by refusing to let them give speeches and toasts.

25. Croly, *Sorosis*, p. 39.

26. Clipping, Sorosis Papers, Smith College Library.

27. The bulk of biographic material is taken from James et al., *Notable American Women*; Frances E. Willard and Mary A. Livermore, *American Women*, 2 vols. (New York: Mast, Crowell and Kirkpatrick, 1897); Phebe Hanaford, *Daughters of America* (Boston: B. B. Russell, 1883); Julia Ward Howe, *Representative Women of New England* (Boston: New England Historical Publishing Co., 1904), and the Sorosis Papers at Smith College and the New England Woman's Club Papers at the Schlesinger Library and in the club's archives in Boston. Membership lists were taken from the Sorosis Papers and New England Woman's Club Papers.

28. Marguerite Dawson Winant, *Century of Sorosis, 1868–1968* (Uniondale, New York: Salisbury Printers, 1968), pp. 16–17.

29. Reaching 137 by 1887, 181 by 1891, 216 by 1900.

30. Croly, *Sorosis*, p. 7.

31. Ibid, pp. 8–9.

32. Jane Cunningham Croly, *The History of the Woman's Club Movement in America* (New York: Henry J. Allen, 1898), p. 21.

33. Ibid.

34. *New York World*, 27 March 1868, p. 4; 5 May 1868, p. 4.

35. For example, on New York Working Women's Association, there was coverage until it died on 23 December 1869. See 27 October 1868, p. 4; and in 1869, 11 February,p. 5; 25 February, p. 5; 8 April, p. 5; 20 May, p. 5; 4 June, p. 4; 18 June, p. 5; 7 October, p. 2; 29 October, p. 5; 6 November, p. 8; 24 December, p. 3; *The Revolution* also covers it extensively. See, for instance, 24 September 1868 and 8 October 1868. See also Ellen C. DuBois, *Feminism and Suffrage* (Ithaca: Cornell University Press, 1976). On Boston, see *New York World*, 1889: 23 April, p. 1; 24 April, p. 4; 17 May, p. 2; 18 May, p. 2; 22 May, p. 5; 23 October, p. 10.

36. 19 October 1868, p. 4. Similar sentiments were expressed on 12 April 1869, p. 4.

37. 24 March 1869, p. 4. The *World* had taken heart temporarily when Sorosis discussed investigating homes for unwed mothers, starting a school for domestic servants, and a Housekeepers Prevention Bureau to test weights and qualities of foods. The paper was relieved. "The New York Woman's Club can hardly in future be charged with doing nothing but having a 'good time.' If it accomplishes half the work cut out at this one meeting, it has employment for a couple of centuries, at least." (5 January 1869, p. 7.) On 11 February 1869, p. 5, the paper reported that the plan for a school for domestic servants was considered too ambitious for the clubwomen. Nothing came of it.

38. *New York World*, 6 November 1868, p. 8.

39. *New York World*, 25 March 1869, p. 4.

40. Croly, *History of the Woman's Club Movement*, p. 18.

41. He recanted in 1874. Sorosis still exists in 1979. Croly, *Sorosis*, p. 14 and Winant, *Century of Sorosis*, p. 10.

42. This article was repeated in *New York World*, June 1868 and by Croly, *Sorosis*, pp. 15–16.

43. Frank Luther Mott, *A History of American Magazines*, vol. 3 (New York: Appleton, 1930), p. 326.

44. Smith College Library, Sorosis clipping, 7 December 1891.

45. Mary K. O. Eagle, *The Congress of Women* (Cincinnati: E. R. Curtis), 1894, p. 87.

46. Smith College Library, Sorosis clipping, 7 December 1891.

47. Eagle, *Congress of Women*, p. 772.

48. Mrs. John Schoonhoven, "Women's Clubs and a New Spirit in Education," *Brooklyn Daily Eagle*, 12 November 1902.

49. Eagle, *Congress of Women*, p. 775.

50. Ibid., p. 589.

51. David Riesman's "Two Generations," in Robert J. Lifton, ed., *The Woman in America* (Boston: Beacon Press, 1965), p. 75.

52. Eagle, *Congress of Women*, p. 775.

53. Ibid.

54. Winant, *Century of Sorosis*, p. 23.

55. Clipping, Sorosis Papers, Smith College Library.

56. Winant, *Century of Sorosis*, p. 23.

57. Sorosis minutes, 16 June 1878.

58. *Sorosis: Its Origin and History*, p. 26.

59. Julia A. Sprague, compiler, *History of the New England Woman's Club from 1868 to 1893* (Boston: Lee and Shepard, 1894), p. 45.

60. Ella Giles Ruddy, *Mother of Clubs: Caroline M. Seymour Severance* (Los Angeles: Baumgart Publishing Co., 1906), p. 22.

61. Ibid., pp. 24–25.

62. Howe's early works were *Passion Flowers* (1854), *Words for the Hour* (1857), *Leonora, or the World's Own* (1857), *Hippolytus* (1857). Later she wrote: *A Trip to Cuba* (1860), *From the Oak to the Olive* (1868), *Memoir of Dr. Samuel Gridley Howe* (1876), *Biography of Margaret Fuller* (1874), and *Reminiscences* (1900). She also edited *Sex in Education* (1874). Additional source material on Howe can be found in Laura E. Richards, *Julia Ward Howe* (Boston: Houghton Mifflin Company, 1925); Louise Hall Tharp, *Three Saints and a Sinner*, (Boston: Little, Brown, 1956); and Deborah Pickman Clifford, *Mine Eyes Have Seen the Glory: A Biography of Julia Ward Howe* (Boston: Little, Brown, 1979).

63. Elizabeth Peabody owned the Boston Bookstore where Fuller's "Conversations" took place. Lucia Peabody had studied at Bronson Alcott's School. Mrs. Lydia Emerson belonged to the club, as did Miss Ellen T. Emerson. Howe, Cheney, and May had been followers of Theodore Parker.

64. The *New York World*, 13 November 1869, pp. 6 and 4, has Mann's article on the cooperative project and a favorable editorial on it. For additional material on the Peabody sisters, see Louise Hall Tharp, *The Peabody Sisters of Salem* (Boston: Little, Brown, 1950); Tharp, *Until Victory: Horace Mann and Mary Peabody* (Boston: Little, Brown, 1953); and Ruth M. Baylor, *Elizabeth Palmer Peabody* (Philadelphia: University of Pennsylvania Press, 1965).

65. She edited *Dress Reform*, a collection of essays by women physicians in Boston on how dress affected the health of women. She also wrote *Women in American Society* and *George Eliot and Her Heroines*.

66. Ruddy, *Mother of Clubs*, p. 42.

67. "Short History," New England Woman's Club Papers, Box 11, Schlesinger Library.

68. 8 April 1872, vol. 9, Schlesinger Library.

69. Cheney had earlier established the Design School for Women, and was still anxious to create new fields for women's talents.

70. Ednah Dow Cheney, *Reminiscences* (Boston: Lee & Shepard, 1902) and NEWC Horticulture Papers, Schlesinger Library; WEIU Minutes, 28 June 1877.

71. "Report of the Committee on Dress," no date, NEWC Papers, Box 10, Schlesinger Library.

72. Ibid.

73. Ibid.

74.  It supported education for women, giving financial support to black students at Hampton Institute, Tuskegee (fifty dollars yearly), Maryville, and Berea. One hundred dollars was given to the Maria Mitchell fund for Vassar scholarships. Money was found for women at Boston University and MIT. In part, Girl's Latin was established in Boston in response to the public opinion the NEWC stirred. Kindergartens were supported. The club provided evening lectures for public school teachers on such topics as physiology, drawing in public schools, and the need for better training of teachers.

75.  Regarding the relationship between the school suffrage project and the Massachusetts State Suffrage, see Sharon Hartman Strom, "Leadership and Tactics in the American Woman Suffrage Movement: A New Perspective from Massachusetts," *Journal of American History*, 62 (September 1975): 299. See also the NEWC Scrapbook, NEWC Papers, Schlesinger Library; Ednah Dow Cheney, *Memoirs of Lucretia Crocker and Abby W. May (Boston: Massachusetts School Suffrage Association, 1893):* and Lois Bannister Merk, "Massachusetts and the Woman Suffrage Movement" (Ph.D. diss., Northwestern University, 1956).

76.  Howe to Cheney, 26 January 1876, Julia Ward Howe Papers, File A, Schlesinger Library.

77.  Cheney, *Reminiscences*, p. 155.

78.  Diary, 17 January 1871. Harriet Hanson Robinson Papers, Schlesinger Library.

79.  *New York World* 23 March 1869.

80.  Winant, *Century of Sorosis*, p. 26.

81.  In addition, Howe began the Saturday Morning Club for young Boston women. Shattuck started Old and New in Malden. Severance started the Friday Morning Club and then the Los Angeles Woman's Club when she moved to California. May Alden Ward began a club in Franklin, Massachusetts, that later became the Alden Club in her honor. Abba Woolson began the Castilian Club.

82.  *New York World*, 23 March 1869.

## Chapter Three

1.  Sorosis Minutes, 20 April 1868, Sorosis Papers, Smith College Library. The *New York World*, reporting on the establishment of Sorosis, emphasized this plan. On 17 April 1869 the paper reported, "The Sorosis is a fixed fact, an institution, and its successful establishment in this city will no doubt lead to the foundation of similar and associated societies in other leading cities in the Union." (p. 6). On 22 April 1869: "Affiliated societies will be formed in other cities, joined to the one in New York." (p. 4). More immediately, Paulina Wright Davis, the abolitionist and suffragist, wrote to Sorosis in March 1868, urging the club to raise money for a Woman's Congress.

2.  "Woman's Parliament," Pamphlet, Sorosis Papers, Smith College Library, 1 June 1869.

3.  Jane Croly, *Sorosis, Its Origin and History* (New York: Press of J. J. Little, 1886), p. 22.

4.  *New York World*, 12 June 1869, p. 11.

5.  *New York World*, 22 October 1869, p. 5.

6.  *New York World*, 31 May 1869, p. 2.

7.  *New York World*, 12 June 1869, p. 11.

8.  *New York World*, 22 October 1869, p. 5.

9.  *New York Tribune*, 6 October 1869, p. 5.

10.  Woman's Parliament, pamphlet, 1 June 1869, Sorosis Papers, Smith College.

11.  Among them were Celia Burleigh, Anna Dinsmore, and Ellen Demorest. Croly, *Sorosis*, p. 23.

12.  Ibid., p. 22.

13.  *New York Tribune,* 5 October 1869, p. 5.

14.  Ibid., 6 October 1869.

15.  *New York World*, 22 October 1869, p. 5.

16.  *New York Tribune*, 6 October 1869, p. 5.

17.  Ibid., 6 October, 1869, p. 4.

18.  Other speakers included Melusina Fay Peirce who spoke on "School Reform," Mary Marwedel on "Industrial Schools for Girls," Miss S. A. Brock on "Southern Women," Celia Burleigh on the "Rights of Children" (*New York Tribune*, 25 October 1869, p. 5; *New York World*, 22 October 1869, p. 5, and 25 October 1869, p. 12).

19.  Woman's Parliament, pamphlet, 1869.

20.  *New York World*, 25 October 1869, p. 12.

21.  *New York Tribune*, 22 October 1869, p. 5.

22.  Ibid.

23.  Croly, *Sorosis*, p. 23.

24.  *New York Tribune*, 30 October 1869, p. 6.

25.  *New York World*, 30 October 1869, p. 12; 15 November 1869, p. 2.

26.  Unidentified clipping, 1873, in Harriet Hanson Robinson scrapbook, Schlesinger Library.

27.  Croly had espoused it at a spring 1870 meeting of Sorosis, but nothing had come of it.

28.  AAW Papers, Fourth Congress of Women, 1876 (Washington, D.C.: Todd Brothers, 1877), p. 121. Croly's term "Women's Parliament" was rejected for Paulina Wright Davis's earlier name, "Woman's Congress." The name "Woman's Congress" had been rejected by Sorosis when the club was selecting a name in the spring of 1868. The term was felt to be too "political and masculine," (Sorosis Minutes, 18 May 1868), but now it perfectly reflected the aims of the founders, who sought to wrest some political power from male legislators by passing their own judgment on social problems.

29.  AAW Papers, Fourth Congress of Women, 1876, p. 123.

30.  Charlotte J. Bell, Fannie L. Baldwin, Laura M. Bronson, Ada M. Brown, Reverend Celia Burleigh, Romelia L. Clapp, Ella M. Clymer, Anna Manning Comfort, Pheobe W. Couzins, J. J. Croly, Ruth O. Delamater, Anna Randall Diehl, Harriet W. Farnsworth, Reverend Phebe A. Hanaford, Adelaide Hastings, Isabella Beecher Hooker, Jane Hull, Hannah M. Jacobs, Henrietta Martin, Isabella Grant Meredith, Ellen E. Miles, Maria Mitchell, Rebecca A. Morse, Zilpah Plumb, Hester M. Poole, Edna M. Price, Dr. Mary Putnam-Jacobi, Margaret D. Ravenhill, Anne M. Rider, Lita Barney Sayles, Caroline Soule, M. Louise Thomas, Charlotte Wilbour.

31.  Julia Ward Howe, Mary Safford, Mrs. Ralph Waldo Emerson, Mrs. Dio Lewis, Mary Livermore, Lucy Stone, Abba Woolson, Louisa May Alcott, Maria Zakrzewska, and Kate Newell Doggett, a Chicago member of the NEWC who became significant in AAW history. Doggett was president of the AAW for three years, from 1878 to 1880. An art patron and art critic (Phebe Hanaford, *Daughters of America* [Boston: B. B. Russell, 1883], p. 286), she helped organize the Fortnightly Club of Chicago and was active in the Sanitary Commission (Muriel Beadle, *The Fortnightly of Chicago* [Chicago: Henry Regnery, 1973]) and was vice-president in the original National Woman Suffrage Association.

32.  *New York Times*, 16 October 1873, p. 5.

33.  Frances E. Willard and Mary A. Livermore, eds., *A Woman of the Century* (New York: Charles Wells Moulton, 1893), pp. 367–368.

34.  Ibid., pp. 308–309.

35.  Sorosis Minutes, 26 September 1873.

36.  "History ," *Souvenir*, Fifth Congress of Women, 1877, AAW Papers, p. 10, says this

first Congress was called by Sorosis but "it was proposed that this convention should organize as an independent association, it not being the intention of the Sorosis to take the lead after the Congress should assemble." Smith College Library.

37. Sorosis Minutes.

38. Croly, *Sorosis*, p. 31.

39. Sorosis Minutes, 6 October 1873.

40. The program: "How Can Women Best Associate Their Efforts for the Amelioration of Society?" by Julia Ward Howe, "The Inviolate Home" by Charlotte Wilbour; five papers on "Enlightened Motherhood," three papers on "The Co-education of the Sexes," one by Mrs. Elizabeth Cady Stanton, five papers on the "Higher Education of Women," by Phoebe Couzins, Maria Mitchell, Frances Willard and others, two papers on women in the church and the pulpit, two papers on women's place in government (euphemism for suffrage), three papers on woman in relation to her dress by Elizabeth Phelps, Abba Woolson and Celia Burleigh, "The Necessities of Woman Professorships in Mixed Colleges" by Reverend Caroline Soule, "Prison Reforms," two papers on the relation of woman to temperance, "Cheering Prospects of Women," by Harriet B. Stowe, "Endowments for Women's Colleges," by C. E. Beecher, "Medical Education for Women," by Dr. Mary Putnam-Jacobi, "Practical Culture" by Emma Marwedel, "Women in Industrial Art," "No Home, and No Home Influences," "Boston University" by Elizabeth Peabody, and "Relation of Women in the Household" by Reverend A. B. Blackwell. Three days of sessions (10 A.M.–1 P.M., 3 P.M.–6 P.M., 8 P.M.–10P.M.) became customary for the delivery of papers, but never again were so many presented. Twelve became the average, leaving more time for comments from panelists and members of the audience.

41. *New York Herald*, 16 October 1873.

42. Sorosis Minutes, 20 October 1873.

43. When the original officers held a mid-year meeting in April 1874, Charlotte Wilbour bulldozed this council into granting approval for plans to meet in New York City again in the fall. But in May, she accompanied her husband, who had just been implicated in the Tweed Ring scandal, to France. Julia Ward Howe used the opportunity to urge the officers to rescind the New York City decision. In June, the officers voted to hold the next Congress in Chicago in October. My thanks to Mary Grant and Wilbour's descendent, Mrs. Deborah McLeod, for this information.

44. The cities to which the AAW went were: New York City, 1873; Chicago, 1874; Syracuse, 1875; Philadelphia, 1876; Cleveland, 1877; Providence, 1878; Madison, 1879; Boston, 1880; Buffalo, 1881; Portland, Maine, 1882; Chicago, 1883; Baltimore, 1884; Des Moines, 1885; Louisville, 1886; New York City, 1887; Detroit, 1888; Denver, 1889; Toronto, 1890; Grand Rapids, 1891; with a supplementary Congress in St. Paul immediately after; Memphis, 1892; Chicago, 1893; Knoxville, 1894; New Orleans, 1895; New Brunswick, St. John's, Canada, 1896; Springfield, Massachusetts, 1897.

45. For example, Sorosis hosted the New York Congresses. In Chicago, the Chicago Women's Club was responsible. In Rhode Island, the Rhode Island Woman's Club, in Buffalo, the Women's Educational and Industrial Union.

46. Harriet A. Townsend, *Reminiscences of Famous Women* (Buffalo: Evans-Penfold Company, 1916), p. 16.

47. Phebe Mitchell Kendall, *Maria Mitchell: Life, Letters and Journals* (Boston: Lee and Shepard, 1896), p. 258.

48. *Buffalo Express*, 20 October 1881, p. 4.

49. *Providence Journal*, 10 October 1878, p. 1.

50. By 1882, the Associated Press was sending daily notices of the annual Congress proceedings to the principal cities in America. AAW, fifteenth *Souvenir*, p. 18.

51. *Chicago Daily Tribune*, 17 October 1874, p. 10.

52. *Providence Journal*, 10 October 1878, p. 1.

53. Anna Garlin Spencer, *The Council Idea and a Tribute to May Wright Sewall* (New Jersey: J. Heidingsfeld Company, 1930), p. 4.

54. Croly, Wilbour, Hanaford, Mitchell, Helen Campbell, Jennie Lozier, Zilpah Plumb.

55. Howe, Cheney, Abby May, Elizabeth Peabody, Harriet Hanson Robinson, Ellen Richards, Kate Gannett Wells, Kate Tannatt Woods.

56. Lesser-known women, also supportive of women's rights, were active in the organization: Dr. Martha Mowry, a Rhode Island physician, Sarah Doyle and Elizabeth K. Churchill, Rhode Island clubwomen, and countless other women active in philanthropy, temperance, education, and suffrage—Lucinda Bannister Chandler, Emma Curtiss Bascom, Kate Parker Cody among them. (Willard and Livermore, *A Woman of the Century*, pp. 61–62, 78, 111.)

57. Julia Ward Howe, AAW, Fourteenth Congress of Women, 1886 (Atlantic Highlands, New Jersey: Leonard and Lingle, 1887), p. 9.

58. "Merits of Women as Educators," "What Agencies Should Women Employ for Uplifting of Society?" and Elizabeth K. Churchill of Rhode Island speaking on "Journalism" in 1878 insisting that women "would report police news with more taste," are other examples.

59. AAW, Fifteenth Congress of Women, 1887, edited by Romelia Llewellyn Clapp and Knight Leffingwell Clapp, Smith College Library, *Souvenir*, p. 3.

60. *Providence Journal*, 14 October 1878, p. 1.

61. Ibid.

62. Grace Appleton, "The Women's Congress," AAW Papers, Fifteenth Congress of Women, 1887 (Fall River, Massachusetts: J. H. Franklin and Co. 1888), p. 55.

63. Julia Ward Howe, "How Can Women Best Associate?" AAW Papers, First Congress of Women, 1873, p. 7.

64. AAW Papers, Fourth Congress of Women, 1876, p. 33. Anna C. Garlin's "Organization of Household Labor." AAW Papers, First Congress of Women, 1873, p. 7.

65. Mrs. Corbin, AAW Papers, First Congress of Women, 1873 (New York: Mrs. William Ballard, Book and Job Printers, 1874), p. 30. Lucinda B. Chandler, "Enlightened Motherhood— How Attainable."

66. *Providence Journal*, 10 October 1878, p. 1.

67. Woolson, "The Relation of Woman to her Dress." AAW Papers, First Congress of Women, 1873, p. 110.

68. Chandler, "Enlightened Motherhood—How Attainable," AAW, First Congress, pp. 17–18.

69. "How Can Women Best Associate?" AAW, First Congress, p. 9.

70. Chandler, "Enlightened Motherhood—How Attainable," AAW, First Congress, p. 17.

71. AAW Papers, Tenth Congress of Women, 1882, Smith College Library, p. viii.

72. Chandler, "Enlightened Motherhood," AAW Papers, First Congress of Women, 1873, p. 24.

73. "Employments Open to Women," AAW Papers, Third Congress of Women, 1875, p. 136.

74. Sewall, AAW Papers, Fourth Congress of Women, 1876, p. 56.

75. AAW Papers, Third Congress of Women, 1875, pp. 91–92.

76. H. H. Robinson, *Massachusetts in the Women Suffrage Movement* (Boston: Roberts Brothers, 1881), p. 158. The NEWC, however, did not dominate the roster of fifty officers and directors that headed the organization. Sorosis had fourteen members on the board, NEWC had seven, and women unaffiliated with either club filled the other twenty-nine positions. As time passed, Sorosis and NEWC domination diminished, although Howe retained the vital presidency from 1879 until the organization disbanded in 1897.

77. Lucy Stone to Mrs. Hussey, 29 November 1876. Blackwell Family Papers, #89 at Library of Congress. Stone's assumptions are false, but even in 1876, President Maria Mitchell

was asked to exclude suffrage from the Philadelphia Congress. (Helen Wright, *Sweeper in the Sky: The Life of Maria Mitchell, First Woman Astronomer in America* [New York: Macmillan, 1949], p. 201).

78. *Buffalo Daily Courier*, 20 October 1881.

79. *Buffalo Express*, 22 October, 1881.

80. *Springfield Republican*, 3 November 1897, p. 3.

81. AAW Report, Nineteenth Women's Congress, 1891 (Syracuse, New York: C. W. Bardeen, 1892), p. 24.

82. Cheney on Suffrage. AAW Papers, Fourteenth Women's Congress, 1886. p. 115.

83. AAW, Fifteenth Women's Congress, 1887, *Souvenir*, p. 18.

84. Cheney, *Reminiscences*, p. 147.

85. 20 October 1881, p. 4.

86. Julia Ward Howe in *Springfield Republican*, 4 November 1887, p. 5, referred to Buffalo.

87. *Springfield Republican*, 3 November 1897, p. 3.

88. Ibid.

89. 12 October 1878, p. 1.

90. "Doubt still lingers in the minds of many as to the exact character and objects of the meeting." *Buffalo Daily Courier*, 17 October 1881, p. 2.

91. *Buffalo Daily Courier*, 20 October 1881, p. 2.

92. *Chicago Daily Tribune*, 17 October 1874, p. 6.

93. 18 October 1874.

94. 14 October 1875.

95. *Providence Journal*, 12 October 1878, p. 1.

96. In Cleveland, in 1877, Mayor Rose welcomed the Congress. In 1879 the Governor and Mrs. Smith welcomed the AAW to Madison, Wisconsin. In Chicago, both Governor and Mayor welcomed the ladies. In Des Moines in 1885, Governor Sherman held a reception for the women at the Capital. In 1891 Senator Washburn gave them a reception in St. Paul. In 1880 Mayor and Governor gave welcoming speeches at the State House.

97. At the fourth Congress, committees were established in Science, Art, Education, Industrial Education, Reform and Statistics, and Finance. By 1887 Finance was dropped·but added were Topics and Papers, Journalism, and Publication.

98. AAW Papers, Sixteenth Women's Congress, 1888. Opening Address by the President, p. 8.

99. Inez Haynes Irwin, *Angels and Amazons* (Garden City: Doubleday, 1933), p. 229, cites personal letter.

100. AAW, Fifteenth Women's Congress, 1887, *Souvenir*, p. 14.

101. Townsend, *Reminiscences of Famous Women*, p. 16.

102. AAW Papers, Tenth Women's Congress, 1882, *History*, p. 22.

103. AAW, Fifteenth Women's Congress, 1887, *Souvenir*, p. 17.

104. AAW, Papers of Tenth Women's Congress, 1882, *History*, by Lita Barney Sayles, p. 38.

105. The clubs were Sorosis, NEWC, RIWC, Women's Club of Chicago, and Fortnightly of Chicago.

106. AAW Papers, Tenth Women's Congress, 1882, *History*, p. 31.

107. AAW Report, Nineteenth Women's Congress, 1891, p. 61.

108. Mary E. Cardwell to Howland, 27 February 1888. Howland Papers, Smith College Library.

109. 20 December 1894, New England Hospital Papers, Box 24, Smith College Library.

110.   A May business meeting in Boston was planned to decide. *Springfield Republican*, 4 November 1897.

111.   New England Hospital Papers, 14 May 1899, Smith College Library.

112.   *Springfield Republican*, November 1897. Charlotte Emerson Brown, president of the General Federation, did not attack the AAW, but assisted it, asking secretary Isabel Howland for announcements of AAW Congresses to send to state federations (1891 letter to Howland, Howland Papers, Smith College Library). 24 September 1891 letter, Brown to Howland, "I wish they (presidents of federation clubs) were all members of the AAW. I shall do all in my power to bring them into the fold."

113.   Townsend, p. 17.

## Chapter Four

1.   Barnard College, *Catalog*, 1890–91, 1900–01; Bryn Mawr College, *Catalog*, 1885–86, 1890, 1900; Buffalo Female Academy, *Catalog*, 1883–84; Elmira College, *Catalog*, 1870, 1880, 1890, 1900; Harvard University, *Catalog*, 1870–71, 1880–81, 1890–91, 1900–01; Mount Holyoke College, *Catalog*, 1870–71, 1880–81, 1890–91, 1900–01; Radcliffe College, *Catalog*, 1894–95; Smith College, *Catalog*, 1872, 1880, 1890, 1900–01; University of Illinois at Urbana-Champaign, *Catalog*, 1870, 1880, 1890, 1900; University of Iowa, Iowa City, *Catalog*, 1869–70, 1880–81, 1890–91, 1900–01; University of Kansas, *Catalog*, 1870, 1880, 1890, 1900; University of Michigan, Ann Arbor, *Catalog*, 1870–71, 1880–81, 1890–91, 1900–01; Vassar College, *Catalog*, 1870–71, 1880–81, 1900–01.

2.   "Women: Yesterday, Today and Tomorrow," Buffalo Seminary Papers, Buffalo, New York.

3.   This feeling precedes the generation of settlement workers in whom Rousmaniere and Jill Conway imply that ambition began. The next generation of women could become settlement workers only because their mothers, the clubwomen, had channeled educational ambition into organizations which stretched the definition of ladydom to include public domesticity. John P. Rousmaniere, "Cultural Hybrid in the Slums: The College Woman and the Settlement House, 1889–1894," *American Quarterly*, 22 (1970): 45–66. Jill Conway, "Jane Addams: An American Heroine," in *The Woman in America,* ed. by Robert Jay Lifton (Boston: Beacon Press, 1967).

4.   Thomas Woody, in vol. 2 of *History of Women's Education in the United States* (New York: Science Press, 1929), reproduces a chart on the express numbers of women in various American cities from *Harper's New Monthly Magazine*, 1868.

5.   Mrs. George Wadsworth to new graduates, Buffalo Female Academy, 1875–1876 *Catalogue*, Buffalo Seminary Papers.

6.   In 1870 there were 873,738 women employed as domestic servants in the United States. In 1880 there were 970,273. Cited in Elizabeth Mickle Bacon, "The Growth of Household Conveniences in the United States from 1865 to 1900" (Ph.D. diss., Radcliffe, 1942), p. 131.

7.   Bacon explores the late nineteenth-century introduction of the potato masher, knife sharpener, sewing machine, cork screw, floor wax, flour sifter, egg beater, kerosene lamp, Ivory soap, Borax, carpet sweeper, wet and dry mop, cooking utensils make of lighter metals than iron, store bought candles, yeast, baking powder, oleomargarine, canned soups, milk and fish, and prepared foods like spices, cereals, and desserts. Cities began to have houses with bathrooms, hot and cold running water, and porcelain tubs. Despite the assistance these products provided there is some debate as to whether they actually eased woman's burden. See Barbara Ehrenreich and Deidre English, "The Manufacture of Housework," *Socialist Revolution*, 5 (October–December 1975): 5–40.

8.   See for instance, Mount Holyoke College Alumnae letters, class of 1869 in 1901.

9.   Buffalo Seminary, 1875–1876 Catalogue, p. 112.

10.   Henriette Greenebaum Frank and Amalie Hofer Jerome, comp., *Annals of the Chicago Women's Club for the First Forty Years of Its Organization, 1876–1916* (Chicago: Chicago Women's Club, 1916, p. 16).

11.   Charlotte Field Dailey, ed., *Rhode Island Woman's Directory for the Columbia Year, 1892* (Providence: Rhode Island Woman's World's Fair Advisory Board, 1893).

12.   This was true of the Charity Organization Society, but women were active as workers in the settlements, Home for the Friendless, District Nursing Association, Ingleside Home for Wandering Girls, Children's Hospital, Salvation Army, Jewish Charities, Buffalo Children's Aid Society, Newsboys and Bootblacks Home, Trinity Cooperative Relief Society of Trinity Episcopal Church, Ladies' Benevolent Association of the First Unitarian Church of Buffalo.

13.   Carrie Niles Whitcomb, *Reminiscences of the Springfield Women's Club, 1884–1924* (Springfield, Mass.: Springfield Women's Club, 1924), p. 8. For observations on American proclivity for joining clubs, see Alexis de Tocqueville, *Democracy in America* (New York: Vintage, 1945), 2:114; Robert Wiebe, *The Search for Order, 1877–1920* (New York: Hill and Wang, 1967), chapter 5; Neil Harris, ed., *Land of Contrasts, 1880–1901* (New York: George Braziller, 1970); Roland Berthoff, "The American Social Order: A Conservative Hypothesis," *American Historical Review*, 65 (April 1960): 495–514. Eric McKitrick and Stanley Elkins, "Institutions in Motion," *American Quarterly*, 12 (Summer 1960): 188–197.

14.   Henrotin Papers, "The Church and the Club," Schlesinger Library, Cambridge. Mass.

15.   Whitcomb, p. 16.

16.   Croly's *History of the Women's Club Movement in America* is a valuable compendium of such detail.

17.   Clipping, Chemung County Historical Society, Elmira, New York, *Star*, 1895.

18.   Rhode Island Woman's Club History, Rhode Island Historical Society, Providence, Rhode Island, p. 54.

19.   For example, Buffalo had a Graduates Association of the Buffalo Seminary. Boston had a club of Mount Holyoke College Alumnae.

20.   New Hampshire Daughters in Boston, National Society of New England Women in New York.

21.   The Scribblers were writers in Buffalo and the Sarah E. Doyle Club members were teachers in Providence.

22.   Mother's Club of Cambridge pamphlet, 13 April 1928, in Schlesinger Library, Cambridge, Mass.

23.   Jane Croly, *History of the Women's Club Movement in America* (New York: Henry G. Allen and Co., 1898), p. 879.

24.   The Rhode Island Woman's Club insisted. "Practically every woman of good moral character is eligible, provided her admission would not be detrimental to the growth of the club." (RIWC, History, p. 48). But as more and more women grew interested in joining, the club was choosing "those who would most advance the interests of the club." (p. 48). This selective process served to reserve membership for the proper Yankee women of the community.

25.   For example, in the 1885 Bluebook, the following husbands were listed: James Tillinghast, F. W. Howe, William Ballou, Dr. F. H. Peckham, Jr., Dr. William Von Gottschalk, Charles Matteson, Charles Hart, Levi W. Russell, and Albert G. Scholfield.

26.   Willard and Livermore, *A Woman of the Century*, pp. 555–556, cites *Home Journal*, *Putnam's Magazine, Peterson's Magazine, Harper's* periodicals and *Galaxy* as publishing Purdy's work.

Rhode Island Woman's Club manuscripts and membership lists, Rhode Island Historical Society and Providence City Directories:

| Date | Number of Members in RIWC | Miss | Mrs. | |
|------|---------------------------|------|------|---|
| 1833–34 | 126 | 41 | 85 | |
| 1889–90 | 217 | 53 | 164 | 79 of these on 1883 list |
| 1885–86 | 244 | 55 | 189 | 155 on a previous list |
| 1903–04 | 266 | 53 | 213 | only 15 are new |
| 1913–14 | 349 | 61 | 288 | only 28 are new |

This information is limited by the accuracy of the printed membership lists and the City Directories.

27. Ardirhebiah membership lists, Rhode Island Historical Society and Providence City Directories.

28. Rhode Island Historical Society manuscripts for Embreaso; Rhode Island Vincent Club; Read, Mark and Learn; Saturday Club; Four-Leaf Clover Club; Fortnightly; Mother's Club; Rhode Island Catholic Women's Club.

29. Croly, *History of the Women's Club Movement in America,* p. 917.

30. 1878 Report, p. 4.

31. Rhode Island Woman's Club, "History," p. 56.

32. In 1909, of eighty members sixty were single.

33. Literary Club of the Church of the Messiah of Buffalo, p. 12.

34. *Woman's Cycle,* 9 January 1890, p. 17.

35. Rhode Island Woman's Club, "History," p. 56.

36. Fortieth Anniversary Address, Sorosis of Elmira, 1938.

37. Frank and Jerome, *Annals of the Chicago Woman's Club,* p. 13.

38. Clippings, Graduates Association, Buffalo Seminary, Buffalo, New York.

39. Literary Club of the Church of the Messiah, p. 11.

40. Croly, *History of the Woman's Club Movement in America,* p. 889.

41. Gilman was well received, recording a trip to Atlanta: "Here I had a charming time, staying with Mrs. Lowe, then President of the GFWC. I lectured for their local club that night: 'Tremendous crowd—standing—lots couldn't get in. Went well. Great enthusiasm. People fainted, went out, recovered and returned.' They were wonderfully kind to me in the South." Gilman, *The Living of Charlotte Perkins Gilman* (New York: Appleton-Century, 1935), p. 254.

42. Other examples: Lorain P. Bucklin of RIWC presented her "Studies of Famous Queens" frequently. Mrs. Mabel Loomis Todd of Amherst spoke widely on Emily Dickinson's poetry, which she edited. H. H. Robinson's daughter Harriet Shattuck went everywhere, teaching clubs to organize along the Parliamentary Law she wrote about. Kate Gannett Wells would not permit the AAW to print her paper at a Congress because she planned to give it again and again. The RIWC in Providence frequently drew on celebrities from Boston. For example, members heard from Ednah Cheney, Mary Eastman, Antoinette Brown Blackwell, Julia Ward Howe, Abby May, Kate Gannett Wells, Mary Livermore, Helen Campbell, Mary Woolley, Ellen Richards, Howe's daughter Julia Anagnos, Jane Addams, and Fanny Merrit Farmer of the Boston Cooking School.

43. Whitcomb, p. 9. Literary Club of the Church of the Messiah, p. 11. Rhode Island Women's Club, "History," p. 51.

44. Topics were art, literature, education, politics, and socioloy, meeting the second and fourth Wednesday morning per month.

45. Literary Club History, p. 6.

46. Croly on Friends in Council, Quincy, Illinois.

47. Mary I. Wood, *The History of the General Federation of Women's Clubs* (New York: Norwood, 1912), p. 29, and A. E. Bostwick, "Club Women's Reading," *Bookman Magazine*, 40 (Jan., Feb., and March, 1915).

48. Sorosis Twenty-first Anniversary Report, pp. 114–115.

49. Harriet Hanson Robinson, Diary, vol. 12, 1888, Schlesinger Library.

50. Julia Green Ferguson, "History," Literary Club of the Church of the Messiah, p. 4.

51. Ibid., p. 5.

52. Croly, *History of the Woman's Club Movement in America*, p. 879.

53. *Brooklyn Daily Eagle*, 13 November 1902. Helen Maria Winslow, clubwoman and novelist, summarized the contributions club life made, in her book *President of Quex* (Boston: Lothrop, Lee and Shepard, 1906), p. 36. "Many are they who shall pursue literature, but few there be who overtake it. Those were the years when we were finding ourselves; when we learned the sound of our own voices; when we learned to tolerate the opinions of other women; when we were growing a desire to do more active and valuable work in the world. Women have not been coming into their own with a jump; we've been working up to it gradually ever since Lucy Stone and Susan B. Anthony and Mrs. Stanton and those others started the ball rolling nearly fifty years ago. You shall not laugh at our little efforts now."

54. *Topeka State Journal*, 13 June 1896. Winslow's novel, *President of Quex*, expressed it this way: "Aside from her few personal friends, she had not cared much for women before and this was the beginning of a new love for and understanding of her sex." p. 40.

55. Literary Club of the Church of the Messiah, p. 10.

56. Rhode Island Woman's Club, *Report*, 1890.

57. *History and Proceedings*, Western New York Federation of Women's Clubs, 1896–1899 (Buffalo: Hubbard Press, 1899), speech of Mrs. Sarah Sumner Teall.

58. Abigail Scott Duniway, *Path-breaking* (New York: Schocken, 1971), chapter 12.

59. Churchill to Cheney, 24 January 1876, New England Hospital Records, Smith College, Northampton, Mass.

60. Rhode Island Woman's Club, March 1878 Annual Report, p. 6.

61. Kate Gannett Wells, "Sphere of Women in Traditional America," *Atlantic Monthly*, 46 (December 1880): 819.

62. G. P. Porter, *Maine Federation of Women's Clubs*, p. 27.

63. Ibid.

64. Mary C. Thurlow, "Encouragement of Serious Reading by Women's Clubs," *Library Journal*, 28 (May 1903): 228. R. Ashmore also records club gossip in "Restlessness of the Age," *Ladies' Home Journal*, 12 (1895): 16. R. Stern indicated that some women used clubs "as cloaks for mere ambition, or as a means of avoiding their domestic or marital duties." (*Home Entertainments*, 1910.)

65. Martha E. D. White, "Work of the Woman's Club," *Atlantic Monthly*, 93 (1903): 614–623. White wrote, "When I gave up teaching after my marriage (1889) I missed the job so much, that I sought another way to teach. Women's clubs offered an opportunity for platform work and I became a 'lecturer.'" In addition to visiting clubs widely, White belonged to the New England Woman's Club, organized the Woman's Club of Arlington, and chaired the Department of Literary and Library Extension in both the General Federation of Women's Clubs and the Massachusetts Federation of Women's Clubs.

E. C. Lee, *Biographical Cyclopedia of American Women.* (New York: Franklin W. Lee, 1925) 2:141.

## Chapter Five

1. Mary P. Ryan, *Womanhood in America from Colonial Times to the Present* (New York:

New Viewpoints, 1975), pp. 225–235. See also Aileen Kraditor, *Ideas of the Woman Suffrage Movement* (Garden City, New York: Doubleday, 1971), p. 53.

2. Mrs. T. J. Bowlker, "Woman's Home-making Function Applied to the Municipality," *American City*, 6 (1912): 863. See also Ida Husted Harper, "Woman's Broom in Municipal Housekeeping," *Delineator*, 73 (February 1909): 213–216 and Sarah Comstock, "Her Town in Order," *Collier's*, 48 (9 March 1912): 38–39.

3. WEIU Report, 1 May 1885, p. 9.

4. Nettie F. Bailey, "Significance of the Women's Club Movement," *Harper's Bazaar* (1905), p. 204.

5. Clisby to Cheney, 8 November 1875. New England Hospital Records, Box 22, Smith College Library.

6. WEIU, 1879 Report, p. 7.

7. S. Agnes Donham, "History of Women's Educational and Industrial Union" (WEIU Papers, Boston), p. 22.

8. WEIU Report, 7 May 1878, p. 11.

9. Among the New England Woman's Club members in the WEIU were: Julia Ward Howe, her daughter Julia R. Anagnos, Edna Dow Cheney, Lucia M. Peabody, Kate Gannett Wells, Abby May, May Alden Ward, Mrs. James Freeman Clarke, Harriet Sewall, Mary Livermore, Mrs. Putnam, Anna Cabot Lodge, and Julia Sprague. All divided their club efforts between the NEWC and the new Women's Educational Industrial Union.

10. Sorosis, which had refused the Working Women's Association direct aid, had also made attempts to cooperate with the working-class woman. Members investigated clubs of working girls (15 October 1881 Sorosis Minutes) and came to the same conclusion. Of Sorosis member Anne Botta it was said, "She was an exquisite needlewoman, making the most artistic and elegant of trifles, and even sewing seams, if need were. But of late years she used laughingly to declare it a kind of irreligion for those women to sew who could afford to hire sewing, because, in every case, it defrauded two persons of their rights." *Memoirs of Anne C. L. Botta* (New York: J. S. Tait, 1894), p. 232. The AAW had also given brief attention to the lives of working women, addressing itself to Factory Girls and Rescue Work in Relation to Prostitution and Reform.

11. Among them: Julia Ward Howe, Mrs. Louis D. Brandeis, Mrs. Charles G. Ames, Mary Morton Kehew, Miss Lucia M. Peabody, Mrs. William L. Putnam, Mrs. Kate Gannett Wells.

12. Laura Spelman Rockefeller gave twenty-five-thousand dollars. Mary Hemenway gave five thousand. Eliza Tiffany gave five hundred.

13. *Report of Progress, 1905*, p. 19.

14. The rooms, open to working-class nonmembers as well as all WEIU members, were located near the Boston Common, in the same location as the NEWC and the *Woman's Journal*, on 4 Park Street. In 1880, the WEIU moved to 157 Tremont Street, to 74 Boylston in 1883 and to 97–98 Boylston in 1899, where it still stood until its recent move to 110 Boylston Street.

15. Donham, "History of Women's Educational and Industrial Union," p. 76. A Committee on Ethics replaced the Moral and Spiritual Committee, distributing leaflets on such topics as "Luxury" and "Responsibility," and providing a blind room for sightless readers in the library, but even this folded by 1908.

16. Eleanor W. Allen, "Boston WEIU," *New England Galaxy* (Spring 1965), p. 33.

17. Donham, "History," p. 94. The WEIU worked with the Moral Education Association, newspapers, clergy, YWCA, Woman's Press Association, Massachusetts Home for Inebriated Women, WCTU. The Massachusetts legislation passed in 1887. Jane Croly, *History of the Woman's Club Movement in America* (New York: Henry G. Allen, 1898) p. 621.

18. Allen, "Boston WEIU," p. 31.

19. She had an ancestor who came over on the Mayflower, another who was the chief justice of the Massachusetts Supreme Court, and still another was Grover Cleveland's first vice-president.

20. "The Life Work of Abby Morton Diaz," *Woman's Journal*, 13 June 1903. Willard on Abby Morton Diaz, p. 240. Frances E. Willard and Mary A. Livermore, *A Woman of the Century* (New York: Charles Wells Moulton, 1893); and Edward T. James et al., *Notable American Women* (Cambridge: Harvard University Press) 1: 471–473.

21. "Life Work of Abby Morton Diaz," *Woman's Journal*, 13 June 1903.

22. The magazines to which she contributed were *Youth's Companion, Wide Awake, St. Nicholas.* In 1867 *Our Young Folks* serialized her *William Henry Letters*, a popular book in 1870. *Lucy Maria* was written in 1872. Other works include *Chronicles of the Stimpcett Family, Schoolmaster's Trunk, A Story Book for Children, A Cat's Arabian Nights, Fireside Chronicles, Jimmyjohns and Other Stories, John Spicer Lectures, Story Free Series, Story of Polly Cologne.* For women, Diaz wrote *Only a Flock of Women, Domestic Problems,* and *By Bury to Beacon Street,* the proceeds of a late edition of the latter going to the suffrage movement. ("Life Work of Abby Morton Diaz," *Woman's Journal.*)

23. "Talk with Mrs. Diaz," Portland (Maine) *Evening Express,* 9 December 1896.

24. Diaz justified her suffragism with morality, urging school suffrage for mothers because they should not yield children after "five or six years of the tenderest solicitude" to "men nominated on party lines, and therefore supposably [sic] under party influences...if women are good, and politics bad, by what logic, or even by what common sense, or what moral sense, does it come about that school education should be given over to the latter?" (Diaz, *Only a Flock of Women* [Boston: D. Lothrop, 1893], p. 126.) Diaz was President of the Belmont Woman Suffrage League.

25. "Talk with Mrs. Diaz," *Portland* (Maine) *Evening Express,* 9 December 1896.

26. Diaz, *Only a Flock of Women* (Boston: D. Lothrop, 1893), pp. 136–137.

27. "Life Work of Abby Morton Diaz," *Woman's Journal.*

28. Diaz, *Only a Flock,* pp. 82–83.

29. Abby Morton Diaz, *A Domestic Problem: Work and Culture in the Household* (Boston: James R. Osgood, 1875), pp. 90, 84, 91, 53–54. Linda Gordon explains these nineteenth-century beliefs about heredity in "Voluntary Motherhood: The Beginning of Feminist Birth Control Ideas in the United States;; in *Clio's Consciousness Raised,* ed. by Mary Hartman and Lois W. Banner (New York: Harper and Row, 1974).

30. Addie Heath, "Abby Morton Diaz," *Women at Work,* 6 (1883): 228.

31. Diaz, *Only a Flock,* p. 102.

32. Diaz, *Domestic Problem,* pp. 85–86.

33. Diaz, *Only a Flock,* pp. 100–101.

34. Whitcomb, *Springfield Women's Club,* p. 11.

35. Consigners paid the WEIU a ten percent commission, but that did not even cover WEIU expenses. The store was a nonprofit service to women.

36. The progress was gradual. In 1882 two thousand dollars was earned. In 1888, thirty thousand. In 1892, thirty-seven thousand. Lucy M. Salmon, "Women's Exchange: Charity or Business," *Forum,* 13 (1892): 394–406.

37. They also studied ventilation in shops, streetcars and schools, examined dangerous trades like rubber, twine and cordage, and developed concern for sweatshops and for enforcing labor laws.

38. 18 January 1878 Minutes.

39. To find employers, they placed ads in the *Woman's Journal* and *Golden Rule,* asked ministers to announce their services from the pulpits, and sent two hundred postcards to those who might hire women. The successor to this job bureau was formed by the WEIU in 1910. Called the Appointment Bureau, it placed trained women in positions of responsibility and power, not just in teaching, but in many ares. It sought places especially for its scholarship students at Radcliffe, Wellesley, Simmons, and Columbia.

40. Among the lawyers were Miss L. J. Robinson, F. A. Franham, H. L. Whittlesey, G. O. Burrage, H. N. Glover, M. L. Willing, and William B. Sewall, said to be among the most distinguished lawyers in the city. WEIU rooms were open for grievances on Wednesday and Saturday afternoons, three to five p.m.

41. *Federation Bulletin*, April 1904, p. 123.

42. WEIU Report, 1879, p. 20.

43. WEIU 1879 Report, Protective Committee, p. 20.

44. James et al., *Notable American Women*, 2: 313–314.

45. Ibid., pp. 335–336.

46. Such topics were investigated as Vocations for the Trained Teacher (1910 and 1914), Boot and Shoe Industry in Massachusetts as a Vocation for Women (1915), Industrial Home Work in Massachusetts (1914), Living Wage of Women Workers–a study of incomes and expenditures of 450 women workers in the city of Boston (1911), Public Schools and Women in Office Service (1914), and Trade School for Girls, a preliminary investigation in typical manufacturing city of Worcester, Mass. (1913).

47. By 1908 they had placed forty-seven graduates. Lucinda W. Prince, "Training for Saleswomen," *Federation Bulletin*, 5 (February 1908): 165–166.

48. Richards wrote many scientific papers, magazine articles, and addresses. In addition, she wrote such books as *The Cost of Living* (1899), *The Cost of Food* (1901), *First Lessons in Food and Diet* and *Art of Right Living* (both in 1904), *Cost of Shelter* (1905), *Sanitation in Daily Life* (1907), *Cost of Cleanliness* (1908), *Industrial Water Analysis* (1908), *Euthenics* (1910), and *Conservation by Sanitation* (1911) and several others.

49. Florence Lockwood, "Working Girls Clubs," *Century Magazine*, 41 (March 1891): 794.

50. "Working Girls Clubs," *Current Opinion*, 29 (August 1900): 195. See also Maude Stanley, "Working Girl's Clubs in Italy," *Living Age*, 254 (28 September 1907): 814–818 and *Clubs for Working Girls* (New York: Macmillan, 1890).

51. Lockwood, "Working Girls Clubs", p. 794.

52. Ibid. Perhaps the working girls conveyed some of their problems to the mill-owners' wives. A congress of working girls in New York City in April 1890 drew two hundred delegates. The Industrial Society of Hoboken urged solidarity. "A working girl is doing other working girls an injury when she consents to work for less than living wages." ("Their Lives Brightened" in *New York Times*, 17 April 1890, p. 2). While most girls revealed that their clubs were a place for amusement, sociability, mutual improvement, an "assemblage of women who meet to discuss various subjects for furthering the interests of womankind," or charity, others saw it as a place for ·· agitation, education and cooperation." ("Working Women's Clubs" in *New York Times*, 13 April 1890, p. 11). Here, at least, was a ready forum for association among working women.

53. *WEIU 1888 Report* (Boston: "Washington Press," George E. Crosby & Co., 1888), p. 9.

54. The WEIU developed branches in the following cities: Buffalo, Syracuse, Auburn, Dunkirk, Watertown, and Rochester, New York; Columbus, Cleveland and Youngstown, Ohio; Saco and Chelsea, Maine; Washington, D.C.; Providence, Rhode Island; Portsmouth, New Hampshire; St. Paul, Minnesota; Brattleboro, Vermont; San Francisco; Brockton, Massachusetts; Cedar Rapids, Iowa; Geneva, Switzerland; and Paris, France.

55. For two years, it met in the rooms of the Fitch Institute on Swan and Michigan. In 1878 the Babcock Mansion on swank Delaware Avenue and Niagara Square downtown was bought for sixteen thousand dollars. In 1894 that mansion was razed and a new structure was built by the club.

56. He was a trustee and treasurer in the Church of the Messiah, trustee of the Buffalo Children's Aid Society and Newsboys' and Boot Blacks' Home, a member of the Decorative Arts Society ("Aid for Art," *Buffalo Morning Express*, 13 February 1884, p. 5), vice-president of the Buffalo Homeopathic Hospital.

57. Harriet A. Townsend, *Reminiscences of Famous Women* (Buffalo: Evans-Penfold, 1916), p. 29.

58. *Buffalo Morning Express*, 25 January 1884; Ibid., "Household Talks," 27 January 1884, p. 9; Ibid., "Hints for Housekeepers," 29 January 1884, p. 6; Ibid., "Diaz Discourses," 31 January 1884, p. 6 and 3 February 1884, p. 9. Almost immediately, the Union idea appealed to Buffalo clubwomen and they acted on Diaz's suggestion by forming a Union of their own.

59. COS Sixth Annual Report, 1884, p. 9.

60. Mrs. Frederick J. (Ellie J.) Shepard, "The Women's Educational and Industrial Union of Buffalo," *Buffalo Historical Society Publications*, 22 (1918): 147.

61. For example, AM&A's department store gave rugs to the Union. Mrs. Meldrum was a member. "The Women's Union" in *Buffalo Morning Express*, 6 April 1884, p. 2. To this day the store attracts customers from clubs via a February public relations campaign Club Day.

62. WEIU, 4 May 1886 Report, Townsend, p. 8.

63. Ibid.

64. Ibid., p. 5.

65. WEIU Report, 1 May 1888, Townsend, p. 7.

66. Emily Huntington, *How to Teach Kitchen Garden* (New York: Doubleday, 1903). Boys also received instruction, but their table-setting and dishwashing was accompanied by making bags for skates and books, and their lessons were adapted to camp life. Shepard, "Women's Educational and Industrial Union," p. 166.

67. Buffalo WEIU, 1892–1893 Handbook, p. 13.

68. Shepard, "Women's Educational and Industrial Union," pp. 167–168.

69. Ibid., p. 169.

70. Buffalo WEIU, 12 May 1891 Report, p. 9.

71. WEIU Report, 1 May 1885, p. 10.

72. 15 March 1904 Minutes of Buffalo Presidents Council for Western New York, Dow folder, New York State Federation of Women's Clubs.

73. Shepard, "Women's Educational and Industrial Union," p. 175.

74. Ibid., p. 157.

75. Ibid., p. 158.

76. The university still maintains a building named Townsend Hall, but like all the civic work these women accomplished, the contribution was swallowed up by the larger society and no one remembers that it came from a movement to improve the lives of women.

## Chapter Six

1. The Council was held from 25 March until 1 April 1888. Representatives from the WCTU, missionary, professional, educational, industrial, Knights of Labor, Granger, peace, moral purity, and charitable associations joined the National Women Suffrage Association suffragists. Their rival suffrage organization, the American Woman Suffrage Association, was also there, represented by Lucy Stone, Henry B. Blackwell, Antoinette Brown Blackwell, Ednah Dow Cheney, Harriet Hanson Robinson, Harriet Robinson Shattuck, and Julia Ward Howe. The formation of the National Council of Women thus looked toward the reunion of the two suffrage camps two years later.

2. Anna Garlin Spencer, *The Council Idea and May Wright Sewall* (New Jersey: J. Heidingsfeld Co., 1930), p. 9.

3. May Wright Sewall, "Genesis of the International Council of Women," p. 6, cited in *International Council of Women: Women in a Changing World* (London: Routledge and Kegan Paul, 1966), p. 12.

4. Spencer, *The Council Idea*, p. 12. For further material on the Council see Countess

Aberdeen, "International Council of Women in Congress," *Nineteenth Century*, 46 (July 1897): 18–25. Aberdeen, "International Council of Women in Congress," *North American Review*, 169 (August 1899): 145–153; Mary Lowe Dickson, "National Council of Women in the United States," *Arena*, 17 (February 1899): 478–493; Gilbert Parker and May Wright Sewall, "International Council of Women," *Fortnightly Review*, 72 (July 1899): 151–159; F. H. Low, "A Woman's Criticism of the Woman's Congress," *Nineteenth Century*, 46 (August 1899): 192–202; F. H. Gaffney, "Reply to a Woman's Criticism of the Woman's Congress," *Nineteenth Century*, 46 (September 1899): 598–611.

5.   *Report of the International Council of Women*, p. 218. Washington D.C.: Rufus H. Darley, 1888.

6.   The New England Woman's Club members had voted to send Abby May as their delegate, "if she was going to Washington and felt able to act in this capacity. If she should decline, it was voted to ask the members of the club present at the Council to make a member represent the NEWC." NEWC Minutes, 3 March 1888, NEWC Papers, Schlesinger Library, Cambridge, Mass. A month later, however, May reported that the NEWC falsely assumed it had been invited to send a delegate. Sorosis, presumed to be the oldest club of its kind, had been invited instead.

7.   Ibid.

8.   *Report of the International Council of Women*, p. 225.

9.   NEWC Minutes, 2 March 1889, NEWC Papers.

10.   Marguerite Dawson Winant, *A Century of Sorosis, 1868–1968* (Uniondale, N.Y.: Salisbury Printers, 1968), p. 27 and Mrs. J. C. Croly, *History of the Woman's Club Movement in America* (New York: Henry G. Allen, 1898), pp. 85–100. Dr. Lelia G. Bedell of Chicago, President of the Chicago Woman's Club, claimed to be the originator of the General Federation of Women's Clubs because she wrote to the *Woman's Journal* in 29 January 1889, urging that women's organizations be coordinated farther than the Association for the Advancement of Women had done. "Herein would be strength and conditions for effective work. But it needs thorough organization, as thorough as that great and noble army of specific workers represented by the WCTU." Cited in Frank and Jerome, comp., *Annals of the Chicago Woman's Club for the First Forty Years of its Organization, 1876–1915*, (Chicago: Chicago Women's Club, 1916), p. 60. Bedell felt Croly had stolen her idea. In fact, it was obvious to many women that the WCTU's success should inspire literary clubs to emulate their structure for greater influence. As Willard herself had said at the ICW, good ideas spring up in many places at once.

11.   Sorosis invited ninety-four clubs. See Mary I. Wood, *The History of the General Federation of Women's Clubs* (New York: Norwood Press, 1912), pp. 315–317. Sorosis intended to invite every woman's literary club, but was able to find out only about these. (*Report of Twenty-First Anniversary of Sorosis* (New York: Styles and Cash, 1890, p. 7.) Among the clubs represented were the NEWC, WEIU of Boston, RIWC, Literary Club of the Church of the Messiah, Springfield Woman's Club, the Old and New of Malden, Massachusetts, and the Woborn Woman's Club, of which Sarah E. Doyle was now president.

12.   Croly, *History of the Woman's Club Movement*, p. 98. *Woman's Cycle*, 7 August 1890, pp. 21–22 cites *New York Sun* of 12 July 1890, p. 22.

13.   Henrotin was an active member of Chicago's two most exclusive clubs, the Fornightly for literary work, and the Chicago Woman's Club for reform. She also founded the Friday Club. (See Muriel Beadle and the Centennial History Committee of Chicago, *The Fornightly* [Chicago: Henry Regnery Company, 1973]), which reports that Jane Addams cooperated with the monied clubwomen of Chicago. No Armours or Swifts belonged to the Fortnightly, but Mrs. George Pullman, Mrs. Samuel Insull, Mrs. Cyrus McCormick, Mrs. Potter Palmer, and Cornelia Gray Hunt, niece of Dr. John Evans, founder of Northwestern University and developer of Evanston, all belonged. Many wives of cabinet officers and diplomats belonged. So did Maria Mitchell's sister-in-law, Emily Mitchell. On the Chicago Woman's Club activities, see William Hard, "The Women of Tomorrow," *Everybody's Magazine*, 24 (January 1911): 98–108.

14.   There were not many clubs in Europe, but in Ceylon, India, and the Panama Canal Zone, where American women settled while their husbands engaged in political or commercial work,

clubs were formed like those at home. A Sorosis member, Dr. Emma Brainerd-Ryder, started the clubs in India and Australia, carrying Croly's message, "Tell them the world was made for women also." See Croly, *History of the Woman's Club Movement*, pp. 193–208.

15. First Biennial in Chicago, 11–13 May 1892; Second in Philadelphia, 9–11 May 1894; Third in Louisville, Kentucky, 27–29 May 1896; Fourth in Denver, 21–27 June 1898; Fifth in Milwaukee, 1900; Sixth in Los Angeles, 1–8 May 1902; Seventh in St. Louis, Missouri, 17–25 May 1904; Eighth in St. Paul, 30 May–7 June 1906; Ninth in Boston, 22–30 June 1908; Tenth in Cincinnati, May 1910; Eleventh in San Francisco, 25 June–5 July 1912; and Twelfth in Chicago, 9–19 June 1914.

16. Georgia Pulsifer Porter, *Maine Federation of Women's Clubs: Historical Sketches, 1892–1924* (Lewiston, Maine: Lewiston Journal Printshop, 1925), pp. 43 and 52.

17. Ninth Biennial Scrapbook, 1908 Massachusetts State Federation of Women's Clubs Archives, Boston.

18. Wood dates all of them, p. 353. The states of Maine, Utah, Iowa, Massachusetts, Kentucky, Illinois, Ohio, New Jersey, and Nebraska all formed federations between the years 1892 and 1894. In 1895 Minnesota, Washington, D.C., Michigan, Colorado, Pennsylvania, Rhode Island, Georgia, Kansas, New Hampshire, and Missouri followed.

19. The annual reports of every state federation contain a copy of the state federation constitutions.

20. Croly, *History of the Woman's Club Movement in America*, p. 184. Regional federations were formed too: the New England Conference in 1902; Western New York Federation of Women's Clubs, 1896; the Buffalo City Federation of Women's Clubs, 1905; the Allegheny County Federation of Women's Clubs, 1895; and even the Women's Educational and Industrial Union talked of federating its own network in 1898, but nothing came of it. (*Buffalo Express*, 29 October 1897, p. 1.) For a history of the New England Conference of State Federations of Women's Clubs, see Mrs. Charles E. Shepard's work by that title, April 1971.

21. The New York State peak was reached in 1930 with five hundred seventy-seven clubs.

22. The highest figure actually recorded during this period, probably accurate because of financial accounts of dues, was about one million six hundred thousand by 1914. (*Chicago Daily Tribune*, 10 June 1914, p. 1.) *Chicago Record Herald* said one million seven hundred thousand (12 June 1914, p. 1). There were eight hundred thousand members in 1908 and one million by 1912. (Wood, pp. 4 and 294).

23. A special, half-fare railroad train went across the country, picking up clubwomen and making it easy and fun for them to attend the Biennials.

24. Among the associations to which she belonged were the Consumers' League, the Portsmouth District Nursing Association, church work, the school board, the New Hampshire Woman's Suffrage Association. H. H. Metcalf, "Mary I. Wood," *Granite Monthly*, 42 (March 1910).

25. See *Directory of Club Speakers and Entertainers* (Lowell, Mass.: Courier–Citizen Company, 1900), for Rhode Island, Massachusetts, and Vermont State Federation speakers.

26. Later, the club magazine went under the names *Home-Maker*, *New Cycle*, *Lotos*, *Club Woman* (1897–1904), *Federation Bulletin* (1903–1920), *Federation Topics* (1921–present). In addition, some state federations dispensed news through a column in a general magazine. In New Hampshire, see the *Granite Monthly*. In Vermont see the *Vermonter*. Still other states formed their own club periodicals. South Carolina had *Keystone*, Georgia had *Southern Woman*, California had *Club Woman* in 1902, *Club Life*, and *Federation Courier*. Oregon and Washington shared *Club Journal*; Massachusetts had *Club Woman* in 1897, *Federation Bulletin* in 1903, and it shared *The Northern* with Vermont and New Hampshire in 1905 (until 1907 when it merged with *Federation Bulletin* to become the General Federation of Women's Clubs organ), the *State Federation Bulletin* from 1915–1916. Syracuse clubs had *Remarques*. The Buffalo WEIU put out *The Lantern*.

27. Croly, *History of the Woman's Club Movement in America*, p. 112.

28. Alice Ames Winter, *The Business of Being a Club Woman* (New York: Century, 1925), pp. 6–7.

29. Helen M. Winslow, *The President of Quex: A Woman's Club Story* (Boston: Lothrop, Lee and Shepard, 1906), pp. 185–186.

30. Wood, *History of the General Federation*, p. 253.

31. For instance, in 1898, at the Massachusetts State Federation of Women's Clubs convention, there was a song from the third act of Wagner's *Lohengrin* and the "Pilgrim's Chorus" from *Tannhäuser*. In 1906 there was a selection of works by woman composers. In 1915 the wife of American composer Edward MacDowell gave a recital/lecture on "MacDowell—His Ideals."

32. A. S. Hall, "Practical Art Among Club Women," *Chautauqua*, 31 (September 1900): 621–624. Miss Purrington, "Emphasis of Literary Work," *The Northern* 1 (April 1905): 55–57.

33. *Yearbook*, Vermont State Federation of Women's Clubs, 1911–1912, p. 33. Vermont State Historical Society, Montpelier, Vermont.

34. Rhode Island Federation Women's Club Papers, RIHS. Maine State Federation Women's Club Papers, Orono, Maine, RISFWC, "A Report of the Traveling Library Work of the Federation from its Beginning," 1909–1910. RISFWC, "A Summary of the Traveling Library Work of the Federation from its Beginning," 1911.

35. Porter, *Maine Federation of Women's Clubs*, pp. 32, 35, 39.

36. Mrs. Finley Shepard and Mrs. Samuel Sherman, comp., *History of the Vermont Federation of Women's Clubs*, April 1971.

37. In 1903 the NYSFWC members contributed forty-one dollars and four hundred fifty books toward the Almond Library. In 1905 the Stony Brook Library was supported by the federation. See NYSFWC Papers, Elmira, New York.

38. RISFWC, "Report of the Traveling Library Work," and "Summary of the Traveling Library Work."

39. Sophonsiba P. Breckinridge, *Women in the Twentieth Century* (New York: McGraw-Hill, 1933), p. 93.

40. Wood, *History of the General Federation*, p. 235.

41. Croly, *History of the Woman's Club Movement in America* p. 176 and Wood, *History of the General Federation*, p. 91. See also General Federation of Women's Clubs, Third Biennial Report, 1896.

42. Wood, *History of the General Federation*, p. 250.

43. Croly, *History of the Woman's Club Movement in America*, pp. 185–188.

44. For example, in Maine in 1908, free tuition was given to one young lady at the Commonwealth School of Art at Boothbay Harbor. In Massachusetts, the Home Club of East Boston sent a woman to MIT. (Croly, *History of the Woman's Club Movement*, p. 627.) In Vermont there were four scholarships for future teachers. In Rhode Island, clubwomen were tremendously supportive of the establishment of Pembroke College for women at Brown University. They provided women with scholarships to attend it and in 1906 raised money for the Woman's College Gymnasium. In Buffalo the WEIU left scholarships for women to attend the University of Buffalo.

45. Wood, *History of the General Federation*, pp. 353–372.

46. Ibid, p. 383.

47. See programs of Friday Culture Club, English-American Reading Club, Women's Investigating Club, Buffalo and Erie County Public Library, Buffalo, New York.

48. "Literature Committee," 1909–1910 Yearbook RISFWC, RISFWC Papers, Providence.

49. Saturday Club, Providence, Rhode Island. Papers, Rhode Island Historical Society, Providence, Rhode Island.

50.  Mrs. Edward Rogerson, "The Teaching of Literature in Public Schools," NYSFWC Scrapbook, NYSFWC Papers, Elmira, New York.

51.  Clippings, NYSFWC Papers. Also, Executive Board Minutes of NYSFWC for 8 December 1898, and 8 November 1899, NYSFWC Papers.

52.  The Progressive men gave credit to contemporary clubwomen for Progressive reforms. See "Men's Views of Women's Clubs," *American Academy of Political and Social Science Annals*, 28 (September 1908): 283–292. This symposium by "Men who are Recognized Leaders in American Institutions," such as representatives from the Institute of Social Service, the United States Civil Service Commissioner, Officers of National Child Labor Commission, Judge of Juvenile Court in Denver, President of the University of Michigan, Chief of the Bureau of Chemistry at the United States Department of Agriculture, expressed praise for club work.

53.  NYSFWC Scrapbook, 1910, p. 129. NYSFWC Papers, Elmira College Library, Elmira, New York.

54.  Croly, *History of the Woman's Club Movement in America*, p. 152.

55.  Wood, *History of the General Federation*, p. 281.

56.  Mrs. Dimies T. S. Dennison, "Federation: Is It Womanly and Worth While?" *Pearson's Magazine*, n.d., pp. 201–208, on preserving Colorado prehistoric cliff dwellings.

57.  The stores refused, but suggested that they might close as early as 6 P.M. on Saturdays in summer. Rhode Island Woman's Club Report, 1909–1910.

58.  Wood, *History of the General Federation*, p. 121.

59.  Mary Ritter Beard, *Women's Work in Municipalities* (New York: D. Appleton, 1915), p. 48.

60.  Marjorie Rosen, *Popcorn Venus* (New York: Avon Books, 1974), p. 59.

61.  Rhode Island's Sarah E. Doyle Club endorsed President Taft's request for fifty thousand dollars to convict and punish those engaged in white slave traffic in 1910. This information on Progressive Reforms was obtained from the records of the GFWC, state federations, magazines of clubs and federations; Wood, *History of the General Federation*; Croly, *History of the Women's Club Movement*; club records; Henrotin, "Attitudes of Women's Clubs and Associations Toward Social Economics," July 1899 for *Bulletin of Department of Labor*. See also *Harper's Bazaar* 1909 series, "The Best Thing Our Club Ever Did," and *Annals of the American Academy of Political and Social Science*, 26 (1906). Caroline French Benton series on women's club programs in *Woman's Home Companion*, 1911–1914, which became *Woman's Club Work and Programs or First Aid to Club Women* (1913), and *Complete Club Book for Women* (1915). Alice Hazen Cass, *Practical Programs for Women's Clubs* (1915), and Kate Louise Roberts, *The Club Woman's Handbook of Programs and Club Management* (1914).

62.  H. L. Johnson, "The Work of the Home Economics Department, General Federation of Women's Clubs," *Journal of Home Economics*, 6 (April 1914): 153–155. By the same author, "Home Economics Work in the General Federation of Women's Clubs," *Journal of Home Economics*, 5 (December 1913): 437–444.

63.  See Ellen Henrotin's address at the 1897 National Education Association Convention on "The Cooperation of Women's Clubs in the Public Schools," *Addresses and Proceedings* (Washington, D.C.: National Education Association of the United States, 1897): 73–83.

64.  Edward T. James et al., *Notable American Women* 2 (Cambridge, Mass.: University of Harvard Press, 1971), pp. 181–183.

65.  Ibid., 1: 451–452.

66.  "Woman's Mission and Women's Clubs," *Ladies' Home Journal*, 22 (May 1905): 3–4.

67.  "My Quarrel with Women's Clubs," *Ladies' Home Journal*, 27 (January 1910): 5–6.

68.  Clipping, NYSFWC Scrapbook, 41, NYSFWC Papers.

69.  Clara Savage, "Man—and Women's Clubs," *Good Housekeeping*, 62 (May 1916): 611.

70.  Winslow, *President of Quex*, pp. 204, 187, 242.

71. Porter, *Maine Federation of Women's Clubs*, p. 72.

72. E. Anne S. May, "Woman Club Movement," *Vermonter*, 3 (August 1897): 169.

73. Gertrude S. Davis, "Vermont Federation of Women's Clubs," *Vermonter*, 7 (December 1901): 413.

74. Mary E. Woolley, Ninth Biennial Scrapbook, Massachusetts State Federation of Women's Clubs Papers, MSFWC, Boston.

75. NHFWC, *Yearbook, 1907–1908*, 29, NHFWC Papers.

76. Helen M. Winslow, *Woman of Tomorrow* (New York: James Pott, 1905), p. 125. Clipping, *Binghamton Republican*, 1905, NYSFWC Scrapbook, NYSFWC Papers.

77. *Milwaukee Daily News*, 4 June 1900, p. 4.

78. "Conservation of Natural Resources," *Federation Bulletin*, 5 (May 1908): 248–249.

79. A.T.G. to Mrs. Croly, *Woman's Cycle*, 7 August 1890, p. 19.

80. MSFWC, Scrapbook, MSFWC Papers. Scrapbook, 1903, p. 9. November 1903 clipping, Miss Grace E. Strachan on "Physical Education, NYSFWC Scrapbook, NYSFWC Papers.

81. NHSFWC, "*Report, 1908–1909*," NHSFWC Papers.

82. Porter, *Maine Federation of Women's Clubs*, p. 55.

83. *Cincinnati Enquirer*, 12 May 1910.

84. *The Northern*, editorial, 1 (June 1905): 98.

85. Zakrzewska to Caroline Severance, 26 January 1899, Severance Papers.

86. Ruffin had achieved in many of the ways clubwomen respected. She was married to a man who had studied law at Harvard, was a member of the Boston City Council and the House of the Massachusetts State Legislature, and in 1883 had become the first black man appointed to a judgeship in the North. Ruffin herself had five children, had worked in the Sanitary Commission, was a Friendly Visitor for charity, was a member of the New England Woman's Club, and worked for woman suffrage and education. (*Notable American Women*, 3, pp. 206–208, Julia Ward Howe, *Representative Women,* pp. 335–339.) Ruffin's Boston Club, The New Era Club, resembled many white clubs in that it gave scholarships, held classes in civics, domestic science, literature and public improvements. It had a newspaper, *Woman's Era*, which Ruffin edited.

87. "The color question, about which so much has been said and written, was not allowed to come on the floor for discussion, owing partially to Mrs. Lowe's tactful guidances and statesmanship, and partly to the efforts of the Massachusetts delegation, who desired harmony and peace with all their hearts." (*The Club Woman*, July 1900, p. 132). The Executive Committee changed its meeting time without notifying the pro-Ruffin members. They decided to table the problem, and since Ruffin was denied a regular accreditation as delegate, she would not be recognized by the chair if she tried to bring it up from the convention floor (*Milwaukee Daily News*, 8 June 1900, p. 1).

88. Ex-president Ellen Henrotin of Chicago favored the Massachusetts plan. See her 1902 position in the papers of the General Federation, Rare Book Room, Boston Public Library.

89. The *Milwaukee Daily News* expected a heated debate. "Mrs. Ruffin will insist upon her rights, however, and there will probably be some exciting scenes before the week is over." (5 June 1900, p. 4.) Ruffin said she had been treated shabbily by the credentials committee, but insisted, "The Southern women don't hate the colored women, they hate the Northern ones. They are hitting the North through us, and they are backed by Southern men, politicians." (*Milwaukee Daily News*, 6 June 1900, p. 1). Black women expressed anger over the incident. Mrs. Fannie Barrier Williams wrote to the *Chicago Record-Herald*, 21 March 1901, to say the General Federation exclusion of black women was typical of racism everywhere in the United States. The New Era Club in Boston expressed the following sentiments: "We felt though that it is our right to say that we shall feel very sorry for the cause of women to see its standard lowered, its accepted ideals repudiated, its power diminished by any declaration that it is the cause of white women for

which it stands, not the cause of women." ("Official Statement from the Women's Era Club to the Members of Clubs in the General Federation of Women's Clubs." 12 November 1900, by Florida Ruffin Ridley, et al.).

90.   The Brighthelmstone Club in Massachusetts was one such club. See Isabelle Williams, *A History of the Brighthelmstone Club of Brighton and Allston* (Cambridge: Harvard University Press, 1923), pp. 53–54.

91.   *Morning Citizen* (Lowell, Massachusetts), 4 March 1902.

92.   Wood, *History of the General Federation*, p. 345. Mary Urqhart Lee of San Francisco wrote to the *Southern Woman* (19 April 1902), p. 4, with "A New Way Out of the Difficulty." She reminded the General Federation that it was growing too fast and ought to ask black clubs to go to their own federation to prevent oversize.

93.   "*Report* of Anna Maxwell Jones to NYSFWC," 1902, Dow Folder, NYSFWC Papers. See also Fannie Barrier Williams, "Club Movement Among Negro Women," in *Progress of a Race* by John W. Gibson and William H. Crogman, (Miami, Florida: Mnemosyne Publishers, 1969), reprint 1902 ed., pp. 197–281. The NEWC was embroiled in debate over whether to withdraw from the General Federation over the Ruffin issue. Cheney, who had prided herself that her New England Hospital for Women and Children "is the only one that admits colored pupils to its training school," (Annie Meyers, Cheney on "Care of the Sick," p. 358), was among those who favored integration. The Board of Directors discussed the problem 4 February 1901 (NEWC Minutes, 5: 6), and supported the Massachusetts plan. The club met on 19 January 1903, when the Massachusetts plan was rejected by the General Federation and Lucia Peabody recommended withdrawal (19 January 1903, 5:88–89). Her view was not the dominant one (Mrs. Perry's comments, p. 126). Two months later, a special meeting was held over the question of resigning, but even Cheney had decided to accept the compromise, trusting the national organization to permit northern state federations to admit black clubs. (Minutes, 9 March 1903, pp. 140–141.)

94.   RISFWC, "Annual Report of Recording Secretary," 23 June 1906, RISFWC Papers.

95.   NYSFWC, Scrapbook, p. 48; *Evening Herald* (Binghamton, New York), 3 November 1905.

96.   Massachusetts SFWC, Ninth Biennial Scrapbook, Boston.

97.   "Report of Delegate of Mother's Club of New York to Sixth Annual Meeting of the NYSFWC, 1900," by Caroline S. Deming, 10 December 1900. NYSFWC Papers, Elmira, New York.

98.   NYSFWC, 1901–1902 Scrapbook, NYSFWC Papers.

99.   Kate Holliday Claghorn, "Social Conscience and the Immigrant Population," NYSFWC Scrapbook, 1902. NYSFWC Papers.

100.   Brooklyn, November 1902.

101.   RIWC discussed suffrage on 23 March 1887.

102.   Belle de Rivera was the founder and president of the New York State Federation of Women's Clubs and president of the New York City Equal Suffrage League. Mary Garrett Hay, friend of Carrie Chapman Catt, was president of the NYSFWC from 1910 until 1912. From 1914 until 1918 she was a director of the General Federation of Women's Clubs. She was also a president of the New York State Equal Suffrage League. Marjorie Shuler, president of the Western New York Federation of Women's Clubs from 1905 to 1909, president of NYSFWC from 1912 until 1914, coauthored with Catt *Woman's Suffrage and Politics* (1923), and was secretary and treasurer of the National American Woman's Suffrage Association.

103.   Suffragists visited conventions frequently. Carrie Chapman Catt often appeared. The president of the Maine Suffrage Association attended the Maine FWC Convention in 1903. Suffragists in Rhode Island talked to the Providence Federation of Women Teachers in 1911. (See RIFWC Scrapbook, 28 May 1911–5 October 1911.) Mrs. Ethel Snowden, author of *The Feminist Movement*, spoke to the NYSFWC in Rochester in 1902. Assuring the clubwomen she

was not a militant, like those making headlines, she said, "I am a suffragist, but not a suffragette. I am terribly respectable." Yet she praised suffragettes and said they would get votes "if they had to tear down the House of Lords." NYSFWC Scrapbook, p. 122, NYSFWC Papers. Snowden kept clubwomen abreast of English suffragism.

104. The committee document was signed by General Federation spokespeople Jane Addams, Maud Nathan, Florence Kelley, Edith M. Howes, and Jean Hamilton.

105. Ida Husted Harper, *The History of Woman Suffrage*, vol. 5 (New York: J. J. Little and Ives, 1922), p. 210.

106. Restricted suffrage, the exclusion of illiterates, was represented by Mr. Rudolph Blankenberg of Pennsylvania. (Wood, p. 266.) See also MSFWC Ninth Biennial Scrapbook.

107. Maria L. Walton, "Lesson of the Last Biennial," *Overland Monthly*, 61 (January 1913): 25–26.

108. RISFWC Scrapbook.

109. Ibid.

110. *Chicago Record-Herald*, 7 June 1914, p. 2.

111. NYSFWC, NYSFWC Papers.

112. Palmer to NYSFWC, 20 November 1912, NYSFWC Papers.

113. *Chicago Record-Herald*, 9 June 1914, p. 2. Richard Jensen, "Family, Career, and Reform: Women Leaders in the Progressive Era," in *The American Family in Social-Historical Perspective*, Michael Gordon, ed. (New York: St. Martin's Press, 1973), found that clubwomen were prone to endorse suffrage.

114. *Glimpses of Fifty Years* (Boston: George M. Smith, 1889), p. 445.

115. Della A. Stewart, "A Record of Golden Years: History of the NYSFWC, 1894–1914," unpublished history, NYSFWC Papers.

116. *Club Woman's Weekly*, 1907.

117. The *Chicago Daily Tribune* found a club president who still insisted, "We are the power behind the throne now, and we find that we get practically everything we want without the power of the franchise." (10 June 1914, p. 1). Other clubwomen, some of them suffragists, simply felt that the GFWC should not take any stand at all. One such woman was Mrs. Andrew P. Coon, recording secretary of the local Biennial board in Chicago (*Chicago Daily Tribune*, 19 June 1914, p. 1). Mrs. Richard S. Lacey, president of the Kentucky Federation, likewise felt the GFWC should not vote on the suffrage question (*Chicago Daily Tribune*, 13 June 1914, p. A13).

118. Anna V. Pennybacker Papers, University of Texas Archives, Austin, Texas.

119. *Chicago Record-Herald*, 14 June 1914, p. 1. For another account of the 1914 Biennial, see Graham Taylor, "The Women's Biennial: Social Sympathy and Public Politics," *Survey*, 32 (July 4, 1914): 358–359.

120. The *Chicago Record-Herald* said as much in an editorial 5 June 1914, p. 6.

121. *Chicago Record-Herald*, 12 June 1914, editorial, p. 5.

122. *Chicago Record-Herald*, 7 June 1914, p. 2.

123. Ibid.

# Bibliography

**Manuscript Collections**

Boston Public Library, Boston, Massachusetts
    General Federation of Women's Clubs Papers
Buffalo and Erie County Historical Society, Buffalo, New York
    Western New York Federation of Women's Clubs Papers
    Women's Educational and Industrial Union of Buffalo Papers
Buffalo Seminary, Buffalo, New York
    Buffalo Seminary Papers
    Graduates Association Papers
Elmira College Library, Elmira, New York
    New York State Federation of Women's Clubs Papers
Elmira Sorosis Collection (private), Elmira, New York
    Miscellaneous materials
Michael Emmett Collection (private), Riverside, California
    Severance Family Papers
Fortnightly Club Collection (private), Northampton, Massachusetts
    Miscellaneous materials
Friday Morning Club, Los Angeles, California
    Miscellaneous materials
General Federation of Women's Clubs (private), Chattanooga, Tennessee
    Miscellaneous materials
Huntington Library, San Marino, California
    Anthony Family Papers
    Caroline M. Severance Papers
Houghton Library, Harvard University, Cambridge, Massachusetts
    Thomas Wentworth Higginson Papers
    Julia Ward Howe Papers
Massachusetts Historical Society, Boston, Massachusetts
    Caroline H. Dall Collection

Massachusetts State Federation of Women's Clubs, Boston, Massachusetts
     Miscellaneous materials
New Hampshire State Historical Society, Concord, New Hampshire
     New Hampshire Federation of Women's Clubs Papers
Ohio Historical Society, Columbus, Ohio
     Woman's Exchange, Columbus, Ohio Papers
     Columbus Female Benevolent Society Papers
     Marietta Reading Club Papers
Ohio State University Archives, Columbus, Ohio
     Starling—Ohio Women's Club Papers
Rhode Island Historical Society, Providence, Rhode Island
     Marie Louise Burge Papers
     Marion M. Burgess Papers
     Lucy D. Carpenter Papers
     Alice Greene Comstock Papers
     Fortnightly Club Papers
     Four-Leaf Clover Club Papers
     Ladies Volunteer Relief Association Papers
     Helen A. Pearce Papers
     Providence Female Charitable Society Papers
     Providence Fortnightly Papers
     Rhode Island State Federation of Women's Clubs Papers
     Rhode Island Woman's Club Papers
     Sarah E. Doyle Club Papers
     Saturday Club Papers
     Wednesday Club Papers
The Arthur and Elizabeth Schlesinger Library of the History of Women,
Cambridge, Massachusetts
     Sarah Knowles Bolton Papers
     Jane Cunningham Croly Letters
     Ellen M. Henrotin Papers
     Julia Ward Howe Papers
     Ladies Physiological Institute Papers
     New England Woman's Club Papers
     Harriet Hanson Robinson Papers
     Harriette Lucy Robinson Shattuck Papers
     Women's Educational and Industrial Union of Boston Papers
Smith College Library, Northampton, Massachusetts
     Helen Tufts Bailie Papers
     Isabel Howland Papers
     New England Hospital Papers
     Ellen S. Richards Papers
     Caroline Maria Severance Papers
     Sorosis Papers

Springfield Public Library, Springfield, Massachusetts
  Springfield Women's Club Papers
State University of Maine at Orono Library, Orono, Maine
  Maine Federation of Women's Clubs Papers
  Women's Club of Orono Papers
University of Texas, Texas Archives, Austin, Texas
  Anna Pennybacker Papers
Vermont Historical Society, Montpelier, Vermont
  Vermont Federation of Women's Clubs Papers
Vermont State Library, Montpelier, Vermont
  Vermont Federation of Women's Clubs Papers
Western Reserve Historical Society, Cleveland, Ohio
  Book and Thimble Club of Cleveland Papers
  Conversational Club of Cleveland, Ohio Papers
  East Cleveland Literary and Scientific Circle Papers
  Morning Musical Club of Cleveland Papers
  Rubenstein Club, Record Book
Women's Educational and Industrial Union, Boston, Massachusetts
  Miscellaneous materials
Women's Literary Union, Portland, Maine
  Miscellaneous materials


## Club Printed Sources

Ardirhebiah, Providence, Rhode Island
  *Programs*. 1908–1909, 1912–1913
  *Yearbooks*. 1900–1920
Association for the Advancement of Women, Smith College, Northampton, Massachusetts
  *Historical Account 1873–1893*. Dedham, Mass.: Transcript Steam Job Print, 1893
  *Papers and Letters of the First Woman's Congress of the Association for the Advancement of Women*. New York: Mrs. William Ballard, Book and Job Printer, 1874.
  *Papers Read at the Third Congress of Women*, 1875.
  *Papers Read at the Fourth Congress of Women*. Held at St. George's Hall, October 4, 5, 6, 1876. Names and addresses of officers and members of the Association for the Advancement of Women. History of the Association. Washington, D.C.: Todd Brothers, 1877.
  *Papers Read at the Tenth Congress of Women.* Portland, Maine: no publisher, 1883.
  *Papers Read at the Twelfth Congress of Women*. Buffalo: Peter, Paul and Brother, Publishers and Printers, 1885.

*Papers Read at the Fourteenth Congress of Women*. Atlantic Highlands, N.J.: Leonard and Lingle, Printers, 1887.

*Papers Read at the Fifteenth Congress of Women*. Fall River, Mass.: J. H. Franklin and Co., Publishers and Printers, 1888.

*Papers Read at the Sixteenth Congress of Women*. Fall River, Mass.: J. H. Franklin and Co., Publishers and Printers, 1889.

*Report of the Fourteenth Congress of Women*. Buffalo: Peter, Paul and Brother, Publishers and Printers, 1887.

*Report of the Nineteenth Congress of Women*. Syracuse, N.Y.: C. W. Bardeen, Publishers and Printers, 1892.

*Souvenir of the Fifteenth Annual Congress of the Association for the Advancement of Women*. No publisher, no date.

*Souvenir of the Nineteenth Annual Congress of the Association for the Advancement of Women*. No publisher, no date.

Buffalo Federation of Women's Clubs, Buffalo, New York
  Convention Programs, 1907, 1908, 1913.

Buffalo Seminary, Buffalo, New York
  Catalogs

Catholic Women's Club, Providence, Rhode Island
  Yearbooks, 1903–1906

Charity Organization Society of Buffalo, Buffalo, New York
  Annual Reports 1882–1920

Colonial Club, Northampton, Massachusetts
  Programs, 1896–1905

Elmira Sorosis (Walnut Street Club), Elmira, New York
  Programs

Embreaso, Providence, Rhode Island
  Programs

English-American Reading Class, Buffalo, New York
  Calendars, 1897–1933

Fortnightly Club, Providence, Rhode Island
  Yearbooks, 1897–1907

Four-Leaf Clover Club, Providence, Rhode Island
  Yearbooks, 1903–1919

Friday Culture Club, Buffalo, New York
  Yearbook, 1890

The Friends, Buffalo, New York
  Programs, 1906–1946

General Federation of Women's Clubs
  *Biennial Convention Program*. Boston: G. H. E. Ellis Co., 1908.
  Biennial Convention Reports. Third (1896); Fourth (1898); Ninth (1908); Tenth (1910); Eleventh (1912).
  Biennial Notebook, 1898.
  *Official Proceedings 1896*. Louisville: John P. Morton and Company, 1896.

*Proceedings*. Louisville: Flexner Brothers, 1896.

*Tenth Biennial Convention: 1910 Official Report*. Newark, N.J.: by the Federation, 1910.

Graduates Association of Buffalo Seminary, Buffalo, New York

Programs

Scrapbooks

Phoebe Hearst Collection, Bancroft Library, University of California at Berkeley, Berkeley, California

Club Reports

Highland Park Literary Club, Buffalo, New York

*History of the Club Movement Among Colored Women of the United States of America as Contained in Minutes of Conventions*. Boston (29 July 1895), Washington, D.C. (20–22 July): National Federation of Afro-American Women, 1902.

International Council of Women

Report. Assembled by National Woman Suffrage Association. Washington, D.C.: Rufus H. Darby, 1888.

Irrepressible Society, Providence, Rhode Island

Miscellaneous publications

Ladies Auxiliary of North Providence Improvement Association, North Providence, Rhode Island

Yearbooks, 1904–1909

Literary Club of the Church of the Messiah, Buffalo, New York

Julia Greene Ferguson. *Club History*. Buffalo: Press of Peter, Paul and Brother, 1890.

*History and Officers: 1880–1890*. Buffalo: Peter, Paul and Brother, 1890.

*Literary Club of the Church of the Messiah, 1880–1890*.

Programs

Literary Review Club, Buffalo, New York

Yearbooks, 1902–1919

Local Council of Women of Rhode Island

Olivia D. Hammill. *Thirty-five Years of Accomplishment: The Story of the Rhode Island Council of Women from 1889–1924*.

List 1897

Maine Federation of Women's Clubs

Annual Reports

Georgia Pulsifer Porter. *Maine Federation of Women's Clubs: Historical Sketches, 1892–1924*. Lewiston, Maine: Lewiston Journal Printshop, 1925.

Massachusetts State Federation of Women's Clubs

Manual, 1898–1904

Manual, 1914–1915. Medford: Tufts College Press, 1914.

Programs

Monday Afternoon Club. Northampton, Massachusetts

Programs, 1889—
Monday Class, Buffalo, New York
  Yearbooks, 1902–1904
Montpelier Women's Club, Montpelier, Vermont
  Programs
  Yearbooks, 1913–1917
The Mother's Club, Cambridge, Massachusetts
  Pamphlet, 13 April 1928
Mount Holyoke College Library, South Hadley, Massachusetts
  Alumnae Newsletters
New England Woman's Club, Boston, Massachusetts
  Report of the Committee on Dress.
  *Report of the Committee on Needlewomen.* Boston: Press of John
    Wilson and Son, 1869.
  Kate Sanborn. "Sketch of Mrs. May Alden Ward."
  *Helen Augusta Whittier (1846–1925) A Memorial.*
New Hampshire Federation of Women's Clubs
  Annual Reports
  History, 1896
New York State Federation of Women's Clubs
  Fanny H. Carpenter and Mary Wood. "Sketch of the History of the
    New York State Federation of Women's Clubs." November 1914.
  Convention Programs, 1901–1922
  *Golden Jubilee: 1894–1944*
  Alice M. Porter. "History of the New York State Federation of Women's
    Clubs, 1894–1957."
  Yearbooks
Nichols, Mary Ellis. *A History of the Cambridge Club.* January 1911.
Norton, Miss Helen Rich. "The Story of the Women's Rest Tour Asso-
    ciation." Published by the Women's Rest Tour Association, circa 1967.
Providence Art Club, Providence, Rhode Island
  Manuals, 1886–1892. Providence: Standard Printing Company, 1906.
Providence Fortnightly, Providence, Rhode Island
  Miscellaneous materials
Providence Medical Association, Providence, Rhode Island
  Constitution and By-laws with a List of Members. Providence:
    Kellogg Printing Company, 1882 and Providence Printing Com-
    pany, 1870.
Providence Mother's Clubs, Providence, Rhode Island
  Constitution
  Yearbooks
Providence Society for Organizing Charity
  Annual Reports
  Circulars
  *The Chronicle*

*Directory of Benevolent Societies and Institutions.* Providence: Continental Printing Company, 1896.

Programs

Providence Women's Christian Temperance Union, Providence, Rhode Island

   Minutes, 1891

   Thirtieth Annual Report, 1903–1904

Read, Mark and Learn Club of Providence, Rhode Island

   Calendars

   Constitution

*Report of the International Council of Women.* Washington, D.C.: Rufus H. Darley, 1888.

Rhode Island Art Association, Providence, Rhode Island. *Circular and Constitution and Officers for 1854.* Providence: Knowles, Anthony and Company, Printers, 1854.

Rhode Island Sanitary Relief, Providence, Rhode Island

   Miscellaneous publications, 1898

Rhode Island State Federation of Women's Clubs, Providence, Rhode Island

   Sarah E. Doyle. *History of the Rhode Island State Federation of Women's Clubs.* Providence, 1893.

   Miscellaneous publications

   Pamphlet on Factory Inspection Law. January, 1909.

   Report of the Traveling Library Work of the Federation from Its Beginning. 1909–1910.

   Summary of the Traveling Library Work of the Federation from Its Beginning. 1911.

   Yearbooks, 1877–1914

Rhode Island Woman Suffrage Association, Providence, Rhode Island

   Reports, 1904–1905

Rhode Island Vincent Club-Chautauqua Literary Society Circle, Providence, Rhode Island

   Reports

Sarah E. Doyle Club, Providence, Rhode Island

   Invitation

   Yearbooks, 1894–1922

Saturday Club, Providence, Rhode Island

   Yearbook, 1907–1908

The Scribblers, Buffalo, New York

   History, Constitution and By-laws, 1907

   Yearbook, 1906–1907

Sewall, May Wright, ed. *National Council of Women.* Indianapolis: Hollenbeck Press, 1898.

Shakespeare Club, Buffalo, New York

   Program, 1875

Shephard, Mrs. Charles E. *History of the New England Conference of*

*State Federations of Women's Clubs, 1909–1970.* Warren, Mass.: printed by the Conference, 1971.

Sorosis, New York, New York
*Fourth Anniversary Program at Delmonico's.* New York: Poole and Maclaughan, Printers, 1872.
Programs
*Report of the Twenty-first Anniversary of Sorosis.* New York: Styles and Cash, Printers, 1890.
Vida Croly Sidney. *Jennie June Croly.*

Spencer, Anna Garlin. *The Council Idea and May Wright Sewall.* New York: J. Heidingsfeld Company, 1930.

Thursday Club of Buffalo, Buffalo, New York
Programs, 1890–1927

Twentieth Century Club (Fortnightly), Buffalo, New York
Programs
Annual Reports, 1894–1939

Tyler, Henry M. *Beginnings of the Northampton Social and Literary Club.* Northampton, Mass.: The Club, 1925.

Vermont Federation of Women's Clubs
Annual Reports
Mrs. Finley Shepard and Mrs. Jeanette Sherman. *History of the Vermont Federation of Women's Clubs.* 5 April 1971.
Yearbooks, 1918–1971

Wednesday Morning Club, Elmira, New York
Programs

Western New York Federation of Women's Clubs, Buffalo, New York
*History and Proceedings.* Buffalo: Hubbard Press, 1898.
Programs

Women's Centennial Executive Committee, Providence, Rhode Island
Report

Women's Club of Orono, Orono, Maine
Programs
Records, 1887–1972

Women's Educational and Industrial Union, Boston, Massachusetts
*The Hours of Labor in Domestic Service.* Boston: Wright and Potter, 1898. Reprint from Massachusetts Labor Bulletin No. 8, October, 1898.
Massachusetts Bureau of Statistics of Labor and Women's Educational and Industrial Union of Boston. "Household Expenses." Boston: Wright and Potter, 1900.
Massachusetts Bureau of Statistics of Labor and Women's Educational and Industrial Union of Boston. "Social Conditions in Domestic Service." Boston: Wright and Potter, 1900.
*Report for Year Ending May 1898.* Cambridge: Cooperative Printing Society, 1898.

*A Report of Progress Made in the Year 1905*, being the twenty-fifth anniversary of the incorporation of the Women's Educational Industrial Union. Boston: 1905.

Women's Educational and Industrial Union, Buffalo, New York
   Circular
   Handbooks, 1885–1913
   Report for the Year Ending May 1, 1885. Also 1906 and 1911–1912.
   Woman's Union Kermess. 1914.

Women's Educational and Industrial Union of Rhode Island, Providence, Rhode Island
   *Annual Reports*.
      First. Providence: J. A. & R. A. Reid, 1885.
      Second. Providence: J. A. & R. A. Reid, 1886.
      Third. Providence: J. A. & R. A. Reid, 1887.
      Fourth. Providence: J. A. & R. A. Reid, 1888.
      Fifth. Providence: The Providence Press, Snow and Farnham, 1889.
   *Constitution and By-laws*. Providence: Livermore and Knight, 1884.
   Journal

Women's Investigating Club, Buffalo, New York
   Program, 1896–1909


**Newspapers and Magazines**

*The Appeal, a National Afro-American Newspaper*. St. Paul and Minneapolis. June 1900.

*Boston Herald*. June 1900; May 1902; July 1912; June 1914.

*Boston Transcript*. October 1880.

*Buffalo Daily Courier*. October 1881.

*Buffalo Express*. October 1881.

*The Bulletin* San Francisco. June–July 1912.

*Chicago Daily Tribune*. October 1874; October 1883; October 1893; June 1914.

*Chicago Record-Herald and the Inter Ocean*. June 1914.

*Club Life*. San Francisco. 1902–1906.

*The Clubwoman*. Lowell, Massachusetts. March 1914.

*Club Woman's Weekly*. New York City. Devoted to the news of women's clubs, societies, and associations. Vol. I, January 12, 1907.

*Commercial Tribune*. Cincinnati. May 1910.

*Demorest's Monthly Magazine*. New York. 1872–1879.

*The Federation Bulletin*. Boston. 1905–1908.

*Godey's Lady's Book and Magazine*. Philadelphia. 1852–1861.

*Granite Monthly*. Manchester, New Hampshire. 1895–1901.

*Guard of Honor Monthly*. Buffalo, New York. 1872.

*Home-Maker Magazine.* New York City. Vol. 6, April 1891–September 1891; Vol. 10, no. 1, April 1893.

*Keystone.* A Monthly Journal devoted to Woman's Work. Vol. 1–14, June 1899–1913.

*Ladies' Companion.* New York City. Vol. 18–19, 1842–1843.

*Ladies' Repository.* Cincinnati. 1856–1859.

*The Lantern.* Buffalo, New York. 1909–1910.

*Los Angeles Times.* May 1902.

*Manchester Union.* New Hampshire. Special Women's Edition. 30 March 1914.

*Milwaukee Daily News.* June 1900.

*Missionary Helper.* Providence, Rhode Island. 1878–1889.

*New Hampshire Magazine.* Concord, New Hampshire. 1904–1905.

*New Orleans Times-Picayune.* June 1900; May 1902; June–July 1912; June 1914.

*New York Times.* October 1869; October 1873; June 1900; May 1902; June–July 1912; June 1914.

*New York Tribune.* October 1869; October 1873; June 1900; May 1902; June–July 1912; June 1914.

*New York World.* 1868–1873.

*The Northern.* Portland, Maine. 1905.

*Providence Journal.* October 1878.

*The Revolution.* New York City. 1868–1871.

*Springfield Republican.* November 1897.

*Vermonter.* St. Albans, Vermont. 1897–1910.

*The Woman's Cycle.* New York City. 1889–1890.

*Woman's Journal.* Boston. 1869–1904.

*Women's Educational and Industrial Union of Rhode Island Journal.* Providence, Rhode Island. 1885–1887.

### Books

Abrahall, Frances H., ed. *Club-Women of New York, 1919–1920.* New York: New York City Federation of Women's Clubs, 1919.

Addams. Jane. *Twenty Years at Hull House.* New York: New American Library, 1960.

Alcott, Louisa May. *Hospital Sketches and Camp and Fireside Stories.* Boston: Roberts Brothers, 1886.

———. *Work: A Story of Experience.* Boston: Roberts Brothers, 1897.

Altbach, Edith Hoshino. *Women in America.* Lexington, Mass.: D. C. Heath, 1974.

Ames, Mary Clemmer. *A Memorial of Alice and Phoebe Cary with Some of Their Later Poems.* New York: Hurd and Houghton, 1894.

Andrews, Wayne, ed. *The Best Short Stories of Edith Wharton.* New York: Scribner's, 1958.

Austin, Anne L. *The Woolsey Sisters of New York, 1860–1900*. Philadelphia: American Philosophical Society, 1971.

Austin, Mary. *Earth Horizon: Autobiography*. New York: The Literary Guild, 1932.

_____. *A Woman of Genius*. Garden City: Doubleday, Page, 1912.

Banner, Lois W. *Women in Modern America: A Brief History*. New York: Harcourt Brace Jovanovich, 1974.

Bayles, Richard Mather, ed. *History of Providence County, Rhode Island*. Vol. 1: *City of Providence*. New York: W. W. Preston, 1891.

Baylor, Ruth M. *Elizabeth Palmer Peabody*. Philadelphia: University of Pennsylvania Press, 1965.

Beadle, Muriel and the Centennial History Committee. *The Fortnightly of Chicago: The City and Its Women, 1873–1973*. Chicago: Henry Regnery, 1973.

Beard, Mary R. *Woman as Force in History*. New York: Macmillan, 1946.

_____. *Woman's Work in Municipalities*. New York: D. Appleton, 1915.

Beauvoir, Simone de. *The Second Sex*. New York: Alfred H. Knopf, 1953.

Beedy, Helen Coffin. *Mothers of Maine*. Portland, Maine: The Thurston Print, 1895.

Benton, Caroline French. *Complete Club Book for Women*. Boston: L. C. Page, 1915.

_____. *Woman's Club Work and Programs or First Aid to Club Women*. Boston: L. C. Page, Inc., 1913.

Blanc, Marie Therese. *The Condition of Woman in the United States: a Traveler's Notes*. Boston: Roberts Brothers, 1895.

Bolton, Sarah K. *Successful Women*. Plainview: Books for Libraries Press, 1974; reprint of 1888 ed. Boston: D. Lothrop.

_____. *Famous Leaders Among Women*. Freeport, New York: Books for Libraries Press, 1972; reprint of 1895 ed.

Boone, Gladys. *The Women's Trade Union League in Great Britain and the United States of America*. New York: Columbia University Press, 1942.

*The Boston Blue Book*. Boston: Sampson and Murdock, 1876.

*The Boston Blue Book*. Boston: Edward E. Clark, 1897.

Bowne, Mrs. Eliza Southgate. *A Girl's Life Eighty Years Ago*. Selections from the Letters of Mrs. Eliza Southgate Bowne. New York: Scribners, 1888.

Brackett, Anna C. *The Education of American Girls*. New York: G. P. Putnam, 1874.

Bradford, Gamaliel. *Portraits of American Women*. Boston: Houghton Mifflin, 1919.

Breault, Judith Colucci. *The World of Emily Howland*. Millbrae, Cal.: Les Femmes, 1976.

Breckinridge, Sophonsiba P. *Women in the Twentieth Century: A Study of Their Political, Social and Economic Activities*. New York: McGraw-Hill, 1933.

Brockett, L. P., MD. *Woman: Her Rights, Wrongs, Privileges and Respon-sibilities.* Freeport, New York: Books for Libraries Press, 1970; reprint of 1869 ed.

Brown, Herbert R. *The Sentimental Novel in America, 1789–1860.* New York: Pageant Books, 1959.

Brown, Rose L. *Cavewoman to Clubwoman: A Primer for Clubwomen.* Philadelphia: Dorrance, 1938.

*Buffalo City Directory.* Buffalo Courier Co., 1875–1914.

Burleigh, Celia. *Poems by William H. Burleigh with a Sketch of His Life.* New York: Hurd and Houghton, 1871.

Campbell, Helen. *Household Economics.* A Course of Lectures in the School of Economics of the University of Wisconsin. New York: G. P. Putnam, 1896.

Cass, Alice Hazen. *Practical Programs for Women's Clubs.* Chicago: A. C. McClurg, 1915.

Catt, Carrie Chapman and Nettie Rogers Shuler. *Woman Suffrage and Politics.* Seattle: University of Washington Press, 1970.

Chace, Elizabeth Buffum and Lucy Buffum Lowell. *Two Quaker Sisters.* New York: Liveright, 1937.

Chambers, Clarke A. *Seedtime of Reform: American Social Service and Social Action, 1918–1933.* Ann Arbor: University of Michigan Press, 1967.

Cheney, Ednah D. *Louisa May Alcott: Her Life, Letters and Journals.* Boston: Roberts Brothers, 1889.

———. *Memoirs of Lucretia Crocker and Abby W. May.* Boston: Massachusetts School Suffrage Association, 1893.

———. *Reminiscence of Ednah Dow Cheney.* Boston: Lee and Shepard, Publishers, 1902.

Churchill, Mrs. Elizabeth K. *Overcoming.* Boston: D. Lothrop, 1870.

Clapp, Roger T. *The Hope Club: A Centennial History, 1875–1975.* Providence: E. A. Johnson, 1975.

Clark, Edward H., MD. *Sex in Education; or, A Fair Chance for the Girls.* Boston: James R. Osgood, 1873.

Clarke, Robert. *Ellen Swallow: The Woman Who Founded Ecology.* Chicago: Follett, 1973.

Clifford, Deborah Pickman. *Mine Eyes Have Seen the Glory: A Biography of Julia Ward Howe.* Boston: Little, Brown, 1979.

*Club Men of New York,* 1898–1899. New York: Republic Printers, 1898.

Conant, Marth Pike, et al. *A Girl of the Eighties at College and at Home: from the Family Letters of Charlotte Howard Conant and from Other Records.* Boston: Houghton Mifflin, 1931.

Cott, Nancy. *The Bonds of Womanhood: "Woman's Sphere" in New England 1780–1835.* New Haven: Yale University Press, 1977.

———. ed. *Root of Bitterness.* New York: E. P. Dutton, 1972.

_____, ed. *Root of Bitterness*. New York: E. P. Dutton, 1972.

Crawford, Mary Caroline. *The College Girl of America*. Boston: L. C. Page, 1905.

_____. *Romantic Days in Old Boston*. Boston: Little, Brown, 1923.

Cremin, Lawrence A. *The Transformation of the School: Progressivism in American Education, 1876–1957*. New York: Alfred A. Knopf, 1968.

Croly, Mrs. Jane Cunningham. *The History of the Woman's Club Movement in America*. New York: Henry G. Allen, 1898.

_____. *Sorosis, Its Origin and History*. New York: Press of J. J. Little, 1886.

Croly, Jennie June, ed. *American Cookery Book*. New York: American News Co., 1866.

_____. *For Better or Worse*. Boston: Lee & Shepard, 1875.

_____. *Knitting and Crochet*. New York: A. L. Burt, 1885.

_____. *Letters and Monograms for Marking on Silk, Linen and Other Fabrics, for Individual and Household Use*. New York; A. L. Burt, 1886.

_____. *Needlework*. New York: A. L. Burt, 1885

_____. *Jennie Juneiana: Talks on Women's Topics*. Boston: Lee & Shepard, 1869.

_____. *Thrown on Her Own Resources or What Girls Can Do*. New York: Thomas Y. Crowell, 1891.

Cross, Barbara M., ed. *The Educated Woman in America*. New York: Teachers College Press, Columbia University, 1965.

Cross, Whitney R. *The Burned-Over District: The Social and Intellectual History of Enthusiastic Religion in Western New York, 1800–1850*. New York: Harper and Row, 1950.

Cunningham, Mary S. *The Woman's Club of El Paso*. El Paso: Texas Western Press, 1978.

Dailey, Charlotte Field, ed. *Rhode Island's Woman's Directory for the Columbian Year 1892*. Providence: Rhode Island Woman's World's Fair Advisory Board, 1893.

Dall, Caroline H., ed. *A Practical Illustration of "Woman's Right to Labor"; or, a lett from Marie E. Zakrzewska, MD*. Boston: Walker, Wise, 1860.

Darling, Flora Adams. *Founding and Organizing of the Daughters of the American Revolution and Daughters of the Revolution*. Philadelphia: Independence Publishing Co., 1901.

Davies, Wallace Evan. *Patriotism on Parade*. Cambridge, Massachusetts: Harvard University Press, 1955.

Davis, Allen F. *American Heroine: the Life and Legend of Jane Addams*. New York: Oxford University Press, 1973.

Diaz, Mrs. Abby Morton. *A Domestic Problem: Work and Culture in the Household*. Boston: James R. Osgood, 1875.

———. *Only a Flock of Women*. Boston: D. Lothrop, 1893.

Dole, Charles F. *Noble Womanhood*. Boston: H. M. Caldwell, 1909.

Dorland, W. A. Newman. *The Sum of Feminine Achievement*. Boston: The Stratford Co., 1917.

Dorr, Rheta Louise (Childe). *What Eight Million Women Want*. Boston: Small, Maynard, 1910.

DuBois, Ellen C. *Feminism and Suffrage*. Ithaca: Cornell University Press, 1978.

Duffey, Mrs. E. B. *No Sex in Education, Or, An Equal Chance for Both Girls and Boys Being a Review of Dr. E. H. Clarke's "Sex in Education."* Philadelphia: J. M. Stoddart, 1874.

Duniway, Abigail Scott. *Path-Breaking: An Autobiographical History of the Equal Suffrage Movement in Pacific Coast States*. New York: Schocken, 1971.

Dunn, Walter S., Jr., Ed. *History of Erie County, 1870–1970*. Buffalo: Buffalo and Erie County Historical Society, 1972.

Eagle, Mary Kavanaugh Oldham. *The Congress of Women: World's Columbian Exposition, Chicago, USA, 1893*. Chicago: W. S. Reeve, 1895.

Earhart, Mary. *Frances Willard: From Prayers to Politics*. Chicago: University of Chicago Press, 1944.

Edelstein, Tilden G. *Strange Enthusiasm: A Life of Thomas Wentworth Higginson*. New York: Atheneum, 1970.

*Elite Blue Book of Providence, Rhode Island, 1895*. Boston: Noyes Brothers, Mens Outfitters, n.d.

Ely, Mary L. and Eve Chappel. *Women in Two Worlds*. New York: American Association for Adult Education, 1938.

Emerson, Edward Waldo. *The Early Years of the Saturday Club, 1855–1870*. Boston: Houghton Mifflin, 1918.

Fairfield, Francis Gerry. *Clubs of New York*. New York: Henry L. Hinton, 1873.

Field, Kate. *Hap-Hazard*. Boston: James R. Osgood, 1873.

———. *Pen Photographs of Charles Dickens's Readings*. Boston: Loring, 1868.

Fisk, Fidelia. *Recollections of Mary Lyon*. Boston: American Tract Society, 1866.

Fletty, Miss Valbourg. *Public Services of Women's Organizations*. University of Syracuse: George Banta, 1951.

Flexner, Eleanor. *Century of Struggle*. Cambridge: Harvard University Press, 1959.

Flexner, Helen Thomas. *A Quaker Childhood*. New Haven: Yale University Press, 1940.

Forcey, Charles. *The Crossroads of Liberalism: Croly, Weyl, Lippmann and The Progressive Era, 1900–1925*. New York: Oxford University Press, 1961.

Frank, Henriette Greenebaum and Amalie Hofer Jerome, comp. *Annals of the Chicago Women's Club for the First Forty Years of Its Organization, 1876–1916*. Chicago: Chicago Women's Club, 1916.

Fredrickson, George M. *The Inner Civil War: Northern Intellectuals and Crisis of the Union*. New York: Harper and Row, 1968.

Fuller, Henry B. *With the Procession*. New York: Harper and Brothers, 1894.

Fulton, Rev. J. D. *Woman as God Made Her; the True Woman*. Boston: Lee and Shepard, 1869.

Gannett, William Channing. *Culture Without College*. Boston: James H. West, 1895.

Garnett, James M. *Lectures on Female Education*. Richmond: Thomas W. White, 1825.

Gibson, Mary S. *A Record of Twenty-five Years of The California Federation of Women's Clubs, 1900–1925*. Printed by California Federation of Women's Clubs, 1927.

Gilchrist, Beth Bradford. *Life of Mary Lyon*. Boston: Houghton Mifflin Co., 1910.

Gilman, Charlotte Perkins. *The Living of Charlotte Perkins Gilman, An Autobiography*. New York: D. Appleton-Century, 1935.

———. *Women and Economics*. Magnolia, Massachusetts: Peter Smith, 1898.

Gordon, Anna A. *The Beautiful Life of Frances E. Willard*. Chicago: Woman's Temperance Publishing Association, 1898.

Graves, Mrs. A. J. *Woman in America; Being an examination into the moral and intellectual condition of American Female Society*. New York: Harper and Brothers, 1858.

Greene, Welcome Arnold. *The Providence Plantations*. Providence: J. A. & R. A. Reid, 1886.

Guild, Reuben A. *Doyle, Thomas Arthur: A Sketch of His Life*. Providence: J. A. & R. A. Reid, n. d.

Gusfield, Joseph R. *Symbolic Crusade*. Urbana: University of Illinois Press, 1972.

Hahn, Emily. *Once Upon a Pedestal*. New York: New American Library, 1975.

Hale, Beatrice Forbes-Robertson. *What Women Want: An Interpretation of the Feminist Movement*. New York: Frederick A. Stokes, 1914.

Hall, Florence Howe. *The Story of the Battle Hymn of the Republic*. New York: Harper and Brothers, 1916.

Halsey, Francis Whiting. *Women Authors of Our Day in Their Homes*. New York: James Pott, 1903.

Hanaford, Phebe A. *Daughters of America*. Boston: B. B. Russell, 1883.

Harland, Marion. *Common Sense in the Household: a Manual of Practical Housewifery*. New York: Scribner, Armstrong, 1874.

Harper, Ida Husted, et al., eds. *The History of Woman Suffrage*. New York: J. J. Little and Ives, 1922.

Harriman, Alice Stratton, et al., comps. and eds. *A History of the New Hampshire Federation of Women's Clubs, 1895–1940*. Bristol, N.H.: Musgrove Printing House, 1941.

Harris, Neil, ed. *Land of Contrasts, 1880–1901*. New York: George Braziller, 1970.

Hart, James D. *The Popular Book: A History of America's Literary Taste*. Berkeley: University of California Press, 1961.

Hays, Frances. *Women of the Day: A Biographical Dictionary of Notable Contemporaries*. Philadelphia: J. B. Lippincott, 1885.

Higginson, Thomas Wentworth. *Women and The Alphabet: A Series of Essays*. New York: Arno Press, 1972; reprints of Boston & New York: Houghton Mifflin, 1881 and 1900.

Higham, John. *Strangers in the Land: Patterns of American Nativism 1860–1925*. New York: Atheneum, 1970.

Hill, Henry Way, ed. *Muncipality of Buffalo, New York: A History, 1720–1923*. Vol. 2; New York: Lewis Historical Publishing Co., 1923.

Hofstadter, Richard. *Anti-Intellectualism in American Life*. New York: Vintage, 1963.

Hokinson, Helen E. *The Ladies, God Bless 'Em!* New York: E. P. Dutton, 1950.

———. *There Are Ladies Present*. New York: E. P. Dutton, 1952.

Horton, John Theodore. *History of Northwestern New York*. New York: Lewis Historical Publishing Co., 3 vols., 1947.

Howe, J. W., ed. *Representative Women of New England*. Boston: New England Historical Publishing Co., 1904.

———. *Sex and Education: A Reply to Dr. E. H. Clarke's "Sex in Education."* Boston: Roberts Brothers, 1874.

Howe, Julia Ward. *Reminiscences, 1819–1899*. Boston: Houghton Mifflin, 1899.

Hunt, Caroline L. *The Life of Ellen H. Richards*. Boston: Whitcomb and Barrows, 1912.

Hunt, Harriot K. *Glimpses and Glances*. Boston: John P. Jewett, 1856.

Huntington, Emily. *How to Teach Kitchen Garden or Object Lessons in Household Work including Songs, Plays, Exercises and Games Illustrating Household Occupations*. New York: Doubleday, Page, 1903.

Ingham, Mrs. W. A. *Women of Cleveland and Their Work*. Cleveland: W. A. Ingham, 1893.

Irwin, Inez Haynes. *Angels and Amazons: A Hundred Years of American Women*. Garden City: Doubleday, Doran, 1933.

James, Edward T., et al. *Notable American Women, 1607–1950*. 3 vols. Cambridge: Harvard University Press, 1971.

James, Henry. *The American Scene*. New York: Harper and Brothers, 1907.

———. *The Bostonians*. New York: Random House, 1956.

Jones, Howard Mumford. *The Age of Energy: Varieties of American*

*Experience, 1865–1915*. New York: Viking Press, 1971.

Kendall, Pheobe Mitchell. *Maria Mitchell: Life, Letters, and Journals*. Boston: Lee and Shepard, 1956.

Kirk, William, ed. *A Modern City: Providence, Rhode Island and Its Activities*. Chicago: University of Chicago Press, 1909.

Knox, Helen. *Mrs. Percy V. Pennybacker: An Appreciation*. New York: Fleming H. Revell, 1916.

Kolko, Gabriel. *The Triumph of Conservatism*. New York: Macmillan, 1963.

Kraditor, Aileen S. *The Ideas of the Woman Suffrage Movement, 1890–1920*. Garden City: Doubleday, Inc., 1971.

_____. *Up from the Pedestal: Selected Writings in the History of American Feminism*. New York: Quadrangle, 1968.

Lansing, Marion F., ed. *Mary Lyon Through Her Letters*. Boston: Books, Inc., 1937.

Larned, Josephus N. *Life and Work of William Pryor Letchworth*. Boston: Houghton Mifflin, 1912.

Larsen, Arthur J., ed. *Crusader and Feminist: Letters of Jane Grey Swisshelm, 1858–1865*. St. Paul, Minnesota: Minnesota Historical Society, 1934.

Lasch, Christopher. *The New Radicalism in America, 1889–1963*. New York: Random House, 1965.

Laws, Annie, ed. *History of Ohio Federation of Women's Clubs 1894–1924*. Cincinnati: Ebbert and Richardson, 1924.

Lee, E. C. *Biographical Cyclopedia of American Women*. Vol. 2. New York: Franklin W. Lee, 1925.

Lerner, Gerda. *Black Women in White America*. New York: Vintage, 1973.

_____. *The Grimke Sisters from South Carolina*. New York: Schocken, 1973.

_____. *The Woman in American History*. Menlo Park, California: Addison-Wesley, 1971.

Lewis, Sinclair. *Main Street*. New York: Harcourt, Brace and World, 1920.

Livermore, Mary A. *The Story of My Life*. Hartford: A. D. Worthington, 1897.

_____. *My Story of the War*. Hartford: A. D. Worthington, 1889.

_____.*What Shall We Do With Our Daughters?* Boston: Lee and Shepard, 1883.

Lockwood, Mary S. and Emily Lee Sherwood. *Story of the Records: DAR*. Washington, D.C.: George E. Howard, 1906.

Lowell, Josephine Shaw. *Public Relief and Private Charity*. New York: G. P. Putnam, 1884.

Luhan, Mabel Dodge. *Intimate Memories*. Vol. 1 (Background). London: Martin Secker, 1933.

Lutz, Alma, *Emma Willard: Pioneer Educator of American Women*. Boston:

Beacon Press, 1964.

Marks, Jeannette. *Life and Letters of Mary Emma Woolley.* Washington, D.C.: Public Affairs Press, 1955.

Martin, Edward Sandford. *The Unrest of Women.* New York: D. Appleton, 1913.

Massey, Mary Elizabeth. *Bonnet Brigades: American Women and the Civil War.* New York: Alfred A. Knopf, 1966.

Mathews, Shailer, ed. *The Woman Citizen's Library: A Systematic Course of Reading and Preparation for the Larger Citizenship.* Vol. 2. Chicago: The Civic Society, 1914.

*The Mayflower Club, 1893–1931.* Cambridge: Riverside Press, 1933.

*Memoirs of Anne C. Botta.* Written by her friends. New York: J. Selwin Tait, 1894.

Meyer, Annie Nathan, ed. *Woman's Work in America.* New York: Henry Holt, 1891; reprint Arno Press, 1972.

Miller, Oliver Thorne. *The Woman's Club: A Practical Guide and Hand-Book.* United States Book Co., 1891.

Miner, George Leland. *Angell's Lane: The History of a Little Street in Providence.* Providence: Akerman-Standard Printers, 1848.

Moore, Frank. *Women of the War.* Hartford: S. S. Scranton, 1867.

Mott, Frank Luther. *A History of American Magazines, 1741–1850.* New York: D. Appleton, 1930.

Nathan, Maud. *The Story of An Epoch-Making Movement.* Garden City: Doubleday, Page, 1926.

Nestor, Agnes. *Woman's Labor Leader: An Autobiography.* Washington, D.C.: Zenger, 1976.

Noffsinger, John S. *Correspondence Schools, Lyceums, Chautauquas.* New York: Macmillan, 1926.

Nye, Russel Blaine. *Society and Culture in America, 1830–1860.* New York: Harper and Row, 1974.

O'Neill, William L. *Everyone Was Brave: The Rise and Fall of Feminism.* New York: Quadrangle, 1969.

*Our Famous Women.* Hartford: A. D. Worthington, 1885.

Papashvily, Helen Waite. *All the Happy Endings.* New York: Harper and Brothers, 1956.

Parton, James, et al. *Eminent Women of the Age.* Hartford: S. M. Betts, 1868.

Parton, Sara Willis. *The Life and Beauties of Fanny Fern.* Philadelphia: T. B. Peterson, 1855.

Paulson, Ross Evans. *Women's Suffrage and Prohibition.* Glenview, Ill.: Scott, Foresman, 1973.

Perkinson, Henry J. *The Imperfect Panacea: American Faith in Education, 1865–1965.* New York: Random House, 1968.

Pivar, David J. *Purity Crusade: Sexual Morality and Social Control, 1868–1900.* Westport, Connecticut: Greenwood Press, 1973.

*Progress and Achievement: A History of the Mass. State Federation of Women's Clubs, 1893–1962*. Lexington: Mass. State Federation of Women's Clubs, 1962.

*The Providence Directory and Rhode Island State Business Directory*. Providence: Sampson and Murdock, 1885–1937.

*The Providence Directory and Rhode Island State Business Directory*. Providence: Sampson, Davenport, 1866–1884.

Putnam, Ruth, ed. *Life and Letters of Mary Putnam Jacobi*. New York: G. P. Putnam, 1925.

Richards, Laura E. and Maud Howe Elliott. *Julia Ward Howe, 1819–1910*. Boston: Houghton Mifflin, 1925.

Roberts, Kate Louise. *The Club Woman's Handybook of Programs and Club Management*. New York: Funk and Wagnalls, 1914.

Robinson, Harriet H. *Mass. in the Woman's Suffrage Movement*. Boston: Roberts Brothers, 1881.

Rosen, Marjorie. *Popcorn Venus*. New York: Avon Books, 1974.

Ross, Ishbel. *Ladies of the Press*. New York: Harper, 1936.

———. *Crusades and Crinolines*. New York: Harper, 1963.
    University of Delaware, 1924.

Ruddy, Ella Giles. *Mother of Clubs: Caroline M. Seymour Severance*. Los Angeles: Baumgart, 1906.

Ryan, Mary P. *Womanhood in America from Colonial Times to the Present*. New York: Franklin Watts, 1975.

Ryden, George H. "Growth of Artistic Appreciation in America in the Nineteenth Century," *Delaware Notes*, 2nd Series. Newark, Delaware: University of Delaware, 1924.

Sandford, Mrs. John. *Woman in her Social and Domestic Character*. (From the 5th London Edition.) Boston: Otis, Broaders, 1838.

Sargent, Mrs. John T., ed. *Sketches and Reminiscences of the Radical Club of Chestnut Street, Boston*. Boston: James R. Osgood, 1880.

Schlesinger, Arthur Meier. *The Rise of the City, 1878–1898*. New York: Macmillan, 1933.

Scott, Anne Firor. *The Southern Lady: From Pedestal to Politics, 1830–1930*. Chicago: University of Chicago Press, 1970.

Scott, J. W. Robertson. *The Story of the Women's Institute Movement in England and Wales and Scotland*. Idbury, Great Britain: The Village Press, 1925.

Seitz, Don C. *Horace Greeley: Founder of the New York Tribune*. Indianapolis: Bobbs-Merrill, 1926.

Shattuck, Harriette R. *The Woman's Manual of Parliamentary Law*. Boston: Lee and Shepard, 1895.

Shaw, Anna Howard, *The Story of a Pioneer*. New York: Harper, 1915.

Sklar, Kathyrn Kish. *Catherine Beecher*. New Haven: Yale University Press, 1973.

Smith, Page. *Daughters of the Promised Land: Women in American History*.

Boston: Little, Brown, 1970.

Smith-Rosenberg, Carroll. *Religion and the Rise of the American City.* Ithaca: Cornell University Press, 1971.

Sochen, June. *Herstory: A Woman's View of American History.* Vols. 1 and 2. New York: Alfred Publishing Co., 1974.

Spencer, Anna Garlin. *Woman's Share in Social Culture.* New York: Arno Press, 1972; reprint of New York: Mitchell Kennerly, 1913.

Spofford, Harriet Prescott, *A Little Book of Friends.* Boston: Little, Brown, 1916.

Sprague, Julia A., comp. *History of the New England Woman's Club from 1868 to 1893.* Boston: Lee and Shepard, 1894.

Stanley, Maude. *Clubs for Working Girls.* New York: Macmillan, 1890.

Stern, Madeleine B. *We the Women: Career Firsts of Nineteenth-Century America.* New York: Schulte, 1963.

Stern, Renee B. *Clubs: Making and Management.* New York: Rand McNally, 1925.

_____. *Neighborhood Entertainments.* New York: Sturgis and Walton, 1913.

*The Story of the Saturday Morning Club of Boston.* Boston: Charles H. Wall, 1932.

Strayer, Martha. *The DAR: An Informal History.* Washington, D.C.: Public Affairs Press, 1958.

Swisshelm, Jane Grey. *Half a Century.* Chicago: Jansen, McClurg and Co., 1880; reprint by New York: Source Book Press, 1970.

_____. *Letters to Country Girls.* New York: J .C. Riker, 1853.

Talbot, Marion. *The Education of Women.* Chicago: University of Chicago Press, 1910.

Talbot, Marion and Lois Kimball Mathews Rosenberry. *The History of the American Association of University Women, 1881–1931.* Boston: Houghton Mifflin, 1931.

Taylor, William R. *Cavalier and Yankee.* New York: Harper, 1961.

Tharp, Louise Hall. *The Peabody Sisters of Salem.* Boston: Little, Brown, 1950.

_____. *Until Victory: Horace Mann and Mary Peabody.* Boston: Little, Brown, 1953.

Thornwell, Emily. *The Lady's Guide to Perfect Gentility.* New York: Derby and Jackson, 1856.

Townsend, Harriet A. *Reminiscences of Famous Women.* Buffalo: Evans-Penfold, Publishers, 1916.

Tyler, Alice Felt. *Freedom's Ferment: Phases of American Social History from the Colonial Period to the Outbreak of the Civil War.* New York: Harper and Row, 1944.

Van Deusen, Glyndon G. *Horace Greeley: Nineteenth-Century Crusader.* Philadelphia: University of Pennsylvania Press, 1953.

Wells, Mildred White. *Unity in Diversity: the History of the General Federation of Women's Clubs*. Washington, D.C.: General Federation of Women's Clubs, 1953.

Welsh, Lilian, MD, LL.D. *Reminiscences of Thirty Years in Baltimore*. Baltimore: The Norman Remington Company, 1925.

Wharton, Edith. "Xingu" in *The Best Short Stories of Edith Wharton*. New York: Scribner's, 1958.

Whitcomb, Carrie Niles. *Reminiscences of the Springfield Women's Club, 1884–1924*. Springfield, Mass.: Springfield Women's Club, 1924.

Whiting, Lilian, *Kate Field, a Record*. Boston: Little Brown, 1899.

*Who Was Who in America*. Vol. 1 (1897–1942). Chicago: A. N. Marquis, 1943.

Wiebe, Robert H. *The Search for Order, 1877–1920*. New York: Hill and Wang, 1967.

Wiggin, Kate Douglas. *My Garden of Memory: An Autobiography*. Boston: Houghton Mifflin, 1923.

Willard, Frances E. *Glimpses of Fifty Years*. Boston: George M. Smith, 1889.

_____. *How To Win*. Chicago and New York: Funk and Wagnalls, 1887.

Willard, Frances E. and Mary A. Livermore. *American Women*. 2 vols. New York: Mast, Crowell and Kirkpatrick, 1897.

Willard, Frances E. and Mary A. Livermore, eds. *A Woman of the Century*. Buffalo, Chicago, New York: Charles Wells Moulton, 1893.

Williams, Isabelle H. *A History of the Brighthelmstone Club of Brighton and Allston*. Cambridge: Harvard University Press, 1923.

Willis, Mrs. Olympia Brown. *Acquaintances, old and new, among reformers by Olympia Brown*. Milwaukee: S. E. Tate, 1911.

Winant, Marguerite Dawson. *Century of Sorosis, 1868–1968*. Uniondale, Long Island, New York: Salisbury Printers, 1968.

Wingate, Charles F. Editor. *Views and Interviews on Journalism*. New York: F. B. Patterson, 1875.

Winslow, Helen M. *The President of Quex: A Woman's Club Story*. Boston: Lothrop, Lee and Shepard, 1906.

_____. *A Woman for Mayor*. Chicago: Reilly and Britton, 1909.

_____. *The Woman of Tomorrow*. New York: James Pott, 1905.

Winslow, Rev. Hubbard. *Woman as She Should Be*. Boston: Otis, Broaders, 1838.

Winsor, Justin, ed. *Memorial History of Boston*. 4 vols. Boston: J. R. Osgood, 1881–1883.

Winter, Alice Ames. *The Business of Being a Club Woman*. New York: Century, 1925.

Wise, Reverend Daniel. *The Young Lady's Counsellor*. New York: Carlton and Porter, 1851.

*The Woman's Book*. New York: Scribner's, 1894.

Woman's Press Club of New York City. *Memories of Jane Cunningham Croly "Jenny June."* New York: G. P. Putnam, 1904.

Women's Literary Club. *Thoughts from Earnest Women*. Syracuse: C. W. Bardeen, 1891.

Wood, Mary I. *The History of the General Federation of Women's Clubs*. New York: Norwood, 1912.

Woody, Thomas A. *History of Women's Education in the United States*. New York: The Science Press, 1929.

Woolson, Abba Goold. *Women in American Society*. Boston: Roberts Brothers, 1873.

Wright, Helen. *Sweeper in the Sky: The Life of Maria Mitchell, First Woman Astronomer in America*. New York: Macmillan, 1949.

Wright, Louis B. *Culture on the Moving Frontier*. New York: Harper, 1955.

Wyman, Lillie Buffum Chace and Arthur Crawford Wyman. *Elizabeth Buffum Chace, 1806–1899*. Boston: W. B. Clarke, 1914.

### Articles and Pamphlets

A.S.B. "Woman's Suffrage." *The Womans' Journal*, 15 (16 February 1884): 54.

Aberdeen, Ishbel. "The Women's International Parliament." *North American Review*, 169 (August 1899): 145–153.

Adams, Florence Bannard. "Fanny Fern or a Pair of Flaming Shoes." West Trenton, N.J.: Hermitage Press, 1966.

Adams, Ida. G. "New Hampshire Club in Lynn, Mass." *Granite Monthly*, 38 (June 1906): 176–177.

_____. "New Hampshire's Daughters: Origins and History of the Club." *Granite Monthly*, 38 (May 1906): 145–146.

Addams, Jane. "Woman's Work for Chicago." *Municipal Affairs*, 2 (September 1898): 502–08.

Akers, Maude V. B. "First Aid to the Club Woman." *Delineator*, 77 (March 1911): 251.

Allen, Eleanor W. "Boston's Women's Educational and Industrial Union." *New England Galaxy*, 7 (Spring 1965): 30–38.

Amos, Mrs. Sheldon. "A Women's Club Movement in London." *American Monthly Review of Reviews*, 16 (October 1897): 440–44.

Anderson, Ellen. *Guide to Woman's Organizations*. Washington, D.C.: Public Affairs Press, 1949–50.

Anstruther, Eva. "Ladies' Clubs." *The Living Age*, 221 (May 27, 1899): 533–44.

Anthony, Julia B. "How a Club Paper Was Written." *Chautauquan*, 32 (October 1900): 30–32.

Ashby, Harriet Wallace. "A Club for the Farmer's Wife." *Ladies' Home Journal*, 29 (June 1912): 48.

Ashmore, Ruth. "The Restlessness of the Age." *Ladies' Home Journal*, 12 (1895): 16.

Ashton, Mrs. Oliver C. "Vermont Federation of Women's Clubs." *Vermonter*, 15 (May 1910): 137–142.

Ault, Nelson A. "The Earnest Ladies: The Walla Walla Women's Club—the Equal Suffrage League of 1886–1889." *Pacific Northwest Quarterly*, 42 (April 1951): 123–137.

Babcock, Louis L. *After Eighty Years—the Buffalo Club, 1867.* Buffalo: printed by the club, 1947.

Bailey, Nettie F. "The Significance of the Woman's Club Movement." *Harper's Bazaar*, 39 (March 1905): 204–209.

Baldwin, Henry. "An Old-Time Sorosis." *Atlantic Monthly*, 74 (December 1894): 748–755.

Bartlett, Mary K. "The Philanthropic Work of the Chicago Women's Club." *The Outlook*, 49 (May 12, 1894): 827–828.

Benton, Caroline French. "A Year of Club-Work." *Woman's Home Companion*, 40 (January): 32; (February): 28; (March): 37+; (April): 30; (May): 38; (September): 26; (October): 29; (November): 41; (December): 37, 1913.

———. "A Page of Club Work." *Woman's Home Companion*, 41 (January): 26; (February): 33–41; (March): 26; (April): 31–32; (May): 33; (June): 45; (September): 30; (October): 39–40; (November): 35; (December): 41, 1914.

———. "The Club Year—Our Own Country." *Woman's Home Companion*, 39 (September 1912): 26.

———. "Ten Woman's Club Programs." *Woman's Home Companion*, 38 (September 1911): 34.

Berthoff, Roland. "The American Social Order: A Conservative Hypothesis." *American Historical Review*, 65 (April 1960): 495–514.

Blackwell, Alice Stone. "Mrs. Abby Morton Diaz—Obituary." *The Woman's Journal*, 35 (9 April 1904): 1+.

———. "Mrs. Ednah D. Cheney—Obituary." *The Woman's Journal*, 35 (November 26, 1904): 1+.

Blair, Emily Newell. "Why Clubs for Women?" *The Forum*, 77 (March 1927): 354–363.

Blauvelt, Mary Taylor. "The Race Problem." *American Journal of Sociology*, 6 (March 1901): 662–672.

Bok, Edward. "My Quarrel with Women's Clubs." *Ladies Home Journal*, 27 (January 1910): 5–6.

Bostwick, Arthur E. "Clubwomen's Reading." 3-part series. *Bookman Magazine*, 40 (January 1915): 575–621; 40 (February 1915): 642–647; 41 (March 1915): 64–70.

Bowlker, Mrs. T. J. "Woman's Home-Making Function Applied to the Municipality." *American City*, 6 (1912): 863–869.

Boyesen, Ajalmar Hjorth. "Why We Have No Great Novelists." *Forum*, 2 (1886–1887): 615–622.

Brackett, J. R. "Work by Women's Clubs and Associations." *Survey*, 8 (7 June 1902): 513–516.

Brooks, E. C. "Women Improving School Houses." *World's Work*, 12 (September 1906): 7937–7938.

Bruere, Martha Bensley and Robert Bruere. "The Revolt of the Farmer's Wife!" *Harper's Bazaar*, 46 (December 1912): 601–602.

Brush, Fred. "Women at the Crossroads." *Survey*, 31 (4 October 1913): 15.

Bryce, Mary E. "The Club as an Ally to Higher Education." *Arena*, 6 (1892): 378–380.

Buenker, John D. "Urban Liberalism in Rhode Island, 1909–1919." *Rhode Island History*, 30 (May or Spring 1971): 35–51.

Buhle, Mari Jo. "Women and the Socialist Party, 1901–1914." *Radical America* (February 1970).

Buhle, Mari Jo, Ann G. Gordon and Nancy Schrom. "Women in American Society: An Historical Contribution." *Radical America*, 4 (July–August 1971): 3–66.

Burdette, Clara B. "The Ex-President of the Federation." *Outlook*, 78 (1 October 1904): 268–269.

Burdette, Mrs. Robert J. "Club Creed." *Chautauquan*, 36 (February 1903): 535.

Burleigh, Elvira Page. "Pemigewasset Women's Club of Plymouth." *Granite Monthly*, 38 (June 1906): 169–172.

Candee, H. C. "Madam President and her Constituents." *Century Magazine*, 62 (October 1901): 851–854.

Cawelti, John G. "America on Display: The World's Fairs of 1876, 1893, 1933." In *The Age of Industrialism in America: Essays in Social Structure and Cultural Values*, pp. 317–363. Edited by Frederic Cople Jaher. New York: Free Press, 1968.

Chase, Lucetta C. "Social Program of the General Federation of Women's Clubs." *Journal of Social Forces*, 2 (May 1923): 465–469.

Cheney, Ednah Dow. *Memorial Meeting for Ednah Dow Cheney, February 20, 1905*. Boston: George H. Ellis Company, 1905.

———. *History of New England Hospital for Women and Children, 1859–1899*.

———. "The Women of Boston," from *Memorial History of Boston*, 1881.

Clarke, Ida Clyde. "A Clubless Woman's World." *The Century Magazine*, 114 (October 1927): 752–759.

Cleveland, Grover. "Woman's Mission and Woman's Clubs." *Ladies' Home Journal*, 22 (May 1905): 3–4.

Clifford, Deborah P. "An Invasion of Strong-Minded Women: The Newspapers and The Woman Suffrage Campaign in Vermont in 1870." *Vermont History*, 43 (Winter 1975): 1–19.

Cobb, Margaret. "Lady Back-Slappers." *American Mercury*, 12 (October 1927): 222–229.

Cobbe, F. P. "Clubs for Women." *Victoria Magazine*, 16 (1870): 569–572.

Colbourne, Carol. "The Luxury of Women's Social Clubs." *Good Housekeeping*, 54 (March 1912): 306–307.

Comstock, Sarah. "Her Town in Order." *Collier's*, 48 (9 March 1912): 38–39+.

Conine, Martha A. B. "Women's Work in Denver." *Municipal Affairs*, 2 (September 1898): 527–531.

Conway, Jill. "Jane Addams: An American Heroine." In *The Woman in America*. Edited by Robert Jay Lifton. Boston: Beacon, 1967.

_____. "Women Reformers and American Culture, 1870–1930." *Journal of Social History*, 5 (Winter 1971–72): 164–182.

Cooke, George Willis. "Mrs. Howe as Poet, Lecturer and Club-woman." *New England Magazine*, 26 (March 1902): 3–21.

_____. "The Saturday Morning Club." *New England Magazine*, 19 (September 1898): 24–34.

Cooley, Winnifred Harper. "The Future of Women's Clubs." *Arena*, 27 (April 1902): 373–380.

Cott, Nancy F. "Young Women in the Second Great Awakening in New England." *Feminist Studies*, 3 (Fall 1975): 15–29.

Cowles, Mrs. Josiah Evans. "A Call to Club Women." *Ladies' Home Journal*, 34 (June 1917): 72.

Cox, Marian. "Marian Cox Tells Why Women Love Music." *Current Opinion*, 68 (March 1920): 349–350.

Crandall, C. H. "What Men Think of Women's Dress." *North American Review*, 161 (1895): 251–254.

Crane, Hattie Elliot. "Woman's Place in the Government and Conduct of Society." *Overland Monthly and Out West Magazine*, 59 (April 1912): 359–366.

Crawford, Evelyn. "The Woman and the Club in California." *Overland Monthly and Out West Magazine*, 53 (February 1909): 120–125.

Crozier, L. Graham. "Women's Clubs and Education." *Educational Review*. 17 (February 1899): 182–186.

Curtis, Isabel Gordon. "A Woman's Club That is Worth While." *Ladies' Home Journal*, 23 (October 1906): 72.

Daggett, Mabel Potter. "Women: the Larger Housekeeping." *The World's Work*, 24 (October 1912): 664–670.

Dailey, Charlotte Field, ed. *Rhode Island Women's Directory for the Columbian Year 1892*. Providence: Rhode Island Women's World's Fair Advisory Board, 1893.

Davis, Gertrude S. "Vermont Federation of Women's Clubs." *Vermonter*, 7 (December 1901): 413–417.

Decker, Sarah Platt. "Mrs. Decker on Equal Suffrage." *Woman Suffrage: Arguments and Results*. National American Woman Suffrage Association, n.d.

_____. "The Meaning of the Woman's Club Movement." *American Academy of Political and Social Science Annals*, 28 (1906): 199–204.

Degler, Carl. "Revolution Without Ideology: The Changing Place of Women in America." *Daedalus*, 93 (1964): 653–670.

Denison, Dimies F. S. "The President of the General Federation of Women's Clubs." *Outlook*, 78 (1 October 1904): 267–269.

DePauw, Linda Grant. *Four Traditions: Women of New York During the American Revolution*. Albany: New York State American Revolution Bicentennial Commission, 1974.

Devine, Edward T. "New View of Charity." *Atlantic Monthly*, 102 (December 1908): 737–744.

Diaz, A. M. "In Time of the Embargo," *The Northern Monthly: Magazine of Literary and Military Affairs*, 1 (1864): 233–240.

_____. "Pink and Blue." *Atlantic Monthly*, 27 (May 1871): 559–574.

_____. "Women's Clubs." *National Magazine*, 2 (1895): 179–183; 288–292; 383–386.

_____. "Women's Clubs: The Castilian Club." *National Magazine*, 3 (1859): 175–180.

_____. "Women's Clubs: The Early Days of the New England Woman's Club." *National Magazine*, 3 (1896): 483–485.

_____. "Women's Clubs: New England Women's Press Club." *National Magazine*, 3 (1896): 367–373.

_____. Women's Clubs: Their True Character." *National Magazine*, 3 (1896): 59–63.

Dickinson, Mary Lowe. "The National Council of Women of the United States." *Arena*, 17 (February 1899): 478–493.

DuBois, Ellen. "The Radicalism of the Woman's Suffrage Movement: Notes Toward the Reconstruction of Nineteenth-Century Feminism." *Feminist Studies*, 3 (Fall 1975): 63–71.

_____. "Struggling Into Existence: The Feminism of Sarah and Angelina Grimke." *New England Free Press*, 1970.

Dunbar, Olivia Howard. "The Newest Woman's Club." *Putnam's Magazine: an Illustrated Monthly of Literature, Art and Life*, 2 (May 1907): 196–206.

_____. "The Woman's University Club." *Harper's Bazaar*, 42 (November 1908): 1111–1114.

Dye, Nancy Schrom. "Creating a Feminist Alliance: Sisterhood and Class Conflict in the New York Women's Trade Union League." *Feminist Studies*, 2 (1975).

E.M.L. "A Word on Women's Clubs." *Victoria Magazine*, 18 (1871): 346–348.

Eastman, Elaine Goodale. "The Mother's Club of St. Paul." *The Outlook*, 58 (19 March 1898): 725–727.

Ehrenreich, Barbara, and Deidre English. "The Manufacture of Housework."

*Socialist Review*, 5 (October–December 1975): 5–40.

Ellis, Mrs. Sarah Stickney. "Education of the Heart, Woman's Best Work." In *The Young Lady's Guide*. New York: American Tract Society, 1870.

Elson, Ruth. "American Schoolbooks and 'Culture' in the Nineteenth Century." *Mississippi Valley Historical Review*, 46 (December 1959): 411–434.

Evans, Miss Margaret J. "Women's Clubs as an Educational Factor." *National Education Association of the United States, Addresses and Proceedings*, 37 (1898): 237–243.

Faragher, Johnny and Christine Stansell. "Women and Their Families on the Overland Trail, 1842–1867." *Feminist Studies*, 2 (1975): 150–166.

Fatout, Paul, "Yarning in the 1850's." *The American Scholar*, 3 (Summer 1934): 281–293.

Forrest, Kate. "Tilton and Northfield Women's Clubs." *Granite Monthly*, 35 (August 1903): 66–76.

Francis, M. C. "The Federation of Women's Clubs." *The Review of Reviews*, 12 (December 1895): 720–721.

Francis, Mary C. "The General Federation of Women's Clubs." *Godey's Magazine*, 131 (December 1895): 575–587.

Frazar, Mrs. M. D. "Clubwomen and Their Work." *National Magazine*, 9 (1898): 185–186.

de Frost, Robert W. "Margaret Olivia Sage, Philanthropist." *Survey*, 34 (November 9, 1918): 151.

Gaffney, Fannie Humphreys. "A Woman's Criticism of the Women's Congress—A Reply." *The Nineteenth Century*, 46 (September 1899): 598–611.

_____. "A Perspective on Women's Clubs." *Chautauquan: A Weekly News Magazine*, 37 (1903): 432–433.

Gardner, Inez J. "Boston and the Woman's Club." *New England Magazine*, 34 (1906): 597–605.

Gilman, Charlotte Perkins. "Women and Social Service." Boston: Equal Suffrage Association for Good Government, 14 November 1907.

Gleason, Arthur Huntington. "Mrs. Russell Sage and her Interests." *World's Work*, 13 (November 1906): 8182–8186.

Gordon, Linda. "Voluntary Motherhood: The Beginnings of Feminist Birth Control Ideas in the United States." In *Clio's Consciousness Raised*. Edited by Mary Hartman and Lois W. Banner. New York: Harper and Row, 1974.

Granger, Mrs. A. O. "The Effect of Club Work in the South." *American Academy of Political and Social Science Annals*, 28 (September 1906): 248–256.

Groff, Frances A. "Mother of Clubs, Caroline Severence." *Sunset Magazine*, 27 (August 1911): 167–170.

Guldin, Mrs. Olaf N. "Suggested Outlines for Club Study." *Journal of Home Economics*, 3 (June 1911): 295–304; (April 1911): 188–189.

Gutman, Herbert G. "Protestantism and the American Labor Movement: Christian Spirit in the Gilded Age." *American Historical Review*, 72 (October 1966): 74–101.

Hall, Adelaide S. "Practical Art among Club-Women." *Chautauquan*, 31 (September 1900): 621–634.

Hammond, Mrs. John Hays. "Woman's Share in Civic Life." *Good Housekeeping*, 54 (May 1912): 593–602.

Hard, William. "The Women of Tomorrow." *Everybody's Magazine*, 24 (January 1911): 98–108.

Harper, Ida Husted. "Woman's Broom in Municipal Housekeeping." *Delineator*, 73 (February 1909): 213–216.

———. "Women's Clubs." *Independent*, 67 (July 22, 1909): 190–192.

Hartmann, Susan M. "The Paradox of Women's Progress 1820–1920." *Forums in History*. St. Charles, Missouri: Forum Press, 1974.

Hartt, Mary Bronson. "Work for Women's Clubs to Do." *Good Housekeeping*, 49 (September 1909): 245–247.

Hastings, C. H., compiler. "Bibliography—Woman's Clubs." *Chautauquan*, 31 (April 1900): 14–15.

Hawksley, Julia M. A. "Influence of Women's Clubs." *Westminister Review*, 153 (1900): 455–457.

Hawthorne, Hildegarde. "The General Federation of Women's Clubs: A Great Altruistic Movement." *The Century Magazine*, 80 (October 1910): 832–837.

Henrotin, Ellen M. "The Attitudes of Women's Clubs and Associations toward Social Economics." *Bulletin of the Department of Labor*, 23 (July 1899): 501–545.

———. "The Church and the Club." *The Advance*, (21 July 1904): 76.

———. "The Co-operation of Women's Clubs in the Public Schools." *National Education Association of the United States, Addresses and Proceedings*, 36 (1897): 73–83.

———. "Evolution of Women's Clubs." *World Today*, 5 (1903): 1308–1314.

———. "Foreword." In *Heroines of Modern Progress*, by Elmer C. Adams and Warren Dunham Foster. New York: Sturgis and Walton, 1913.

———. "General Federation of Women's Clubs." *Outlook*, 55 (February 1897): 442–446.

———. "The General Federation of Women's Clubs." *The Review of Reviews*, 6 (March 1896): 291–293.

———. "State Federations of Women's Clubs." *American Monthly Review of Reviews*, 16 (October 1897): 437–440.

Hess, M. Whitcomb. "Conversations in Boston, 1839." *Catholic World*. 149 (1939): 309–317.

Higginson, Thomas Wentworth. "Ought Women to Learn the Alphabet?" *Atlantic Monthly*, 3 (February 1859): 137–150.

Hogeland, Ronald W. "Coeducation of the Sexes at Oberlin College: A Study of Social Ideas in Mid-Nineteenth-Century America." *Journal of Social History*, 6 (Winter 1972–1973): 160–176.

_____. "'The Female Appendage': Feminine Life-Styles in America, 1820–1860." *Civil War History*, 17 (1971): 101–114.

Horton, Mrs. Thaddeus. "An Order of Old-Fashioned Women." *Ladies' Home Journal*, 23 (July 1906): 5–6.

Hosmer, Katherine. "What women have done in Washington's City Affairs." *Municipal Affairs*, 2 (September 1898): 514–522.

Howe, Julia Ward. "A Chronicle of Boston Clubs." *New England Magazine*, 34 (July 1906): 610–615.

_____. "Dress and Undress." *Forum*, 3 (1887): 313–320.

Ives, Alice E. "A Very New Woman: A Woman's Suffrage Drama." Women's Suffrage Leaflet. Boston: *Woman's Journal*, 7.

Jacoby, Robin. "The Women's Trade Union League and American Feminism." *Feminist Studies*, 3 (Fall 1975).

James, Isabel Vaughan. "The Pan-American Exposition." Buffalo: Buffalo and Erie County Historical Society, 6, 1961.

Jensen, Richard. "Family, Career, and Reform: Women Leaders in the Progressive Era." In *The American Family in Social-Historical Perspective*. Edited by Michael Gordon. New York: St. Martin's Press, 1973.

Johnson, Helen Louise. "The Work of the Home Economics Department, General Federation of Women's Clubs." *Journal of Home Economics*, 6 (April 1914): 153–155.

_____. "Home Economics Work in the General Federation of Women's Clubs." *Journal of Home Economics*, 5 (December 1913): 437–441.

June, Jennie. "Talks with Women." *The Revolution* (reprinted from *Demorest's Monthly Magazine*, 23 September 1869): 182–183.

Kenealley, James. "Women and the Trade Unions, 1870–1920: The Quandry of the Reformer." *Labor History*, 14 (1973): 42–55.

Kern, May Root. "Dressing Without the Corset." *Ladies' Home Journal*, 10 (1893): 17.

Kirkbride, Mrs. Eliza B. "Women's Clubs in the United States, a Significant Sign of our Time." *Der Internationale Kongress fur Frauenwerke und Frauenbestribungen*, Berlin, 1896, 96–99.

Knobe, Bertha Damaris. "Club Houses Owned by American Women." *Harper's Bazaar*, 42 (August 1908): 790–796.

_____. "New York Women's Colony Club." *Harper's Bazaar*, 40 (April 1906): 340–346.

Kohlstedt, Sally Gregory. "Maria Mitchell: The Advancement of Women in Science" *New England Quarterly*, 51 (March 1978): 39–63.

Kroll, R. "The Inter-American Committee of the Sorosis Club." *The Pan-American Magazine*, 29 (August 1919): 217–218.

L.M. "National Obstacles to Culture of Women." *Victoria Magazine*, 23 (1874): 95–105.

Laut, Agnes C. "The New Spirit among Women who Work." *The Century Magazine*, 89 (April 1915): 927–933.

Le Bosquet, Maurice. "Women's Clubs and the Introduction of Domestic Science into Schools." *Journal of Home Economics*, 1 (April 1909): 178–181.

Lerner, Gerda. "Early Community Work of Black Club Women." *Journal of Negro History*, 59 (April 1974): 158–167.

Lewis, Miss Bertha. "The Civic Club of Philadelphia." *Der Internationale Kongress fur Frauenwerke und Frauenbestribungen,* Berlin, 1896, pp. 93–96.

Lindsay, Malvina. "The Hen Party." *North American Review*, 236 (December 1933): 525–530.

Livermore, Mary. A. "Cooperative Womanhood in the State." *North American Review*, 153 (September 1891): 283–295.

———. "Mass. Women in the Civil War." In Thomas Wentworth Higginson, *Mass. in the Army and Navy During the War of 1861–65.* Vol. 2. Boston: Wright and Potter Printing Company. 1865.

———. "What Has the Woman Suffrage Reform Accomplished?" *National Magazine*, 1 (1859): 81–86.

Lockwood, Florence. "Working Girl's Clubs." *Century Magazine*, 41 (March 1891): 793–794.

Low, Frances H. "A Woman's Criticism of the Women's Congress." *The Nineteenth Century*, 46 (August 1899): 192–202.

Lowe, Rebecca Douglas. "Women's Opportunity for Social Service." *Gunton's Magazine*, 23 (July 1902): 58–65.

Lummis, Charles F. "The Skin Question." *Out West*, 16 (1901): 524–525.

Lyon, Dore. "A Plea for Women's Clubs." *Current Opinion*, 34 (June 1903): 739–740.

McCracken, Elizabeth. "The Women of America—Fifth Paper—The Woman in Her Club." *The Outlook*, 76 (February 13, 1904): 419–426.

McGovern, James. "The American Women's Pre-World War I Freedom in Manners and Morals." *Journal of American History*, 55 (September 1968): 315–333.

McGriff, Jessie Atkinson. "Making Your Club Effective." *Delineator*, 77 (May 1911): 406.

McKitrick, Eric and Stanley Elkins. "Institutions in Motion." *American Quarterly*, 12 (Summer 1960): 188–197.

MacLean, Annie Marion. "A Progressive Club of Working Women." *Survey*, 15 (December 2, 1905): 299–302.

Mason, Amelia Gere. "Woman's Clubs." (From *Woman in the Golden Ages*, The Century Company, 1901.) In *Living Age*, 231 (1901): 656–658.

Matthews, S. "The Woman's Club and the Church." *Independent*, 103 (3 July 1920): 12–13.

May, E. Anne S. "The Woman's Club Movement." *The Vermonter*, 3 (August 1897): 167–172.

"Medical Man." "The Ways of Women in Their Physical, Moral and Intellectual Relations." New York: John P. Jewett, 1873.

Melder, Keith. "Ladies Bountiful: Organized Women's Benevolence in Early Nineteenth-Century America." *New York History*, 47 (July 1967): 231–254.

_____. "Mask of Oppression: the Female Seminary Movement in the United States." *New York History*, 55 (July 1974): 261–279.

Melius, Marion. "A Woman's Club that was Helpful." *Ladies' Home Journal*, 25 (November 1908): 65.

Merk, Lois Bannister. "Boston's Historic Public School Crisis." *New England Quarterly*, 31 (June 1958): 172–199.

Merrill, Margaret Manton. "Sorosis." *Cosmopolitan*, 15 (May–October 1893): 153–158.

Metcalf, H. H. "Mary I. Wood." *Granite Monthly*, 42 (March 1910): 89–91.

Millspaugh, Mrs. Charles F. "Women as a Factor in Civic Improvement." *Chautauquan*, 43 (June 1906): 312–319.

Mitchell, Mary C. "Consigning to Women's Exchanges." *Woman's Home Companion*, 44 (November 1917): 27.

Moody, Helen Watterson. "The Unquiet Sex." *Scribner's Magazine*, 22 (1897): 486–491.

Moore, Dorothea. "The Work of the Women's Clubs in California." *American Academy of Political and Social Science Annals*, 28 (September 1909): 257–260.

Moore, Eva Perry. "What We Will Work for in 1910." *Delineator*, 75, (June 1910): 41+.

Moore, Isabel N. "The Woman's Club of Penacook." *The Granite Monthly*, 30 (January 1901): 3–7.

Moore, Mrs. Philip N. "What Women's Clubs Expect To Do." *Ladies' Home Journal*, 30 (January 1913): 30.

Moran, Mary H. and Julia Pulsifer. "Boston's Public School Lunches." *The Federation Bulletin*, 5 (June 1908): 269–271.

Moulton, Louise Chandler. "Two London Clubs." *Arena*, 6 (August 1892): 384–387.

Mulligan, Charlotte. "Report of Memorial Meeting at Twentieth Century Club," 9 November 1914.

Mumford, Mary E. "The Civic Club of Philadelphia." *Outlook*, 52 (13 October 1894): 588–589.

_____. "Clubs in Conservative Philadelphia." *Arena*, 6 (1892): 371–373.

Murray, Margaret Polson. "Women's Clubs in America." *Nineteenth Century*, 47 (May 1900): 847–854.

National Council of Women. *Women Through the Century. A Souvenir of the National Council of Women Exhibit: A Century of Progress, 1833, Chicago, 1933.*

————. "Symposium on Women's Dress." *Arena*, 6 (September 1892): 488–507.

Nobles, Katherine. "Club Life in the South." *Arena*, 6 (1892): 374–378.

*Old Anti-Slavery Days. Proceedings of Commemorative Meeting.* Danvers Historical Society, 26 April 1893.

Park, Julian. "A History of the University of Buffalo." *Publications of Buffalo Historical Society*, 22 (1918).

Parker, Gilbert and May Wright Sewall. "The International Council of Women." *Fortnightly Review*, 72 (July 1899): 151–159.

Parmelee, Anne. "Newport Women's Club." *Granite Monthly*, 41 (February 1909): 47–52.

Pennybacker, Mrs. Percy V. "Eighth Biennial Convention of the General Federation of Women's Clubs." *American Academy of Political and Social Science Annals*, 28 (September 1909): 277–282.

————. "The Business of Saving Time." *Ladies' Home Journal*, 32 (April 1915): 27.

————. "The Immigrant Among Us." *Ladies' Home Journal*, 32 (May 1915): 27.

————. "A Message to Club Mothers." *Ladies' Home Journal*, 32 (July 1915): 21.

————. "Patriotism That Makes for Peace." *Ladies' Home Journal*, 32 (June 1915): 21.

————. "What the Woman's Club Has Done." *Ladies' Home Journal*, 31 (May 1914): 26.

Peterson, M. Jeanne. "The Victorian Governess: Status Incongruence in Family and Society." *Victorian Studies*, 14 (September 1970): 7–26.

Poole, Hester M. "Club Life in New York." *Arena*, 6 (1892): 368–369.

Prince, Lucinda W. "Training for Salewomen." *The Federation Bulletin*, 5 (February 1908): 165–166, 184.

Purrington, Miss. "Emphasis of Literary Work." *The Northern*, I (April 1905): 55–57.

Quimby, Mary D. "Laconia Women's Club." *Granite Monthly*, 38 (April 1906): 103–108.

Read, Leslie Stringfellow. "Clubwomen in Council." *The Woman Citizen*, 10 (June 13, 1925): 9, 26–27.

————. "A Great American Institution." *Delineator*, 98 (June 1917): 20.

Rhine, Alice Hyneman. "The Work of Women's Clubs." *Forum*, 12 (December 1891): 519–528.

Richards, Ellen H. "Domestic Science: What It Is and How to Study It at Home." *Outlook*, 55 (April 1897): 1078–1080.

————. "The Place of Science in Women's Education." *The American Kitchen Magazine*, 7 (1897): 224–226.

————. "The Social Significance of the Home Economics Movement." *Journal of Home Economics*, 3 (April 1911): 117–125.

_____. "Waste of Energy in Organizations." *Outlook*, 63 (December 1899): 928–930.

Richardson, Anne Steese. "The After-the-War Clubwoman." *Woman's Home Companion*, 47 (February 1920): 26+.

Richmond, Mary E. "Working Women's Clubs." *Charities Review*, 6 (June 1897): 351–352.

Rickert, Edith. "What Women's Clubs Have Really Done." *Ladies' Home Journal*, 27 (October 1912): 12.

Riegal, Robert E. "The Split of the Feminist Movement in 1869." *Mississippi Valley Historical Review*, 49 (1962): 485–496.

Riesman, David. "Two Generations." In *The Woman in America*. Edited by Robert Jay Lifton. Boston: Beacon, 1965.

Riley, Glenda. "Origins of the Argument for Improved Female Education." *History of Education Quarterly*, 9 (Winter 1969): 455–470.

_____. "The Origins of the Feminist Movement in America." *Forums in History*. St. Charles, Mo.: Forum, 1973.

_____. "The Subtle Subversion: Changes in the Traditionalist Image of the American Woman." *The Historian*, 30 (1970): 210–219.

Roberts, Josephine. "Horace Mann and the Peabody Sisters." *New England Quarterly*, 18 (1945): 164–180.

Rose, Flora. "Forty Years of Home Economics at Cornell University." *Fifteenth Annual Report*. New York State College of Home Economics at Cornell University, 1940.

Rotch, Mrs. Grace M. "Milford Women's Club," *Granite Monthly*, 38 (May 1906): 137–144.

Rousmaniere, John P. "Cultural Hybrid in the Slums: The College Woman and the Settlement House, 1889–1894." *American Quarterly*, 22 (1970): 45–66.

Ruhl, Arthur. "Discovering the Club Woman." *Collier's*, 48 (9 December 1911): 2031.

Ruoff, John C. "Frivolity to Consumption: Or, Southern Womanhood in Antebellum Literature." *Civil War History*, 18 (1971): 213–229.

Sage, Mrs. Russell. "Opportunities and Responsibilities of Leisured Women." *North American Review*, 161 (November 1905): 712–721.

Salmon, Lucy M. "Women's Exchange: Charity or Business." *Forum*, 13 (1892): 394–406.

Sands, Alexander H. "Intellectual Culture of Women." *Southern Literary Messenger*, 28 (May 1859): 321–332.

Savage, Clara. "Men—and Women's Clubs." *Good Housekeeping*, 62 (May 1916): 610–616.

Schlesinger, Elizabeth Bancroft. "Fanny Fern: Our Grandmother's Mentor." *New York Historical Society Quarterly*, 38 (1954): 500–519.

_____. "The Nineteenth Century Women's Dilemma and Jennie June." *New York History*, 62 (October 1961): 365–379.

Severance, Mrs. Caroline M. "The Genesis of the Club Idea." *Woman's Journal*, 33 (31 May 1902): 174.

Sewall, May Wright. "Women's Clubs—A Symposium." *Arena*, 6 (1892): 362–368.

Shepard, Mrs. Frederick J. (Ellie J.) "The Women's Educational and Industrial Union of Buffalo." *Buffalo Historical Society Publications*, 22 (1918): 147–200.

Sherman, Mrs. John Dickinson. "The Women's Clubs in the Mid West States." *American Academy of Political and Social Science Annals*, 28 (1906): 227–247.

———. "What the General Federation Can Do for the Individual Clubwoman." *Woman's Home Companion*, 51 (September 1924): 16+.

Shuler, Marjorie. "Getting Things Done." *Woman's Home Companion*, 48 (September 1921): 16.

Simpson, Lola Jean. "Woman and the Dominant Male." *The Independent Woman*, 6 (November 1927): 10–11.

Slocomb, Mrs. George A. "The Clubwoman and the Corner Grocery." *Collier's*, 51 (14 June 1913): 20–21.

Slosson, Edwin E. "A Man and the Woman's Club." *Current Opinion*, 30 (May 1891): 600–602.

———. "Why I Do Not Belong to the Woman's Club." *Independent*, 53 (14 February 1904): 387–389.

Smith, C. C. "Self-Culture of Women." *Christian Examiner*, 51 (September 1851): 185–194.

Smith, Daniel Scott. "Family Limitation, Sexual Control and Domestic Feminism in Victorian America." In *Clio's Consciousness Raised*. Edited by Mary S. Hartmann and Lois Banner. New York: Harper and Row, 1974.

Smith, Henry Ladd. "The Beauteous Jennie June: Pioneer Woman Journalist." *Journalism Quarterly*, 40 (Spring 1963): 169–174.

Smith-Rosenberg, Carroll. "Beauty, the Beast, and the Militant Woman: A Case Study in Sex Roles and Social Stress in Jacksonian America." *American Quarterly*, 23 (1971).

———. "The Female World of Love and Ritual: Relations between Women in Nineteenth-Century America." *Signs*, 1 (Autumn 1975): 1–29.

———, and Charles Rosenberg. "The Female Animal: Medical and Biological Views of Woman and Her Role in Nineteenth-Century America." *Journal of American History*, 60 (1973): 332–356.

Spooner, Mrs. Charles H. "Vermont Art Problem." *Vermonter*, 15 (May 1910): 143–157.

Stanley, Caroline H. "A Successful Women's Club." *New England Magazine*, 2 (March 1890): 54–62.

Stanley, Maude. "Working-Girls' Clubs in Italy." *Living Age*, 254 (September 28, 1907): 814–818.

Stearns, Bertha M. "Early New England Magazines for Ladies." *New England Quarterly*, 12 (1929): 420–457.

_____. "Early Factory Magazines in New England." *Journal of Economic and Business History*, 2 (August 1930): 685–705.

_____. "Early Philadelphia Magazines for Ladies." *Pennsylvania Magazine of History and Biography*, 64 (October 1940): 479–491.

_____. "New England Magazines for Ladies, 1830–1860." *New England Quarterly*, 3 (1930): 627–656.

_____. "Southern Magazines for Ladies, 1819–1860." *Southern Quarterly*, 31 (January 1932): 70–87.

_____. "Early Western Magazines for Ladies." *Mississippi Valley Historical Review*, 18 (December 1931): 319–330.

Stern, Madeleine B. "House of Expanding Doors: Anne Lynch's Soirees, 1846." *New York History*, 23 (January 1942): 42–51.

Stewart, Jane A. "National Patriotic Societies." *Chautauquan*, 59 (June 1910): 142–146.

Stone, Ellen Foster. "What the Woman's Club Can Do This Year." *Ladies' Home Journal*, 36 (October 1919): 53.

Strom, Sharon Hartman. "Leadership and Tactics in the American Woman's Suffrage Movement: A New Perspective from Massachusetts." *Journal of American History*, 42 (September 1975): 296–315.

Taylor, Graham. "The Women's Biennial: Social Sympathy and Public Policies." *Survey*, 32 (July 4, 1914): 358–359.

Taylor, Kate Kittridge. *Biographical Sketch of Elizabeth Kittredge Churchill.* Read in Churchill Memorial Course, Providence, March 30, 1883.

Taylor, William R. and Christopher Lasch. "Two Kindred Spirits: Sorority and Family in New England, 1839–1846." *New England Quarterly*, 36 (1963).

Thayer, Katherine M. "The Nashaway Women's Club." *Granite Monthly*, 30 (May 1901): 263–269.

Thomas, Rose Fay. "Women's Amateur Muscial Clubs." *Music*, 20 (June 1901): 90–95.

Thurlow, Mary C. "Encouragement of Serious Reading by Women's Clubs." *Library Journal*, 28 (May 1903): 227–229.

Tillett, Wilbur Fish. "Southern Womanhood as Affected by the War." *Century*, 43 (1891–92): 9–16.

Toombs, Elizabeth O. "The Golden-Prairie Biennial." *Good Housekeeping*, 71 (September 1920): 23, 172+.

Townsend, Harriet A., President of the Union. "The Buffalo Educational and Industrial Union." *Harper's Bazaar*, 30 (October 23, 1897): 889–890.

Underhill, Carolyn A. "The Club-woman's Guide." *Ladies' Home Journal*, 32 (September 1915): 34; 32 (November 1915): 76; 33 (January 1916): 30.

_____. "The Club-woman's Guide: How to Organize a Club Properly."

*Ladies' Home Journal*, 32 (October 1915): 54.

Underwood, Sara A. "A Woman's Case." *Arena*, 6 (1892): 344–360.

Uttrachi, Patricia Branca and Peter N. Stearns. "Modernization of Women in the Nineteenth Century." *Forums in History*. St. Charles, Mo.: Forum Press, 1973.

Van Rensallaer, M. G. "The Waste of Women's Intellectual Forces." *Forum*, 13 (1892): 616–628.

Walton, Marie L. "Lesson of the Last Biennial." *Overland Monthly and Out West Magazine*, 61 (January 1913): 16–26.

Ward, May Alden. "The Influence of Women's Clubs in New England and in the Mid-Eastern States." *American Academy of Political and Social Science Annals*, 28 (1906): 205–226.

Warren, John. "The Women Who Are Making a Musical America." *Delineator*, 76 (September 1910): 164–210.

Watson, Annah Robinson. "Attitude of the Typical Southern Woman to Clubs." *Arena*, 6 (1892): 373–374.

Welch, Margaret Hamilton. "Club Life in Women's Colleges." *Harper's Bazaar*, 33 (June 16, 1900): 436–438.

Wells, Kate Gannett. "Boston Club Women." *Arena*, 6 (1892): 369–371.

_____. "Sphere of Woman in Transitional America." *Atlantic Monthly*, 46 (December 1880): 817–823.

_____. "The Transitional American Woman." *Atlantic Monthly*, 46 (December 1880): 817–818.

_____. "Women in Organizations." *Atlantic Monthly*, 46 (September 1880): 360–367.

Wells, Mildred White. "Know Your General Federation: Brave Steps Into a New World." *General Federation Club Woman* (October 1965).

_____. "Know Your General Federation: A Guide Around the Globe." *General Federation Club Woman* (February 1966).

_____. "Know Your General Federation: The Great House of Womanhood." *General Federation Club Woman* (November 1965).

Welter, Barbara. "Anti-Intellectualism and the American Woman, 1800–1860." *Mid-America*, 48 (October 1966): 258–270.

_____. "The Cult of True Womanhood: 1820–1860." *American Quarterly*, 18 (Summer 1966): 151–174.

_____. "The Feminization of American Religion; 1800–1860." In *Clio's Consciousness Raised*. Edited by Mary Hartman and Lois W. Banner. New York: Harper and Row, 1974.

Wheeler, Candace, "A Tribute to Kate Field," *The Critic*, 29 (18 July 1896).

Whitaker, Mrs. Hobart K., ed. "Vermont Federation of Women's Clubs." *Vermonter*, 10 (Summer 1905).

Whitcomb, Caroline E. "The Women's Clubs of Keene." *The Granite Monthly*, 30 (February 1901): 228–235.

White, Martha E. D. "The Case of the Woman's Club." *The Outlook*, 59 (June 25, 1898): 479–481.

_____. "Work of the Woman's Club." *Atlantic Monthly*, 93 (1903): 614–623.

_____. "The Work of Women's Clubs in New England." *New England Magazine*, 28 (June 1903): 447–463.

Wilbour, Charlotte B. "Mrs. Wilbour's Address Before the Judiciary Committee of the Assembly of the State of New York. 3 April 1872." New York: G. W. Carleton, 1872.

Wilkinson, Charlotte Coffyn. "Working-Women's Clubs." *Gunton's Magazine*, 18 (June 1900): 520–527.

Willard, Frances E. "The Dawn of Woman's Day." *Our Day*, 2 (1888): 345–360.

Williams, Fannie Barrier. "Club Movement among Negro Women." In *Progress of a Race*. Edited by John W. Gibson and William H. Crogman. Miami: Mnemosyne, 1969; reprint of 1902 ed.

Wilson, John B. "Elizabeth Peabody and Other Transcendentalists on History and Historians." *The Historian*, 30 (November 1967): 72–86.

Winslow, Helen M. "Literary Club Women." *Critic*, 44 (April 1904): 333–338.

_____. "Literature via the Women's Club." *Critic,* 44 (1904): 237–244.

_____. "The Massachusetts State Federation: What It Has Accomplished." *Delineator*, 64 (August 1904): 295–296.

_____. "At Spinster Farm," *Delineator*, 66 and 67 (August 1905–January 1906).

_____. "Club Women and Civics." *Delineator*, 67 (January 1906): 174–175.

_____. "Club Programmes." *Delineator*, 67 (February 1906): 374–375.

_____. "The Story of the Women's Club Movement." *New England Magazine*, 38 (1908): 543–557.

_____. "Where the Modern Club Woman Has 'Won Out'." *Delineator*, 80 (October 1912): 262.

_____. "The Modern Club Woman: How Women First Began to Organize." *Delineator*, 80 (November 1912): 370–371.

_____. "The Modern Club Woman: The Story of Organized Womanhood." *Delineator*, 80 (December 1912): 473.

_____. "The Modern Club Woman: What Women's Clubs Really Stand For." *Delineator*, 81 (January 1913): 57.

_____. "Here's Work Worthwhile." *Delineator*, 81 (March 1913): 202–203.

_____. "Work for the Club Year." *Delineator*, 82 (April 1913): 302, 312.

_____. "What Club Loyalty Means." *Delineator*, 82 (May 1913): 388.

_____. "New Topics for Club Study." *Delineator*, 82 (June 1913): 482–487.

_____. "What One Woman Did in Flatville." *Delineator*, 83 (November 1913): 52.

_____. "Some Real Work in Civics." *Delineator*, 84 (April 1914): 46.

Winter, Alice Ames, "The General Federation of Women's Clubs." *Ladies'*

*Home Journal*, 43 (June 1926): 25.

_____. "The Salt Lake City Council." *Good Housekeeping*, 73 (September 1921): 73.

_____. "Women's Clubs To-Day." *North American Review*, 214 (November 1921): 636–640.

Wood, Ann D. "The 'Scribbling Women' and Fanny Fern: Why Women Wrote." *American Quarterly*, 23 (Spring 1971): 3–24.

Wood, Mary I. "Civic Activities of Women's Clubs." *American Academy of Political and Social Science Annals*, 28 (September 1906): 78–87.

_____. "The Woman's Club Movement." *Chautauquan*, 59 (June 1910): 13–64.

_____. "Federation Educational Work." *Ladies' Home Journal*, 32 (July 1915): 21.

_____. "How to Serve Rural Communities." *Ladies' Home Journal*, 32 (June 1915): 21.

_____. "Our Part in Conservation." *Ladies' Home Journal*, 32 (April 1915): 27.

_____. "What We Can Do for Her." *Ladies' Home Journal*, 32 (May 1915): 27.

_____. "What Women's Clubs Do for Christmas." *Ladies' Home Journal*, 30 (December 1913): 28.

Woodruff, Clinton Rogers. "Woman and Her Larger Home." *Good Housekeeping*, 48 (January 1909): 3–10.

Woodworth, Mrs. Mary P. "Concord Women's Club." *The Granite Monthly*, 18 (June 1895): 395–407.

Woolley, Mary E. "The Woman's Club Woman." *Good Housekeeping*, 50 (May 1910): 559–565.

Wyman, Katharine. "Inspiring Examples of Rural Uplift." *Good Housekeeping*, 48 (March 1909): 289–293.

Young, Rose. "A Leader of Women: Mrs. Percy Pennybacker." *Good Housekeeping*, 57 (November 1913): 634–635.

_____. "What Next for Women's Clubs?" *Good Housekeeping*, 58 (June 1914): 739–747.

Zakrzewska, Maria Elizabeth. *Memoir*. Boston: New England Hospital for Women and Children, 1903.

## Unattributed Articles

"Are Women's Clubs a Menace to the Church?" *Current Opinion*, 41 (September 1906): 325–326.

"As to Woman's Clubs." *Atlantic Monthly*, 103 (January 1909): 135–136.

"The Best Thing Our Club Ever Did." (series) *Harper's Bazaar*, 43 (February 1909): 156–157; (March 1909): 279; (April 1909): 407; (June 1909): 614–616; (July 1909): 716–718; (August 1909): 812–814;

(September 1909): 915–917; (October 1909): 1038–1040; (November 1909): 1125–1127.

"Browning or the Budget." *Independent*, 71 (30 November 1911): 1218–1220.

"Canadian Women Show Awakening." *The Survey*, 27 (24 February 1912): 1796–1797.

"Child Labor—A National Disgrace." *American Academy of Political and Social Science Annals*, 28 (September 1909): 301–303.

"Clubs—and Clubs." *Living Age*, 271 (16 December 1911): 697–699.

"Communications—Report of the Civic Committee." *American Academy of Political and Social Science Annals*, 28 (September 1909): 293–300.

"Contributors' Club." *Atlantic Monthly*, 46 (1880): 724–725.

"Contributors' Club." *Atlantic Monthly*, 92 (December 1903): 860–863.

"Eight Week Clubs." *Independent*, 77 (9 March, 1914): 352.

"An English View of American Organizations." *London Daily Mail*, November 1909.

"The General Federation of Women's Clubs." *The Outlook*, 107 (July 4, 1914): 512–513.

"General Federation of Women's Clubs." *The Outlook*, 113 (June 17, 1916): 295–297.

"The Gentle Patriot." *Scribner's Monthly*, 42 (October 1907): 506–507.

"Glimpses of the General Federation of Women's Clubs Biennial." *The Woman Citizen*, 11 (July 1926): 35–36.

"How They Have Grown." *The Independent*, 85 (February 28, 1916): 313.

"Intellectuality of Woman." *International Review*, 13 (1883): 123–136.

"Larger Opportunity." *The Outlook*, 48 (August 12, 1893): 305–306.

"Men's Views of Women's Clubs." *American Academy of Political and Social Science Annals*, 28 (September 1909): 283–292.

"The Object of Women's Clubs." *The North American Review*, 185 (19 July 1907): 684–686.

"The Place of the Present Organizations of Women." *Delineator*, 74 (July 1909): 33.

"Reading Course in Domestic Science." *Journal of Home Economics*, 3 (December 1911): 493–494.

"Recent Novels." *The Nation*, 17 (July–December 1873), 73.

"Recreation and a Southern Business Women's Club." *Survey*, 32 (July 11, 1914): 396.

"Report of Pure food Committee." *American Academy of Political and Social Science Annals*, 28 (September 1909): 296–301.

"Table-Talk." *Putnam's Magazine*, 13 (May 1869), 639–640.

"Thirty-Five Years of Federation." *The Woman Citizen*, 10 (May 30 1925), 8–9; 27–28.

"Vermont Federation of Women's Clubs." *Vermonter*, 9 (November 1903): 120–122.

"Woman's Club of Durham." *Granite Monthly*, 38 (November 1906): 531–534.

"A Woman's Club with a Brand-new Idea." *Woman's Home Companion*, 47 (September 1920): 66+.

"Women's Club Scholarship Funds." *Chautauquan*, 42 (October 1905): 166–168.

"The Women's Clubs." *Atlantic Monthly*, 101 (June 1908): 864–866.

"Women's Clubs." *Nation*, 91 (20 October 1910): 356–357.

"Working-Girls' Clubs." *Current Opinion*, 29 (August 1900): 195.

"Workingwomen's Association." *The Revolution*, (24 September 1868): 181–182.

"Workingwomen's Association." *The Revolution*, (October 8, 1868): 214–215.

**Unpublished Manuscripts**

Bacon, Elizabeth. "The Growth of Household Conveniences in the United States, 1865–1900." Ph.D. dissertation, Radcliffe College, 1942.

Beldon, Gertrude May. "A History of the Woman Suffrage Movement in Illinois." M.A. thesis, University of Chicago, 1913.

Bolquerin, M. James. "An Investigation of the Contributions of David, June, and Herbert Croly to American Life—with Emphasis on the Influence of the Father on the Son." M.A. thesis, University of Missouri, July 1948.

Brown, Sherry and Debra Goldman. "A Study of the Buffalo Chapter of the United States Sanitary Commission During the Civil War." Paper, State University of New York at Buffalo Archives, 1975.

Cochran, Eva Owen. "A Sketch of the Colonial Club of Northampton, Massachusetts, 1890–1938." Paper delivered to members, 4 April 1938.

Cott, Nancy Falik. "In the Bonds of Womanhood: Perspectives on Female Experience and Consciousness in New England, 1780–1830." Ph.D. dissertation, Brandeis University, April 1974.

Donham, S. Agnes. "History of Women's Educational and Industrial Union." Paper, Women's Educational and Industrial Union, Boston.

DuBois, Ellen, "A New Life: The Development of an American Woman Suffrage Movement, 1860–1869." Ph.D. dissertation, Northwestern University, 1975.

Fields, Emma L. "The Women's Club Movement in the United States, 1877–1900." M.A. thesis, Howard University, 1948.

Filiaci, Anne. "Female Anti-Suffragists and the Separate but Equal Ideology in the Woman Movement." Paper, 1975.

Giele, Janet A. "Social Change in the Feminine Role: A Comparison of Woman Suffrage and Woman's Temperance, 1870–1920." Ph.D. dissertation, Radcliffe, 1961.

Greenberg, Brian. "Worker and Community: Fraternal Orders in Albany, New York, 1845–1885." Paper presented at State University College at Brockport, October, 1975.

Hamilton, Tullia. "The National Association of Colored Women, 1896–1920." Paper presented at Third Berkshire Conference, 11 June 1976.

Jacoby, Robin M. "Women's Trade Union League and American Feminism." Paper presented at Second Berkshire Conference, Radcliffe, October 27, 1974.

Jones, Grace Anstice. "The Woman Question: A Study of Feminism in the United States, 1830–1850." M.A. thesis, Mount Holyoke College, 1959.

Kneeland, Miss Harriet J. "Northampton Social and Literary Clubs." Paper, Folger Library, Northampton, 1923.

McLeod, Mrs. Henry M. "Charlotte B. Wilbour." Address given to Sorosis, 1975.

Merk, Lois Bannister. "Massachusetts and the Woman Suffrage Movement." Ph.D. dissertation, Northwestern University, 1956; Copyright 1961.

Mulligan, Charlotte, B. "Autobiography." Buffalo and Erie County Historical Society, Buffalo, New York, 1894.

Ranlett, Judith Becker. "Sorority and Community: Women's Answer to a Changing Massachusetts, 1865–1895." Ph.D. dissertation, Brandeis University, 1974.

Shelton, Brenda K. "Social Reform and Social Control in Buffalo, 1890–1900." Ph.D. dissertation, State University of New York at Buffalo, 1970.

Stanley, Sara Marie, "Caroline M. Severance: Feminist and Reformer 1820–1914." B.A. thesis, Scripp's College, 1978.

Stewart, Della A. and Cornelia F. Bedell. "A Record of Golden Years, 1894–1944: The History of the New York State Federation of Women's Clubs," 1944.

Stiver, Marylou Reed, "Public Speaking of Caroline M. Severance." M.A. Thesis, California State College at Long Beach, 1969.

Walter, Francis Joseph. "A Social and Cultural History of Buffalo, New York 1865–1901." Ph.D. dissertation, Western Reserve University, January 1958.

Wilbour, Charlotte Beebe. "Honor Among Women." An address delivered on the Third Anniversary of Sorosis by its President, Charlotte B. Wilbour at Delmonico's, New York, 20 March, 1871.

———. "Of Egyptian Women." Association for the Advancement of Women Fifteenth Congress, New York, 1887.

———. "Why We Ask the Ballot." An Address given before the Judiciary Committee of the Assembly of the State of New York, 3 April 1872.

# Index

F-H

Blair, K

THE CLUB

Holmes &

(1968)99 pages